STEP *1*

WORD
Bridge
3600

Intro

Word Bridge 3600의 수준별 학습
중학교 필수 단어에서 특목고 대비를 위한 단어까지 총 3,600 단어가 단계별로 레벨업되어 있습니다. 자신의 수준에 맞추어서 차근차근 어휘력을 다져나갈 수 있도록 하였습니다.

귀로 듣고, 입으로 따라하기
단어마다 문법과 구문법칙이 응용된 모범예문을 원어민의 정확한 발음으로 듣고 따라하다 보면 암기 효과를 두 배로 올릴 수 있도록 하였습니다.

영영정의를 통한 의미 이해
단어의 주요 의미를 영영으로 정의해 놓고 연관된 예문을 제시함으로써 그 의미를 더욱 정확하게 이해할 수 있도록 하였습니다.

반복, 반복 쏙쏙 암기
눈으로 암기하는 단어는 오래 기억되지 못합니다. 듣기, 말하기, 쓰기 등을 활용한 다양한 연습 형태를 통해 반복적으로 단어를 학습할 수 있도록 하였습니다.

교재의 구성

본 교재는 단계별로 총 5권으로 구성되어 있습니다.

각 권은 10 Part로, 각 Part는 모두 4 unit으로 구성되어 있습니다.

Listen and repeat
주요 학습 파트로 새로운 단어 18개와 단어를 활용한 모범예문이 수록되어 있으며 듣기 학습이 포함되어 있습니다.

Exercise / Review
주요 학습에서 익힌 단어와 예문을 활용하여 문제를 풀어보고 암기합니다.

▼ Step 5

B. Fill in the word and meaning.

Word	Meaning		Meaning	Word
01 able		01 ~할 수 있는	
02 bicycle		02 ~에 대하여	
03 above		03 ~의 위쪽에	
04 big		04 ~을 가로질러서	
05 black		05 ~후에	
06 airplane		06 비행기	
07 city		07 띠, 벨트	
08 bird		08 자전거	
09 blanket		09 큰	
10 clock		10 새	
11 across		11 검정색, 검정색의	
12 class		12 담요	
13 about		13 턱	
14 church		14 교회	

▼ Step 6

🎧 C. Listen, write the word and meaning. (Track 3)

Word	Meaning		Word
01		10	
02		11	
03		12	
04		13	
05		14	
06		15	
07		16	
08		17	
09		18	

▼ Step 7

A. Read and fill in the word and meaning.

word	definition	meaning
	a creature with feathers and wings which can fly	
	an instrument that shows you what time it is	
	not dirty	
	a large and important town	
	from one side of something to the other	
	of the darkest color, like night or coal	
	on the subject of	
	in a higher place	
	a cover made of wool to keep people warm	

교재의 학습방법

- **Step 1 – 새 단어 귀로 들으며 익히기**
  새 단어와 예문을 원어민의 발음으로 들으며 익힌다.

- **Step 2 – 단어 뜻 암기하기**
  영영 정의를 익히면서 단어의 정확한 의미를 이해하고, 예문을 해석하면서 예문 속에서 단어의 쓰임을 학습합니다.

- **Step 3 – 입으로 따라하며 암기하기**
  다시 한 번 CD를 들으면서 큰 소리로 따라합니다. 예문을 따라하면서 통째로 암기합니다.

- **Step 4 – 문장 완성하기**
  주어진 단어 힌트를 이용하여 암기한 예문을 완성합니다.

- **Step 5 – 단어와 뜻 채우기**
  제시된 영어 단어는 뜻을 우리 말로 쓰고, 단어의 뜻이 제시되어 있으면 영어 단어를 쓰면서 복습합니다.

- **Step 6 – 듣고 단어와 뜻 채우기**
  CD를 듣고 정확한 발음을 익히며 영어 단어와 뜻을 쓰면서 반복 학습합니다.

- **Step 7 – 단어 암기 확인**
  영영 정의를 읽고 암기한 영어 단어와 뜻을 쓰면서 확인 학습을 합니다.

Contents

part 1

Unit 1	6
Unit 2	10
Review 1	14
Unit 3	16
Unit 4	20
Review 2	24

part 2

Unit 5	26
Unit 6	30
Review 3	34
Unit 7	36
Unit 8	40
Review 4	44

part 3

Unit 9	46
Unit 10	50
Review 5	54

Unit 11	56
Unit 12	60
Review 6	64

part 4

Unit 13	66
Unit 14	70
Review 7	74
Unit 15	76
Unit 16	80
Review 8	84

part 5

Unit 17	86
Unit 18	90
Review 9	94
Unit 19	96
Unit 20	100
Review 10	104

WORD BRIDGE 3600

part 6

Unit 21	…………………………	106
Unit 22	…………………………	110
Review 11	………………………	114
Unit 23	…………………………	116
Unit 24	…………………………	120
Review 12	………………………	124

part 7

Unit 25	…………………………	126
Unit 26	…………………………	130
Review 13	………………………	134
Unit 27	…………………………	136
Unit 28	…………………………	140
Review 14	………………………	144

part 8

Unit 29	…………………………	146
Unit 30	…………………………	150
Review 15	………………………	154

Unit 31	…………………………	156
Unit 32	…………………………	160
Review 16	………………………	164

part 9

Unit 33	…………………………	166
Unit 34	…………………………	170
Review 17	………………………	174
Unit 35	…………………………	176
Unit 36	…………………………	180
Review 18	………………………	184

part 10

Unit 37	…………………………	186
Unit 38	…………………………	190
Review 19	………………………	194
Unit 39	…………………………	196
Unit 40	…………………………	200
Review 20	………………………	204
Total Test	………………………	207
Answer Key	………………………	229

Unit 1

🎧 Listen and repeat. Track 1

01 able — a ~할 수 있는 — to have the ability to do something
[éibəl]
I was **able** to solve the problem.
나는 그 문제를 풀 수 있었다.

02 about — prep ~에 대하여 — on the subject of
[əbáut]
She knew a lot **about** food.
그녀는 음식에 관하여 많은 것을 알았다.

03 above — ad ~위에 / prep ~의 위쪽에 — in a higher place
[əbʌ́v]
He's lifting the books **above** his head.
그는 머리 위로 책들을 들어 올리고 있다.

04 across — prep ~을 가로 질러서 — from one side of something to the other
[əkrɔ́ːs]
He walked **across** the field.
그는 들판을 가로질러 걸었다.

05 after — ad ~후에 — later than something; at a later time
[ǽftər]
They arrived at the station **after** the train left.
그들은 기차가 떠난 후에 역에 도착했다.

06 airplane — n 비행기 — a vehicle with wings and engines that can fly through the air
[έərplèin]
I lost my **airplane** ticket.
나는 비행기 표를 잃어버렸다.

07 belt — n 띠, 벨트 — a thin piece of cloth that you wear around your waist
[belt]
He bought a new **belt**.
그는 새 벨트를 하나 샀다.

08 bicycle — n 자전거 — a vehicle which you sit on and ride by moving your legs
[báisikəl]
He taught his sister how to ride a **bicycle**.
그는 여동생에게 자전거 타는 법을 가르쳤다.

09 big — a 큰 — large; not small
[big]
This dress is too **big** for me.
이 드레스는 나에게 너무 크다.

key words
ability n 능력 / solve v 풀다 / subject n 주제 / arrive v 도착하다 / vehicle n 탈 것 / through prep ~을 통하여 / cloth n 천, 옷감 / wear v 입다 / ride v (탈 것을) 타다

🎧 Listen and repeat. Track 2

10 bird [bəːrd]
n 새   a creature with feathers and wings which can fly
Some **birds** are making their nests on the tree.
몇 마리의 새들이 나무 위에 둥지를 만들고 있다.

11 black [blæk]
n 검정색 / a 검정색의   of the darkest color, like night or coal
He was dressed all in **black**.
그는 모두 검정색으로 차려 입었다.

12 blanket [blǽŋkit]
n 담요   a cover made of wool to keep people warm
He bought me a **blanket**.
그가 나에게 담요를 사다 주었다.

13 chin [tʃin]
n 턱   the part of your face below your mouth
Don't touch your **chin**.
턱을 만지지 말거라.

14 church [tʃəːrtʃ]
n 교회   a building where Christians go to pray
Do you go to **church** regularly?
너는 정기적으로 교회에 가니?

15 city [síti]
n 도시   a large and important town
Venice is a beautiful **city** to travel.
베니스는 여행하기에 아름다운 도시이다.

16 class [klæs]
n 수업, 학급   a group of students who are taught together
I have many friends in my **class**.
나는 우리 반에 친구가 많다.

17 clean [kliːn]
a 깨끗한   not dirty
Cats are very **clean** animals.
고양이는 매우 깨끗한 동물이다.

18 clock [klɑk]
n 시계   an instrument that shows you what time it is
I set the alarm **clock** before sleeping.
나는 자기 전에 알람시계를 맞춰 놓았다.

---

key words
creature n 생물 / feather n 깃털 / nest n 둥지 / cover n 덮개 / touch v 만지다 / pray v 기원하다
regularly ad 정기적으로 / important a 중요한 / dirty a 더러운 / instrument n 기계, 도구

Exercise

A. Complete the sentence.

1. He's lifting the books _____ his head.
   그는 머리 위로 책들을 들어 올리고 있다.

2. I lost my _____ ticket.
   나는 비행기 표를 잃어버렸다.

3. This dress is too _____ for me.
   이 드레스는 나에게 너무 크다.

4. I have many friends in my _____.
   나는 우리 반에 친구가 많다.

5. He taught his sister how to ride a _____.
   그는 여동생에게 자전거 타는 법을 가르쳤다.

6. Don' touch your _____.
   턱을 만지지 말아라.

7. He bought a new _____.
   그는 새 벨트를 하나 샀다.

8. Do you go to _____ regularly?
   너는 정기적으로 교회에 가니?

9. Venice is a beautiful _____ to travel.
   베니스는 여행하기에 아름다운 도시이다.

10. He walked _____ the field.
    그는 들판을 가로질러 걸었다.

11. They arrived at the station _____ the train left.
    그들은 기차가 떠난 후에 역에 도착했다.

12. Some _____ are making their nests on the tree.
    몇 마리의 새들이 나무 위에 둥지를 만들고 있다.

13. He was dressed all in _____.
    그는 모두 검정색으로 차려 입었다.

14. I was _____ to solve the problem.
    나는 그 문제를 풀 수 있었다.

15. He bought me a _____.
    그가 나에게 담요를 사다 주었다.

16. She knew a lot _____ food.
    그녀는 음식에 관하여 많은 것을 알았다.

17. Cats are very _____ animals.
    고양이는 매우 깨끗한 동물이다.

18. I set the alarm _____ before sleeping.
    나는 자기 전에 알람시계를 맞춰 놓았다.

Hint

| clock | above | chin | class | after | black | big | bicycle | airplane |
| across | bird | able | church | blanket | belt | about | clean | city |

Exercise

B. Fill in the word and meaning.

	Word	Meaning
01	able	
02	bicycle	
03	above	
04	big	
05	black	
06	airplane	
07	city	
08	bird	
09	blanket	
10	clock	
11	across	
12	class	
13	about	
14	church	
15	belt	
16	chin	
17	clean	
18	after	

	Meaning	Word
01	~할 수 있는	
02	~에 대하여	
03	~위에, ~의 위쪽에	
04	~을 가로 질러서	
05	~후에	
06	비행기	
07	띠, 벨트	
08	자전거	
09	큰	
10	새	
11	검정색, 검정색의	
12	담요	
13	턱	
14	교회	
15	도시	
16	수업, 학급	
17	깨끗한	
18	시계	

C. Listen, write the word and meaning. (Track 3)

	Word	Meaning		Word	Meaning
01			10		
02			11		
03			12		
04			13		
05			14		
06			15		
07			16		
08			17		
09			18		

Unit 2

🎧 Listen and repeat. (Track 4)

01 dolphin [dálfin] — **n** 돌고래 — a mammal with a pointed mouth that lives in the sea
A **dolphin** helped the drowning people.
돌고래가 물에 빠진 사람을 구했다.

02 door [dɔːr] — **n** 문 — a piece of wood that you open and close to get in or out of a room
I heard someone knocking on the **door**.
나는 누군가 문을 두드리는 소리를 들었다.

03 draw [drɔː] — **v** 그리다 — to do a picture or diagram of something with a pencil, pen
Can you **draw** a picture well?
너는 그림을 잘 그릴 수 있니?

04 dry [drai] — **a** 마른 / **v** 말리다 — without liquid in it or on it; not wet
The paint is **dry** now.
색칠한 것이 이제 다 말랐다.

05 duck [dʌk] — **n** 오리 — a water bird with short legs, a short neck, and a large flat beak
I saw a lot of **ducks** near the river.
나는 강가에서 많은 오리들을 보았다.

06 ear [iər] — **n** 귀 — the part of the body which is on each side of the head to hear
He whispered something in her **ear**.
그는 그녀의 귀에 무엇인가 속삭였다.

07 fun [fʌn] — **n** 재미 — pleasure and enjoyment
We had a lot of **fun** at the party.
우리는 파티에서 즐거운 시간을 보냈다.

08 garden [gáːrdn] — **n** 정원 — a piece of land next to a house where flowers and vegetables can be grown
The **garden** is full of grass.
정원에 풀이 무성하다.

09 gentleman [dʒéntlmən] — **n** 신사 — a man is polite and behaves well towards other people
He's a real **gentleman**.
그는 진정한 신사이다.

---

key words
mammal n 포유동물 / drown v 물에 빠지다 / knock v 치다, 두드리다 / diagram n 그림, 도형
liquid a 액체의 / flat a 납작한 / beak n 부리 / whisper v 속삭이다 / polite a 공손한, 예의 바른
behave v 행동하다

🎧 Listen and repeat. Track 5

10 get
[get]
v 사다, 얻다   to receive, obtain or buy something
I **got** a letter from my sister.
나는 여동생에게서 편지를 받았다.

11 girl
[gə:rl]
n 소녀, 여자아이   a female child
Is the baby a boy or a **girl**?
아기가 남자아이 인가요, 여자아이 인가요?

12 give
[giv]
v 주다   to make somebody have something
My parents **gave** me a big present.
부모님이 나에게 큰 선물을 주셨다.

13 house
[haus]
n 집   a building that is made for people to live in
She has moved to a smaller **house**.
그녀는 더 작은 집으로 이사했다.

14 how
[hau]
ad 어떻게, 얼마나   use this to ask about the degree, amount or age
How do you spell your name?
네 이름의 철자는 어떻게 쓰니?

15 hungry
[hʌ́ŋgri]
a 배고픈   wanting to eat
I want to help **hungry** children.
나는 굶주린 아이들을 도와주고 싶다.

16 idea
[aidí:ə]
n 생각, 의견   a plan or thought about what to do
He has a good **idea**.
그에게 좋은 생각이 있다.

17 ill
[il]
a 병든   not in good health; not well
My mother was **ill** yesterday.
어제 엄마가 편찮으셨다.

18 inside
[ínsáid]
ad 안쪽에, 안쪽으로   in, on or to the inner part
Is there anything **inside** the box?
상자 안에 무엇인가 들어있니?

---

key words
receive v 받다 / obtain v 얻다 / female a 여성의 / present n 선물 / degree n 정도 / amount n 양 / spell v 철자를 쓰다 / thought n 사고, 생각 / health n 건강 / inner a 안의, 내부의

Exercise

A. Complete the sentence.

1. A _____ helped the drowning people.
   돌고래가 물에 빠진 사람을 구했다.

2. I want to help _____ children.
   나는 굶주린 아이들을 도와주고 싶다.

3. Can you _____ a picture well?
   너는 그림을 잘 그릴 수 있니?

4. My mother was _____ yesterday.
   어제 엄마가 편찮으셨다.

5. I saw a lot of _____ near the river.
   나는 강가에서 많은 오리들을 보았다.

6. The paint is _____ now.
   색칠한 것이 이제 다 말랐다.

7. _____ do you spell your name?
   네 이름의 철자는 어떻게 쓰니?

8. Is there anything _____ the box?
   상자 안에 무엇인가 들어있니?

9. He whispered something in her _____.
   그는 그녀의 귀에 무엇인가 속삭였다.

10. We had a lot of _____ at the party.
    우리는 파티에서 즐거운 시간을 보냈다.

11. He's a real _____.
    그는 진정한 신사이다.

12. Is the baby a boy or a _____?
    아기가 남자아이 인가요, 여자아이 인가요?

13. I heard someone knocking on the _____.
    나는 누군가 문을 두드리는 소리를 들었다.

14. My parents _____ me a big present.
    부모님이 나에게 큰 선물을 주셨다.

15. She has moved to a smaller _____.
    그녀는 더 작은 집으로 이사했다.

16. I _____ a letter from my sister.
    나는 여동생에게서 편지를 받았다.

17. He has a good _____.
    그에게 좋은 생각이 있다.

18. The _____ is full of grass.
    정원에 풀이 무성하다.

Hint

| ill | door | dry | duck | ear | girl | gentleman | garden | idea |
| fun | inside | hungry | dolphin | draw | give | how | house | get |

Unit 2

Exercise

B. Fill in the word and meaning.

	Word	Meaning
01	draw	
02	ear	
03	door	
04	get	
05	fun	
06	dolphin	
07	dry	
08	how	
09	idea	
10	duck	
11	give	
12	girl	
13	garden	
14	house	
15	inside	
16	ill	
17	hungry	
18	gentleman	

	Meaning	Word
01	돌고래	
02	문	
03	그리다	
04	마른, 말리다	
05	오리	
06	귀	
07	재미	
08	정원	
09	신사	
10	사다, 얻다	
11	소녀, 여자아이	
12	주다	
13	집	
14	어떻게, 얼마나	
15	배고픈	
16	생각, 의견	
17	병든	
18	안쪽에, 안쪽으로	

C. Listen, write the word and meaning. (Track 6)

	Word	Meaning		Word	Meaning
01			10		
02			11		
03			12		
04			13		
05			14		
06			15		
07			16		
08			17		
09			18		

Review 1

A. Read and fill in the word and meaning.

word	definition	meaning
	a creature with feathers and wings which can fly	
	an instrument that shows you what time it is	
	not dirty	
	a large and important town	
	from one side of something to the other	
	of the darkest color, like night or coal	
	on the subject of	
	in a higher place	
	a cover made of wool to keep people warm	
	a thin piece of cloth that you wear around your waist	
	to have the ability to do something	
	a group of students who are taught together	
	a vehicle with wings and engines that can fly through the air	
	later than something; at a later time	
	large; not small	
	a vehicle which you sit on and ride by moving your legs	
	a building where Christians go to pray	
	the part of your face below your mouth	

Hint
across bird chin able after clean belt city above
church clock black bicycle blanket class about big airplane

B. Read and fill in the word and meaning.

word	definition	meaning
	not in good health; not well	
	a water bird with short legs, a short neck, and a large flat beak	
	to receive, obtain or buy something	
	pleasure and enjoyment	
	without liquid in it or on it; not wet	
	the part of the body which is on each side of the head to hear	
	a piece of wood that you open and close to get in or out of a room	
	to make somebody have something	
	a mammal with a pointed mouth that lives in the sea	
	to do a picture or diagram of something with a pencil, pen	
	in, on or to the inner part	
	a female child	
	a plan or thought about what to do	
	a man is polite and behaves well towards other people	
	use this to ask about the degree, amount or age	
	a piece of land next to a house where flowers and vegetables can be grown	
	wanting to eat	
	a building that is made for people to live in	

Hint

| door | hungry | fun | inside | ear | draw | dry | gentleman | get |
| dolphin | ill | give | duck | girl | how | garden | house | idea |

Unit 3

🎧 Listen and repeat. Track 7

01 listen [lísən] — v 듣다 — to pay attention in order to hear him / her / it
Now please **listen** carefully.
이제 집중해서 들어주세요.

02 live [liv] — v 살다 — to have your home in a place; to be or stay alive
He still **lives** with his parents.
그는 여전히 그의 부모님과 함께 살고 있다.

03 long [lɔːŋ] — a 길이가 긴 — measuring a large amount in distance or time
We had to wait a **long** time.
우리는 오랜 시간 기다려야 했다.

04 look [luk] — v 보다 — to turn your eyes in a particular direction
Look carefully at this picture.
이 그림을 주의해서 보세요.

05 love [lʌv] — v 사랑하다 — a strong feeling when you like somebody very much
You should **love** each other.
너희들은 서로 사랑해야 한다.

06 name [neim] — n 이름 — a word by which somebody / something is known
Do you know the **name** of this flower?
너는 이 꽃의 이름을 알고 있니?

07 neck [nek] — n 목 — the part of your body that joins your head to your shoulders
She has pain in her **neck**.
그녀는 목이 아프다.

08 nephew [néfjuː] — n 조카 — the son of your brother or sister
I had a birthday party for my **nephew**.
나는 조카를 위해 생일 파티를 열었다.

09 new [njuː] — a 새로운 — that has recently been built, made
I need **new** shoes.
나는 새 신발이 필요하다.

---

key words
attention n 주의 / carefully ad 주의 깊게 / stay v 머무르다 / measure v 측정하다
distance n 거리, 간격 / particular a 특정한, 특별한 / join v 결합하다, 연결하다
pain n 아픔 / recently ad 최근

🎧 Listen and repeat. (Track 8)

10 nice [nais]
a 좋은, 기쁜   pleasant, enjoyable or attractive
I want to spend a **nice** time with you.
너와 함께 좋은 시간을 보내고 싶어.

11 night [nait]
n 밤   the part of the day when it is dark
I had a strange dream last **night**.
지난밤에 이상한 꿈을 꾸었다.

12 poor [puər]
a 가난한   not having enough money
The girl was too **poor** to buy new clothes.
그 소녀는 너무 가난해서 새 옷을 살 수 없었다.

13 pork [pɔːrk]
n 돼지고기   meat from a pig
We had dishes of **pork**.
우리는 돼지고기 요리를 먹었다.

14 potato [pətéitou]
n 감자   a round vegetable that grows under the ground
My mother made me peel **potatoes**.
엄마가 나에게 감자 껍질을 벗기라고 시키셨다.

15 pretty [príti]
a 예쁜, 꽤   attractive and pleasant to look at or hear
She is a very **pretty** girl.
그녀는 매우 귀여운 소녀이다.

16 problem [prábləm]
n 문제   a thing that is difficult to deal with
I have a big **problem**.
나는 큰 문제가 생겼다.

17 pull [pul]
v 당기다, 끌다   to use force to move something towards yourself
I **pulled** on the rope strongly.
나는 밧줄을 힘껏 당겼다.

18 room [ruːm]
n 방   a part of a house that has its own walls and floor
He left the **room** in anger.
그는 화가 나서 방을 떠났다.

---

key words
enjoyable **a** 즐거운 / attractive **a** 매력적인 / spend **v** (때를) 보내다 / strange **a** 이상한
nough **a** 충분한 / too~to 너무 ~해서 ~할 수 없다 / meat **n** 고기 / peel **v** 껍질을 벗기다
deal **v** 다루다 / own **a** 자기자신의 / anger **n** 노염, 화

Exercise

A. Complete the sentence.

1. He still _____ with his parents.
   그는 여전히 그의 부모님과 함께 살고 있다.

2. My mother made me peel _____.
   엄마가 나에게 감자 껍질을 벗기라고 시키셨다.

3. We had to wait a _____ time.
   우리는 오랜 시간 기다려야 했다.

4. Now please _____ carefully.
   이제 집중해서 들어주세요.

5. I had a birthday party for my _____.
   나는 조카를 위해 생일 파티를 열었다.

6. We had dishes of _____.
   우리는 돼지고기 요리를 먹었다.

7. I want to spend a _____ time with you.
   너와 함께 좋은 시간을 보내고 싶어.

8. She is a very _____ girl.
   그녀는 매우 귀여운 소녀이다.

9. _____ carefully at this picture.
   이 그림을 주의해서 보세요.

10. Do you know the _____ of this flower?
    너는 이 꽃의 이름을 알고 있니?

11. He left the _____ in anger.
    그는 화가 나서 방을 떠났다.

12. I need _____ shoes.
    나는 새 신발이 필요하다.

13. I had a strange dream last _____.
    지난밤에 이상한 꿈을 꾸었다.

14. The girl was too _____ to buy new clothes.
    그 소녀는 너무 가난해서 새 옷을 살 수 없었다.

15. I have a big _____.
    나는 큰 문제가 생겼다.

16. She has pain in her _____.
    그녀는 목이 아프다.

17. You should _____ each other.
    너희들은 서로 사랑해야 한다.

18. I _____ on the rope strongly.
    나는 밧줄을 힘껏 당겼다.

Hint

| live | long | neck | night | poor | problem | love | pork | nephew |
| look | room | name | listen | pull | nice | new | potato | pretty |

Exercise

B. Fill in the word and meaning.

	Word	Meaning
01	live	
02	neck	
03	pork	
04	room	
05	listen	
06	nice	
07	nephew	
08	pull	
09	long	
10	night	
11	problem	
12	poor	
13	new	
14	pretty	
15	potato	
16	look	
17	name	
18	love	

	Meaning	Word
01	듣다	
02	살다	
03	길이가 긴	
04	보다	
05	사랑하다	
06	이름	
07	목	
08	조카	
09	새로운	
10	좋은, 기쁜	
11	밤	
12	가난한	
13	돼지고기	
14	감자	
15	예쁜, 꽤	
16	문제	
17	당기다, 끌다	
18	방	

C. Listen, write the word and meaning. Track 9

	Word	Meaning		Word	Meaning
01			10		
02			11		
03			12		
04			13		
05			14		
06			15		
07			16		
08			17		
09			18		

Unit 4

🎧 Listen and repeat. Track 10

01 **shoe** — **n** 신, 구두 — object which you wear on your feet
[ʃuː]
What is your **shoe** size?
너는 신발 사이즈가 몇이니?

02 **short** — **a** 키가 작은 — less than the average height
[ʃɔːrt]
He's **short** and fat.
그는 키가 작고 뚱뚱하다.

03 **shoulder** — **n** 어깨 — the part of your body between your neck and the top of your arm
[ʃóuldər]
He just lifted his **shoulders**.
그는 그저 어깨를 으쓱거렸다.

04 **sick** — **a** 아픈 — not well; ill
[sik]
Yesterday I was very **sick**.
어제 나는 많이 아팠다.

05 **sign** — **n** 신호, 표지 / **v** 서명하다 — something that shows a present thing
[sain]
I couldn't see the **sign**.
나는 그 신호를 보지 못했다.

06 **sugar** — **n** 설탕 — a sweet substance that you get from certain plants
[ʃúgər]
Do you take **sugar** in tea?
너는 커피에 설탕을 넣니?

07 **sun** — **n** 태양 — the star that shines in the sky during the day
[sʌn]
The **sun** rises in the east.
해는 동쪽에서 뜬다.

08 **supper** — **n** 저녁 식사 — the main meal eaten in the early part of the evening
[sápər]
I invited my friends for **supper**.
나는 친구들을 저녁 식사에 초대했다.

09 **swim** — **v** 수영하다 — to move your body through water
[swim]
How far can you **swim**?
너는 얼마나 멀리까지 수영할 수 있니?

---

key words
size n 크기 / average n 평균 / height n 높이, 고도 / lift v 들어올리다 / substance n 물질
during prep ~하는 동안 / rise v 해가 떠오르다, 일어서다 / meal n 식사 / invite v 초대하다 / far ad 멀리

🎧 Listen and repeat. (Track 11)

10 switch [swɪtʃ]
n 스위치 / v 스위치를 켜다, 끄다　a small button that you press up or down to turn on electricity
She pressed the **switch** of the dishwasher.
그녀는 접시 닦는 기계의 스위치를 눌렀다.

11 table [téibəl]
n 탁자　a piece of furniture with a top and legs
Let me help you clear the **table**.
내가 탁자 닦는 일을 도와줄게.

12 ugly [ʌ́gli]
a 추한, 못생긴　unpleasant to look at or listen to
The hat is **ugly**.
그 모자는 예쁘지 않다.

13 uncle [ʌ́ŋkəl]
n 삼촌　the brother of your father or mother
I don't know about my **uncle**.
나는 내 삼촌에 대해 아는 것이 없다.

14 under [ʌ́ndər]
prep ~의 아래에　in or to a position that is below something
We found the cat **under** the table.
우리는 탁자 아래에서 고양이를 찾았다.

15 understand [ʌ̀ndərstǽnd]
v 이해하다　to know or realize the meaning of something
I didn't **understand** the book.
나는 그 책을 이해하지 못했다.

16 use [ju:z]
v 사용하다　to do something with a machine or a method
Can I **use** your pen?
네 펜을 사용해도 되겠니?

17 vegetable [védʒətəbəl]
n 야채　a plant or part of a plant that we eat
I had **vegetable** soup for dinner.
나는 저녁으로 야채 스프를 먹었다.

18 zoo [zu:]
n 동물원　a park where many kinds of wild animals are kept
He took his grandson to the **zoo** last Sunday.
그는 지난 일요일 손자를 동물원에 데려갔다.

---

key words
press v 누르다 / electricity n 전기 / dishwasher n 접시 닦는 기계 / position n 위치, 장소
realize v 깨닫다 / method n 방법, 순서 / plant n 식물 / kind n 종류 / wild a 야생의 / grandson n 손자

Unit 4　21

Exercise

A. Complete the sentence.

1. He's _____ and fat.
   그는 키가 작고 뚱뚱하다.

2. What is your _____ size?
   너는 신발 사이즈가 몇이니?

3. I didn't _____ the book.
   나는 그 책을 이해하지 못했다.

4. The _____ rises in the east.
   해는 동쪽에서 뜬다.

5. I don't know about my _____.
   나는 내 삼촌에 대해 아는 것이 없다.

6. How far can you _____?
   너는 얼마나 멀리까지 수영할 수 있니?

7. We found the cat _____ the table.
   우리는 탁자 아래에서 고양이를 찾았다.

8. She pressed the _____ of the dishwasher.
   그녀는 접시 닦는 기계의 스위치를 눌렀다.

9. He just lifted his _____.
   그는 그저 어깨를 으쓱거렸다.

10. I couldn't see the _____.
    나는 그 신호를 보지 못했다.

11. He took his grandson to the _____ last Sunday.
    그는 지난 일요일 손자를 동물원에 데려갔다.

12. The hat is _____.
    그 모자는 예쁘지 않다.

13. Do you take _____ in tea?
    너는 커피에 설탕을 넣니?

14. I invited my friends for _____.
    나는 친구들을 저녁 식사에 초대했다.

15. Let me help you clear the _____.
    내가 탁자 닦는 일을 도와줄게.

16. I had _____ soup for dinner.
    나는 저녁으로 야채 스프를 먹었다.

17. Yesterday I was very _____.
    어제 나는 많이 아팠다.

18. Can I _____ your pen?
    네 펜을 사용해도 되겠니?

Hint

| under | short | sun | supper | zoo | sugar | uncle | table | understand |
| sick | sign | swim | shoe | switch | ugly | shoulder | use | vegetable |

Exercise

B. Fill in the word and meaning.

	Word	Meaning
01	shoulder	
02	uncle	
03	sun	
04	under	
05	shoe	
06	understand	
07	supper	
08	ugly	
09	short	
10	swim	
11	use	
12	sugar	
13	zoo	
14	vegetable	
15	sign	
16	table	
17	switch	
18	sick	

	Meaning	Word
01	신, 구두	
02	키가 작은	
03	어깨	
04	아픈	
05	신호, 표지, 서명하다	
06	설탕	
07	태양	
08	저녁 식사	
09	수영하다	
10	스위치, 스위치를 켜다, 끄다	
11	탁자	
12	추한, 못생긴	
13	삼촌	
14	~의 아래에	
15	이해하다	
16	사용하다	
17	야채	
18	동물원	

🎧 C. Listen, write the word and meaning. (Track 12)

	Word	Meaning		Word	Meaning
01			10		
02			11		
03			12		
04			13		
05			14		
06			15		
07			16		
08			17		
09			18		

Review 2

A. Read and fill in the word and meaning.

word	definition	meaning
	a thing that is difficult to deal with	
	measuring a large amount in distance or time	
	a part of a house that has its own walls and floor	
	to have your home in a place; to be or stay alive	
	a strong feeling when you like somebody very much	
	the son of your brother or sister	
	to use force to move something towards yourself	
	the part of your body that joins your head to your shoulders	
	to pay attention in order to hear him / her / it	
	a word by which somebody / something is known	
	to turn your eyes in a particular direction	
	attractive and pleasant to look at or hear	
	pleasant, enjoyable or attractive	
	meat from a pig	
	not having enough money	
	a round vegetable that grows under the ground	
	that has recently been built, made	
	the part of the day when it is dark	

Hint

| new | room | name | look | neck | problem | pull | pork | potato |
| night | long | poor | listen | love | pretty | live | nephew | nice |

B. Read and fill in the word and meaning.

word	definition	meaning
	a sweet substance that you get from certain plants	
	the star that shines in the sky during the day	
	less than the average height	
	unpleasant to look at or listen to	
	the main meal eaten in the early part of the evening	
	object which you wear on your feet	
	a plant or part of a plant that we eat	
	not well; ill	
	something that shows a present thing	
	the part of your body between your neck and the top of your arm	
	a piece of furniture with a top and legs	
	a small button that you press up or down to turn on electricity	
	to do something with a machine or a method	
	in or to a position that is below something	
	to move your body through water	
	a park where many kinds of wild animals are kept	
	the brother of your father or mother	
	to know or realize the meaning of something	

Hint
under short sun supper zoo sugar uncle table understand
sick sign swim shoe switch ugly shoulder use vegetable

Unit 5

🎧 Listen and repeat. Track 13

01 afternoon
[æ̀ftərnúːn]
n 오후   the day between lunchtime and about 6 o'clock.
He stayed in his room all **afternoon**.
그는 오후 내내 그의 방안에 있었다.

02 again
[əgén]
ad 다시   to indicate something that happens a second time
Again it started to rain.
다시 비가 오기 시작했다.

03 always
[ɔ́ːlweiz]
ad 항상, 언제나   at all times; regularly
I **always** get up at 7 o'clock.
나는 항상 7시에 기상한다.

04 angel
[éindʒəl]
n 천사   a spiritual being that some people believe
My daughter likes a book of **angel** stories.
내 딸은 천사들의 이야기가 담긴 책을 좋아한다.

05 animal
[ǽnəməl]
n 동물   a living creature such as a dog, lion, or rabbit
A dog is a faithful **animal**.
개는 충실한 동물이다.

06 apple
[ǽpl]
n 사과   a fruit with green or red skin and white flesh.
To eat an **apple** in the morning is good for health.
아침에 사과를 먹는 것은 건강에 좋다.

07 bike
[baik]
n 자전거   a cycle that has two wheels; moved by foot pedals
Children like to ride **bikes**.
아이들은 자전거 타는 것을 좋아한다.

08 blue
[bluː]
n 파란색 / **a** 파란색의   the color of the sky on a sunny day
Look at the cloudless **blue** sky.
구름 한 점 없는 파란 하늘을 보렴.

09 boat
[bout]
n 보트, 배   a small vehicle that is used for going across water
I can go to the island by **boat**.
나는 보트를 타고 섬에 갈 수 있다.

---

key words
stay **v** 머무르다 / indicate **n** 가리키다 / regularly **ad** 일정하게 / spiritual **a** 정신의, 영적인
faithful **a** 충실한 / flesh **n** 과육, 육체 / wheel **n** 바퀴 / cloudless **a** 구름 없는 / island **n** 섬

🎧 Listen and repeat. (Track 14)

10 body [bádi]
n 몸   a whole physical form of a person
She has a healthy **body**.
그녀는 건강한 몸을 가지고 있다.

11 book [buk]
n 책   a collection of sheets of paper
Read many good **books**.
좋은 책을 많이 읽어라.

12 bottle [bátl]
n 병   a glass or plastic container in which drinks are kept
The **bottle** is made of glass.
그 병은 유리로 만들어졌다.

13 close [klouz]
v 닫다   to shut something to cover a hole or opening
She **closed** the door quietly.
그녀는 문을 조용히 닫았다.

14 clothes [klouðz]
n 옷, 의복   the things that you wear
Take off those wet **clothes**.
젖은 옷을 벗으렴.

15 cloud [klaud]
n 구름   a mass that floats in the sky
The sun disappeared behind a **cloud**.
해가 구름 뒤로 사라졌다.

16 coat [kout]
n 외투, 코트   an outer clothes fitting the upper part of the body
I'd like to wear that green **coat**.
나는 저 녹색 코트를 입고 싶어요.

17 cold [kould]
a 추운   having a low temperature
Is it **cold** outside?
밖이 춥나요?

18 early [ə́ːrli]
a 일찍, 이른   before the usual time that an activity happens
I got up **early** today.
나는 오늘 일찍 일어났다.

key words
whole a 전체의 / physical a 육체의 / collection n 수집(물) / sheet n 장(매) / container n 용기 / shut n 닫다 / wet a 젖은 / mass n 덩어리 / float v 떠돌다, 뜨다 / disappear v 사라지다 / fit v 적합하다 / temperature n 기온 / activity n 활동, 행동

Unit 5   27

Exercise

A. Complete the sentence.

1. She _____ the door quietly.
   그녀는 문을 조용히 닫았다.

2. _____ it started to rain.
   다시 비가 오기 시작했다.

3. I _____ get up at 7 o'clock.
   나는 항상 7시에 기상한다.

4. My daughter likes a book of _____ stories.
   내 딸은 천사들의 이야기가 담긴 책을 좋아한다.

5. She has a healthy _____.
   그녀는 건강한 몸을 가지고 있다.

6. He stayed in his room all _____.
   그는 오후 내내 그의 방안에 있었다.

7. Take off those wet _____.
   젖은 옷을 벗으렴.

8. I got up _____ today.
   나는 오늘 일찍 일어났다.

9. The sun disappeared behind a _____.
   해가 구름 뒤로 사라졌다.

10. I can go to the island by _____.
    나는 보트를 타고 섬에 갈 수 있다.

11. A dog is a faithful _____.
    개는 충실한 동물이다.

12. To eat an _____ in the morning is good for health.
    아침에 사과를 먹는 것은 건강에 좋다.

13. I'd like to wear that green _____.
    나는 저 녹색 코트를 입고 싶어요.

14. Children like to ride _____.
    아이들은 자전거 타는 것을 좋아한다.

15. Is it _____ outside?
    밖이 춥나요?

16. Read many good _____.
    좋은 책을 많이 읽어라.

17. Look at the cloudless _____ sky.
    구름 한 점 없는 파란 하늘을 보렴.

18. The _____ is made of glass.
    그 병은 유리로 만들어졌다.

Hint

| coat | body | always | cold | animal | bike | cloud | clothes | book |
| blue | again | boat | afternoon | bottle | close | apple | early | angel |

Exercise

B. Fill in the word and meaning.

	Word	Meaning
01	always	
02	boat	
03	animal	
04	body	
05	close	
06	afternoon	
07	cloud	
08	blue	
09	cold	
10	bike	
11	coat	
12	early	
13	again	
14	book	
15	clothes	
16	apple	
17	bottle	
18	angel	

	Meaning	Word
01	오후	
02	다시	
03	항상, 언제나	
04	천사	
05	동물	
06	사과	
07	자전거	
08	파란색, 파란색의	
09	보트, 배	
10	몸	
11	책	
12	병	
13	닫다	
14	옷, 의복	
15	구름	
16	외투, 코트	
17	추운	
18	일찍, 이른	

C. Listen, write the word and meaning. Track 15

	Word	Meaning		Word	Meaning
01			10		
02			11		
03			12		
04			13		
05			14		
06			15		
07			16		
08			17		
09			18		

Unit 6

🎧 Listen and repeat. Track 16

01 foot [fut]   **n** 발   the parts of your body that are at the ends of your legs
Let's go on **foot** to the bank.
은행까지 걸어가자.

02 free [fri:]   **a** 한가한, 자유로운   not controlled, or limited by rules or other people
There was **free** movement of people.
사람들의 자유로운 이동이 있었다.

03 friend [frend]   **n** 친구, 벗   someone who you know well and like
We are old **friends**.
우리는 오랜 친구들이다.

04 from [frʌm]   **prep** ~로부터   showing the place that something starts
He moved here **from** the east.
그는 동부에서 이사 왔다.

05 fruit [fru:t]   **n** 과일   the part of a tree that contains seeds
Eat more fresh **fruit** and vegetables.
신선한 과일과 채소를 많이 드세요.

06 full [ful]   **a** 배부른, 가득한   holding or contains as much (many) as possible
The bus was **full** of people.
그 버스는 사람들이 가득 타고 있었다.

07 help [help]   **v** 돕다   to make something easier to do
Let me **help** you with those packages.
짐 드는 것을 도와드릴게요.

08 here [hiər]   **ad** 여기에   in the place where the speaker is
If you want to swim, you must come **here** by two.
너는 수영을 하고 싶다면, 여기에 2시까지 와야 한다.

09 high [hai]   **a** 높은   a large distance between the bottom and the top
What's the **highest** mountain in the world?
세계에서 가장 높은 산이 무엇이니?

key words
on foot 걸어서 / controlled **a** 제어할 수 있는 / rule **n** 규칙, 법칙 / movement **n** 이동, 운동
contain **v** 포함하다 / package **n** 짐, 꾸러미 / bottom **n** 바닥

🎧 Listen and repeat. Track 17

10 home [houm]
n 집 / ad 집으로   the place where you live
She is going back **home** next week.
그녀는 다음 주에 집으로 돌아갈 것이다.

11 horse [hɔːrs]
n 말   a large animal that is used for riding on
A man rides on a big **horse**.
한 남자가 큰 말을 타고 있다.

12 jeans [dʒiːnz]
n 청바지   casual trousers that are usually made of blue cotton cloth
He is wearing **jeans**.
그는 청바지를 입고 있다.

13 lesson [lésn]
n 수업, 과   a period of teaching
She gives a **lesson** in music.
그녀는 음악 수업을 한다.

14 let [let]
v ~시키다   to allow something
My parents **let** me clean the car.
부모님께서 나에게 자동차 청소를 시키셨다.

15 lie [lai]
n 거짓말 / v 드러눕다   untrue thing that someone says; not standing or sitting
She can't tell a **lie**.
그녀는 거짓말 할 줄 모른다.

16 light [lait]
n 등불, 빛   the energy to see things from the sun or a lamp
The **light** was too dim to see it.
빛이 너무 흐려서 그것을 볼 수 없었다.

17 like [laik]
v 좋아하다   to find somebody / something pleasant
I **like** to talk with friends.
나는 친구들과 대화하는 것을 좋아한다.

18 lion [láiən]
n 사자   a large animal of the cat family that lives in Africa
The **lion** has a big mouth.
사자는 큰 입을 가지고 있다.

---

key words
ride v 타다 / casual a 평상시의 / trousers n 바지 / period n 수업시간, 기간
allow v ~하게 하다 / untrue a 거짓의 / dim a 희미한, 흐린

Unit 6   31

Exercise

A. Complete the sentence.

1. There was _____ movement of people.
   사람들의 자유로운 이동이 있었다.

2. A man rides on a big _____.
   한 남자가 큰 말을 타고 있다.

3. The bus was _____ of people.
   그 버스는 사람들이 가득 타고 있었다.

4. Let me _____ you with those packages.
   짐 드는 것을 도와드릴게요.

5. Let's go on _____ to the bank.
   은행까지 걸어가자.

6. If you want to swim, you must come _____ by two.
   너는 수영을 하고 싶다면, 여기에 2시까지 와야 한다.

7. He is wearing _____.
   그는 청바지를 입고 있다.

8. She gives a _____ in music.
   그녀는 음악 수업을 한다.

9. We are old _____.
   우리는 오랜 친구들이다.

10. My parents _____ me clean the car.
    부모님께서 나에게 자동차 청소를 시키셨다.

11. She can't tell a _____.
    그녀는 거짓말 할 줄 모른다.

12. He moved here _____ the east.
    그는 동부에서 이사 왔다.

13. The _____ has a big mouth.
    사자는 큰 입을 가지고 있다.

14. Eat more fresh _____ and vegetables.
    신선한 과일과 채소를 많이 드세요.

15. What's the _____ mountain in the world?
    세계에서 가장 높은 산이 무엇이니?

16. She is going back _____ next week.
    그녀는 다음 주에 집으로 돌아갈 것이다.

17. The _____ was too dim to see it.
    빛이 너무 흐려서 그것을 볼 수 없었다.

18. I _____ to talk with friends.
    나는 친구들과 대화하는 것을 좋아한다.

Hint

friend	lion	foot	lie	full	help	here	free	home
from	horse	jeans	let	fruit	lesson	like	high	light

Unit 6

Exercise

B. Fill in the word and meaning.

	Word	Meaning
01	help	
02	friend	
03	jeans	
04	home	
05	fruit	
06	lie	
07	here	
08	lesson	
09	foot	
10	light	
11	high	
12	like	
13	free	
14	lion	
15	let	
16	from	
17	horse	
18	full	

	Meaning	Word
01	발	
02	한가한, 자유로운	
03	친구, 벗	
04	~로부터	
05	과일	
06	배부른, 가득한	
07	돕다	
08	여기에	
09	높은	
10	집, 집으로	
11	말	
12	청바지	
13	수업, 과	
14	~시키다	
15	거짓말, 드러눕다	
16	등불, 빛	
17	좋아하다	
18	사자	

C. Listen, write the word and meaning. Track 18

	Word	Meaning		Word	Meaning
01			10		
02			11		
03			12		
04			13		
05			14		
06			15		
07			16		
08			17		
09			18		

Review 3

A. Read and fill in the word and meaning.

word	definition	meaning
	to indicate something that happens a second time	
	a collection of sheets of paper	
	a fruit with green or red skin and white flesh	
	the day between lunchtime and about 6 o'clock	
	a living creature such as a dog, lion, or rabbit	
	to shut something to cover a hole or opening	
	a whole physical form of a person	
	at all times; regularly	
	a glass or plastic container in which drinks are kept	
	a spiritual being that some people believe	
	the color of the sky on a sunny day	
	having a low temperature	
	before the usual time that an activity happens	
	a small vehicle that is used for going across water	
	a mass that floats in the sky	
	a cycle that has two wheels; moved by foot pedals	
	an outer clothes fitting the upper part of the body	
	the things that you wear	

Hint

angel   again   close   cold   body   bike   bottle   clothes   afternoon
blue   animal   book   boat   cloud   always   early   apple   coat

B. Read and fill in the word and meaning.

word	definition	meaning
	to make something easier to do	
	to allow something	
	untrue thing that someone says; not standing or sitting	
	in the place where the speaker is	
	someone who you know well and like	
	a large animal that is used for riding on	
	a large distance between the bottom and the top	
	not controlled, or limited by rules or other people	
	the energy to see things from the sun or a lamp	
	the place where you live	
	a period of teaching	
	the parts of your body that are at the ends of your legs	
	to find somebody / something pleasant	
	the part of a tree that contains seeds	
	casual trousers that are usually made of blue cotton cloth	
	showing the place that something starts	
	a large animal of the cat family that lives in Africa	
	holding or contains as much (many) as possible	

Hint
light   lion   fruit   full   lie   high   here   free   lesson
jeans   home   from   like   foot   horse   let   help   friend

Unit 7

🎧 Listen and repeat. Track 19

01 mouse [maus] **n** 생쥐   a small furry animal with a long tail
The **mouse** is behind the hat.
생쥐가 모자 뒤에 숨어 있다.

02 mouth [mauθ] **n** 입   the area of your face where your lips are
Open your **mouth**.
입을 벌려라.

03 movie [múːvi] **n** 영화   a moving picture
The **movie** was a blockbuster.
그 영화는 크게 히트 쳤다.

04 much [mʌtʃ] **ad** (양이) 많은   a large amount of something
Did she say **much**?
그녀가 너무 많이 말했니?

05 music [mjúːzik] **n** 음악   pleasing, harmonious or melodic sound
My hobby is listening to **music**.
내 취미는 음악을 듣는 것이다.

06 must [mʌst] **v** ~해야 한다   used to express necessity that something happens
You **must** clean your room today.
너는 오늘 반드시 방 청소를 해야 한다.

07 people [píːpl] **n** 사람들   any group of human beings
Some **people** believe in superstitions.
어떤 사람들은 미신을 믿는다.

08 pepper [pépər] **n** 후추   a hot-tasting spice which is used to flavor food
Will you pass me the **pepper**?
그 후추 좀 건네주시겠습니까?

09 pick [pik] **v** 따다, 꺾다   break flowers or fruit off the plant or tree
She **picked** strawberries.
그녀는 딸기를 땄다.

key words
furry **a** 털로 덮인 / blockbuster **n** 대히트작 / harmonious **a** 가락이 맞는 / melodic **a** 가락이 아름다운
superstition **n** 미신 / spice **n** 양념 / flavor **v** ~에 맛을 내다 / pass **v** 건네다

🎧 Listen and repeat. Track 20

10 play
[pleɪ]
v 연주하다, 놀다   to spend time doing enjoyable things
We **played** all day and were very tired.
우리는 하루 종일 놀아서 완전히 지쳤다.

11 pocket
[pákit]
n 호주머니   a kind of small bag in clothing
You have something in your **pocket**.
주머니 안에 무엇인가 가지고 있구나.

12 point
[pɔint]
n 끝, 점수 / **v** 가리키다   the thin sharp end of something
The **point** of a pencil can hurt you.
연필 끝에 상처 입을 수도 있다.

13 run
[rʌn]
v 달리다   to move more quickly than walking
The dog is **running** around the apartment.
그 개는 아파트 주위를 달리고 있다.

14 sad
[sæd]
a 슬픈   feeling unhappy or sorrowful
He looked **sad** because he failed the test.
그는 시험이 떨어져서 슬퍼 보였다.

15 say
[seɪ]
v 말하다   to speak words
Don't **say** it to her.
그녀에게 말하지 마.

16 school
[skuːl]
n 학교   a place where children are educated
We have no **school** tomorrow.
내일은 학교가 쉰다.

17 sea
[siː]
n 바다   the salty water that covers large parts of the earth
Do you live by the **sea**?
당신은 바닷가에 사나요?

18 see
[siː]
v 보다, 만나다   to notice something using your eyes
I will **see** you later.
나중에 또 보자.

---

key words
spend **v** 소비하다 / tired **a** 피로한 / sharp **a** 날카로운 / hurt **v** 상처 내다 / quickly **ad** 빨리
sorrowful **a** 슬픈 / fail **v** 실패하다 / educate **v** 교육하다 / notice **v** ~을 인지하다

Exercise

A. Complete the sentence.

1. You _____ clean your room today.
   너는 오늘 반드시 방 청소를 해야 한다.

2. We _____ all day and were very tired.
   우리는 하루 종일 놀아서 완전히 지쳤다.

3. Do you live by the _____?
   당신은 바닷가에 사나요?

4. The _____ of a pencil can hurt you.
   연필 끝에 상처 입을 수도 있다.

5. My hobby is listening to _____.
   내 취미는 음악을 듣는 것이다.

6. The dog is _____ around the apartment.
   그 개는 아파트 주위를 달리고 있다.

7. He looked _____ because he failed the test.
   그는 시험이 떨어져서 슬퍼 보였다.

8. Did she say _____?
   그녀가 너무 많이 말했니?

9. Don't _____ it to her.
   그녀에게 말하지 마.

10. Open your _____.
    입을 벌려라.

11. The _____ was a blockbuster.
    그 영화는 크게 히트 쳤다.

12. Some _____ believe in superstitions.
    어떤 사람들은 미신을 믿는다.

13. She _____ strawberries.
    그녀는 딸기를 땄다.

14. We have no _____ tomorrow.
    내일은 학교가 쉰다.

15. You have something in your _____.
    주머니 안에 무엇인가 가지고 있구나.

16. Will you pass me the _____?
    그 후추 좀 건네주시겠습니까?

17. The _____ is behind the hat.
    생쥐가 모자 뒤에 숨어 있다.

18. I will _____ you later.
    나중에 또 보자.

Hint

| mouse | play | pocket | sad | school | run | sea | must | movie |
| see | mouth | pick | much | music | point | people | say | pepper |

Unit 7

Exercise

B. Fill in the word and meaning.

	Word	Meaning
01	people	
02	play	
03	run	
04	movie	
05	pick	
06	school	
07	mouse	
08	pocket	
09	see	
10	music	
11	sea	
12	mouth	
13	point	
14	say	
15	must	
16	sad	
17	pepper	
18	much	

	Meaning	Word
01	생쥐	
02	입	
03	영화	
04	(양이) 많은	
05	음악	
06	~해야 한다	
07	사람들	
08	후추	
09	따다, 꺾다	
10	연주하다, 놀다	
11	호주머니	
12	끝, 점수, 가리키다	
13	달리다	
14	슬픈	
15	말하다	
16	학교	
17	바다	
18	보다, 만나다	

C. Listen, write the word and meaning. (Track 21)

	Word	Meaning		Word	Meaning
01			10		
02			11		
03			12		
04			13		
05			14		
06			15		
07			16		
08			17		
09			18		

Unit 8

🎧 Listen and repeat. Track 22

01 stay [stei]
v 머무르다   to continue to be there and do not leave
I **stayed** at home all day.
나는 하루 종일 집에 머물렀다.

02 stop [stap]
v 멈추다   to no longer do something
He **stopped** talking.
그는 이야기를 멈췄다.

03 story [stɔ́:ri]
n 이야기   a description of imaginary people and events
I'll tell you a funny **story**.
내가 재미있는 이야기 해줄게.

04 strong [strɔ(:)ŋ]
a 힘센, 강한   having great physical power to act
He wants to be a **strong** man.
그는 강한 남자가 되고 싶다.

05 student [stjú:dənt]
n 학생   a person who is studying at a school
I became a middle school **student**.
나는 중학생이 되었다.

06 study [stʌ́di]
v 공부하다   to spend time learning about some subjects
If you **study** hard, you will pass the exam.
열심히 공부한다면 시험에 통과할 것이다.

07 towel [táuəl]
n 타월, 수건   a piece of thick soft cloth to dry yourself
Give me a clean **towel**.
깨끗한 수건 주세요.

08 town [taun]
n 도시   a place where people live and work
I lived in a small **town**.
나는 작은 도시에 살았다.

09 train [trein]
n 기차   a type of transport that is pulled by an engine along a railway line
Hurry up or we'll miss the **train**.
서두르지 않으면 기차를 놓치겠어.

key words
continue v 계속하다 / description n 기술, 묘사 / imaginary a 상상의 / funny a 재미있는
physical a 신체의 / exam n 시험 / transport n 수송기구 / hurry v 서두르다 / miss v 놓치다

🎧 Listen and repeat. Track 23

10	**tree**	**n** 나무	a tall plant that has a hard trunk, branches, and leaves
	[tri:]		There are many **trees** around the park.
			공원 주위에는 나무들이 많이 있다.

11	**try**	**v** 시도하다	to experience something new or different
	[trai]		**Try** one more time.
			한번만 더 시도해 봐.

12	**turn**	**v** 돌리다	to move something to face in a different direction
	[tə:rn]		She **turned** the key in the lock.
			그는 자물쇠의 열쇠를 돌렸다.

13	**window**	**n** 창문	an opening in the wall
	[wíndou]		Please open the **window**.
			창문 좀 열어주세요.

14	**woman**	**n** 여자	an adult female person
	[wúmən]		Would you prefer to see a **woman** doctor?
			여의사에게 진찰 받으시겠어요?

15	**year**	**n** 해, 년	the period from 1 January to 31 December
	[jiə:r]		She worked here for twenty **years**.
			그녀는 여기서 20년을 일했다.

16	**yellow**	**n** 노란색 / **a** 노란색의	the color of lemons or butter
	[jélou]		She wears a light **yellow** dress.
			그녀는 밝은 노란색의 드레스를 입고 있다.

17	**young**	**a** 짊은, 어린	in the first part of life and growth; not old
	[jʌŋ]		You are **young** and smart.
			너는 젊고 똑똑해.

18	**zebra**	**n** 얼룩말	an African wild horse which has black and white stripes
	[zí:brə]		A **zebra** has black and white lines on its body.
			얼룩말은 몸에 까맣고 하얀 줄무늬가 있다.

key words

trunk **n** 줄기 / branch **n** 가지 / experience **v** 경험하다 / lock **n** 자물쇠 / adult **n** 성인
female **a** 여성의 / period **n** 기간 / growth **n** 성장 / stripe **n** 줄무늬

Exercise

A. Complete the sentence.

1. If you _____ hard, you will pass the **exam**.
   열심히 공부한다면 시험에 통과할 것이다.

2. There are many _____ around the park.
   공원 주위에는 나무들이 많이 있다.

3. He wants to be a _____ man.
   그는 강한 남자가 되고 싶다.

4. She _____ the key in the lock.
   그는 자물쇠의 열쇠를 돌렸다.

5. He _____ talking.
   그는 이야기를 멈췄다.

6. She wears a light _____ dress.
   그녀는 밝은 노란색의 드레스를 입고 있다.

7. I became a middle school _____.
   나는 중학생이 되었다.

8. _____ one more time.
   한번만 더 시도해 봐.

9. You are _____ and smart.
   너는 젊고 똑똑해.

10. A _____ has black and white lines on its body.
    얼룩말은 몸에 까맣고 하얀 줄무늬가 있다.

11. I _____ at home all day.
    나는 하루 종일 집에 머물렀다.

12. I'll tell you a funny _____.
    내가 재미있는 이야기 해줄게.

13. Would you prefer to see a _____ doctor?
    여의사에게 진찰 받으시겠어요?

14. I lived in a small _____.
    나는 작은 도시에 살았다.

15. Please open the _____.
    창문 좀 열어주세요.

16. Hurry up or we'll miss the _____.
    서두르지 않으면 기차를 놓치겠어.

17. Give me a clean _____.
    깨끗한 수건 주세요.

18. She worked here for twenty _____.
    그녀는 여기서 20년을 일했다.

Hint

| town | student | tree | try | woman | young | study | stop | towel |
| story | window | train | zebra | yellow | stay | turn | strong | year |

Exercise

B. Fill in the word and meaning.

	Word	Meaning
01	story	
02	train	
03	window	
04	young	
05	stay	
06	tree	
07	study	
08	yellow	
09	stop	
10	woman	
11	town	
12	year	
13	towel	
14	zebra	
15	turn	
16	student	
17	try	
18	strong	

	Meaning	Word
01	머무르다	
02	멈추다	
03	이야기	
04	힘센, 강한	
05	학생	
06	공부하다	
07	타월, 수건	
08	도시	
09	기차	
10	나무	
11	시도하다	
12	돌리다	
13	창문	
14	여자	
15	해, 년	
16	노란색, 노란색의	
17	젊은, 어린	
18	얼룩말	

C. Listen, write the word and meaning. (Track 24)

	Word	Meaning		Word	Meaning
01			10		
02			11		
03			12		
04			13		
05			14		
06			15		
07			16		
08			17		
09			18		

Review 4

A. Read and fill in the word and meaning.

word	definition	meaning
	a large amount of something	
	a moving picture	
	a small furry animal with a long tail	
	any group of human beings	
	a hot-tasting spice which is used to flavor food	
	the area of your face where your lips are	
	to move more quickly than walking	
	used to express necessity that something happens	
	to notice something using your eyes	
	feeling unhappy or sorrowful	
	pleasing, harmonious or melodic sound	
	a kind of small bag in clothing	
	to speak words	
	to spend time doing enjoyable things	
	the salty water that covers large parts of the earth	
	break flowers or fruit off the plant or tree	
	a place where children are educated	
	the thin sharp end of something	

Hint

movie   people   music   sad   mouth   much   sea   pick   mouse
say   school   must   run   pocket   point   play   see   pepper

B. Read and fill in the word and meaning.

word	definition	meaning
	an opening in the wall	
	to continue to be there and do not leave	
	having great physical power to act	
	an adult female person	
	to move something to face in a different direction	
	to no longer do something	
	the period from 1 January to 31 December	
	a description of imaginary people and events	
	the color of lemons or butter	
	a piece of thick soft cloth to dry yourself	
	to experience something new or different	
	a place where people live and work	
	a person who is studying at a school	
	a tall plant that has a hard trunk, branches, and leaves	
	in the first part of life and growth; not old	
	to spend time learning about some subjects	
	a type of transport that is pulled by an engine along a railway line	
	an African wild horse which has black and white stripes	

Hint

| year | town | tree | story | woman | stop | try | young | window |
| study | towel | stay | zebra | yellow | train | turn | strong | student |

Unit 9

🎧 Listen and repeat. Track 25

01 **arm** — n 팔 — one of the two long parts of body attached to shoulders
[ɑːrm]
I hurt my **arms**.
나는 양팔을 다쳤다.

02 **around** — ad ~의 주위에, ~의 둘레를 — in or to various places or directions
[əráund]
They sat **around** a table.
그들은 테이블 주위에 앉았다.

03 **arrive** — v 도착하다 — to reach the place
[əráiv]
I **arrived** here 3 days ago.
나는 여기에 3일전에 도착했다.

04 **aunt** — n 숙모 — the sister of your father or mother
[ænt]
Her **aunt** is an announcer.
그녀의 숙모는 아나운서다.

05 **back** — ad 뒤로 / n 등 — behind you; the opposite side to the chest
[bæk]
I have a problem in my **back**.
등에 문제가 있어요.

06 **backwards** — ad 뒤로, 거꾸로 — in the direction that your back is facing
[bǽkwərdz]
I walked **backwards**.
나는 뒷걸음질 쳤다.

07 **bowl** — n 사발, 공기 — a deep round dish without a lid
[boul]
The **bowl** is full of peanuts.
그릇에 땅콩이 가득해요.

08 **boy** — n 소년, 남자아이 — a male child or young man
[bɔi]
A **boy** was dancing.
한 소년이 춤을 추고 있었다.

09 **bread** — n 빵 — a type of food made from flour, water, and yeast
[bred]
Would you like jam on your **bread**?
빵에 잼을 발라 드릴까요?

---

key words
attached **a** 붙어 있는 / various **a** 여러 방면의 / opposite **a** 정반대의 / chest **n** 가슴
deep **a** 깊은 / without **prep** ~없이 / lid **n** 뚜껑 / male **a** 남자의 / flour **n** 밀가루

🎧 Listen and repeat. Track 26

10 break
[breik]
v 깨다   to be damaged and separated into two or more parts
This dish **breaks** easily.
이 접시는 깨지기 쉽다.

11 breakfast
[brékfəst]
n 아침 식사   the first meal of the day
I had a good **breakfast**.
나는 아침을 맛있게 먹었어요.

12 bring
[briŋ]
v 가져오다, 데려오다   to come to a place with somebody or something
Bring me the alarm clock.
그 자명종 시계를 가져다 주세요.

13 can
[kæn]
v ~할 수 있다   to have an ability to do something
Can you speak English?
당신은 영어로 말할 수 있습니까?

14 day
[dei]
n 날, 하루   a period of 24 hours
It's a cold and windy **day**.
오늘은 춥고 바람이 부는 날이다.

15 desk
[desk]
n 책상   a piece of furniture like a table
The **desk** is full of books.
그 책상은 책으로 가득하다.

16 dinner
[dínər]
n 저녁 식사, 정찬   the main meal of the day
Let's go out for **dinner** tonight.
오늘 저녁은 외식해요.

17 dirty
[də́:rti]
a 더러운   to need to be clean; not clean
There is a **dirty** doll.
더러운 인형이 있어요.

18 everybody
[évribàdi]
pron 모두   all people; every person
Everybody likes to receive mail.
모두 편지 받는 것을 좋아합니다.

key words
damage v 손해를 입히다 / separate v 분리하다 / alarm n 자명종 / ability n 능력
furniture n 가구 / main a 주요한 / receive v 받다 / mail n 우편물

Unit 9 47

Exercise

A. Complete the sentence.

1. I hurt my _____.
   나는 양팔을 다쳤다.

2. The _____ is full of peanuts.
   그릇에 땅콩이 가득해요.

3. I _____ here 3 days ago.
   나는 여기에 3일전에 도착했다.

4. A _____ was dancing.
   한 소년이 춤을 추고 있었다.

5. They sat _____ a table.
   그들은 테이블 주위에 앉았다.

6. Would you like jam on your _____?
   빵에 잼을 발라 드릴까요?

7. _____ you speak English?
   당신은 영어로 말할 수 있습니까?

8. Let's go out for _____ tonight.
   오늘 저녁은 외식해요.

9. Her _____ is an announcer.
   그녀의 숙모는 아나운서다.

10. There is a _____ doll.
    더러운 인형이 있어요.

11. I have a problem in my _____.
    등에 문제가 있어요.

12. This dish _____ easily.
    이 접시는 깨지기 쉽다.

13. _____ likes to receive mail.
    모두 편지 받는 것을 좋아합니다.

14. I had a good _____.
    나는 아침을 맛있게 먹었어요.

15. It's a cold and windy _____.
    오늘은 춥고 바람이 부는 날이다.

16. I walked _____.
    나는 뒷걸음질 쳤다.

17. _____ me the alarm clock.
    그 자명종 시계를 가져다 주세요.

18. The _____ is full of books.
    그 책상은 책으로 가득하다.

Hint

| everybody | arm | desk | bowl | dirty | bread | can | dinner | around |
| breakfast | aunt | backwards | break | boy | arrive | bring | day | back |

Exercise

B. Fill in the word and meaning.

	Word	Meaning
01	aunt	
02	back	
03	bring	
04	can	
05	arrive	
06	break	
07	day	
08	arm	
09	bread	
10	dirty	
11	boy	
12	everybody	
13	dinner	
14	bowl	
15	around	
16	breakfast	
17	desk	
18	backwards	

	Meaning	Word
01	팔	
02	~의 주위에, ~의 둘레를	
03	도착하다	
04	숙모	
05	뒤로, 등	
06	뒤로, 거꾸로	
07	사발, 공기	
08	소년, 남자아이	
09	빵	
10	깨다	
11	아침 식사	
12	가져오다, 데려오다	
13	~할 수 있다	
14	날, 하루	
15	책상	
16	저녁 식사, 정찬	
17	더러운	
18	모두	

🎧 **C. Listen, write the word and meaning.** (Track 27)

	Word	Meaning		Word	Meaning
01			10		
02			11		
03			12		
04			13		
05			14		
06			15		
07			16		
08			17		
09			18		

Unit 10

🎧 Listen and repeat. Track 28

01	**fine**	a 좋은, 훌륭한	very good; high quality
	[fain]		The end of the movie was **fine**. 영화의 결말은 훌륭했다.

02	**finger**	n 손가락	one of the five long thin parts at the end of each hand
	[fíŋgər]		My little **finger** hurts. 내 새끼손가락이 아프다.

03	**finish**	v 끝내다	to stop doing something
	[fíniʃ]		I **finished** the homework. 나는 숙제를 끝냈다.

04	**flower**	n 꽃	the part of a plant which is often brightly colored
	[fláuər]		She is making paper **flowers**. 그녀는 종이 꽃을 만들고 있어요.

05	**fly**	v 날다 / n 파리	to move through the air; a small insect with two wings
	[flai]		How can they **fly** to the moon? 그들은 어떻게 달까지 날아갈 수 있을까요?

06	**food**	n 식량, 식품	what people and animals eat
	[fu:d]		Korean **food** is superior to American. 한국 음식이 미국 음식보다 뛰어나다.

07	**hard**	a 어려운	difficult to do, understand or answer
	[ha:rd]		It is a **hard** question to answer. 그것은 대답하기 어려운 질문이네요.

08	**hate**	v 몹시 싫어하다	to dislike something very much
	[heit]		I **hate** snakes. 나는 뱀을 싫어한다.

09	**have**	v 가지고 있다	to own or to hold something; to possess
	[hæv]		I **have** no money. 나는 돈이 한 푼도 없다.

key words
quality n 질, 품질 / thin a 가는 / end n 끝 / brightly ad 밝게 / insect n 곤충, 벌레
superior a 뛰어난 / answer v 대답하다 / dislike v 싫어하다 / particular a 각자의

🎧 Listen and repeat. Track 29

10	**head**	**n** 머리	the top part of your body
	[hed]		He hit my **head**. 그가 나의 머리를 때렸다.

11	**into**	**prep** ~안으로	moving to a position in or inside something
	[íntu]		A boy and his mom came **into** the shop. 한 소년이 엄마와 가게 안으로 들어왔다.

12	**jacket**	**n** 재킷, 윗옷	a short coat with long sleeves
	[dʒǽkit]		Put on your life **jacket**. 구명 재킷을 입으세요.

13	**lamp**	**n** 램프	a light that works by using electricity
	[læmp]		There is a **lamp** on the desk. 책상 위에 전등이 있어요.

14	**late**	**a** 늦은 / **ad** 늦게	near the end of a period of time
	[leit]		I get up **late** every morning. 난 매일 아침 늦게 일어난다.

15	**laugh**	**v** 웃다	to make a sound with your throat while smiling
	[læf]		We **laughed** together. 우리는 함께 웃었다.

16	**learn**	**v** 배우다	to obtain knowledge or a skill through studying or training
	[ləːrn]		You have to **learn** good table manners. 너는 올바른 식탁 예법을 배워야 한다.

17	**left**	**n** 왼쪽	on the side where your heart is in the body
	[left]		Move it to the **left**. 그걸 왼쪽으로 움직이세요.

18	**leg**	**n** 다리	one of the parts of body that connect the feet
	[leg]		I have no feeling in my **legs**. 나는 다리에 감각이 없다.

key words

sleeve **n** 소매 / life jacket **n** 구명 재킷 / electricity **n** 전기 / knowledge **n** 지식 / manner **n** 예의, 풍습

Unit 10 51

Exercise

A. Complete the sentence.

1. How can they _____ to the moon?
   그들은 어떻게 달까지 날아갈 수 있을까요?

2. I _____ no money.
   나는 돈이 한 푼도 없다.

3. I have no feeling in my _____.
   나는 다리에 감각이 없다.

4. She is making paper _____.
   그녀는 종이 꽃을 만들고 있어요.

5. He hit my _____.
   그가 나의 머리를 때렸다.

6. Put on your life _____.
   구명 재킷을 입으세요.

7. Korean _____ is superior to American.
   한국 음식이 미국 음식보다 뛰어나다.

8. Move it to the _____.
   그걸 왼쪽으로 움직이세요.

9. The end of the movie was _____.
   영화의 결말은 훌륭했다.

10. You have to _____ good table manners.
    너는 올바른 식탁 예법을 배워야 한다.

11. My little _____ hurts.
    내 새끼손가락이 아프다.

12. It is a _____ question to answer.
    그것은 대답하기 어려운 질문이네요.

13. We _____ together.
    우리는 함께 웃었다.

14. I _____ snakes.
    나는 뱀을 싫어한다.

15. A boy and his mom came _____ the shop.
    한 소년이 엄마와 가게 안으로 들어왔다.

16. There is a _____ on the desk.
    책상 위에 전등이 있어요.

17. I _____ the homework.
    나는 숙제를 끝냈다.

18. I get up _____ every morning.
    난 매일 아침 늦게 일어난다.

Hint

| flower | food | have | fly | head | left | jacket | fine | hate |
| finish | late | hard | into | lamp | finger | laugh | leg | learn |

Unit 10

Exercise

B. Fill in the word and meaning.

	Word	Meaning
01	finish	
02	hard	
03	food	
04	head	
05	fine	
06	learn	
07	have	
08	leg	
09	finger	
10	lamp	
11	left	
12	laugh	
13	jacket	
14	late	
15	flower	
16	into	
17	hate	
18	fly	

	Meaning	Word
01	좋은, 훌륭한	
02	손가락	
03	끝내다	
04	꽃	
05	날다, 파리	
06	식량, 식품	
07	어려운	
08	몹시 싫어하다	
09	가지고 있다	
10	머리	
11	~안으로	
12	재킷, 윗옷	
13	램프	
14	늦은, 늦게	
15	웃다	
16	배우다	
17	왼쪽	
18	다리	

C. Listen, write the word and meaning. Track 30

	Word	Meaning
01		
02		
03		
04		
05		
06		
07		
08		
09		

	Word	Meaning
10		
11		
12		
13		
14		
15		
16		
17		
18		

Review 5

A. Read and fill in the word and meaning.

word	definition	meaning
	to have an ability to do something	
	one of the two long parts of body attached to shoulders	
	a period of 24 hours	
	the main meal of the day	
	to reach the place	
	in or to various places or directions	
	a piece of furniture like a table	
	behind you; the opposite side to the chest	
	to need to be clean; not clean	
	all people; every person	
	the sister of your father or mother	
	a male child or young man	
	a type of food made from flour, water, and yeast	
	the first meal of the day	
	in the direction that your back is facinig	
	to come to a place with somebody or something	
	a deep round dish without a lid	
	to be damaged and separated into two or more parts	

Hint
everybody arm desk bowl aunt bread can dinner backwards
breakfast dirty around day boy arrive bring break back

B. Read and fill in the word and meaning.

word	definition	meaning
	moving to a position in or inside something	
	one of the parts of body that connect the feet	
	near the end of a period of time	
	to stop doing something	
	a short coat with long sleeves	
	very good; high quality	
	to make a sound with your throat while smiling	
	a light that works by using electricity	
	the part of a plant which is often brightly colored	
	one of the five long thin parts at the end of each hand	
	to dislike something very much	
	what people and animals eat	
	to obtain knowledge or a skill through studying or training	
	difficult to do, understand or answer	
	to move through the air; a small insect with two wings	
	the top part of your body	
	on the side where your heart is in the body	
	to own or to hold something; to possess	

Hint

hate   fly   fine   food   into   hard   flower   have   jacket
finish   leg   left   head   lamp   finger   laugh   late   learn

Review 5

Unit 11

🎧 Listen and repeat. Track 31

01 **miss**   v 놓치다   to fail to catch or reach something
[mis]
She tried to catch the ball but she **missed**.
그녀는 공을 잡으려고 했지만 놓쳤다.

02 **money**   n 돈   the coins or bank notes to use to buy things
[mʌ́ni]
I have some **money**.
나에게 돈이 조금 있습니다.

03 **monkey**   n 원숭이   an animal with a long tail which climbs trees
[mʌ́ŋki]
A **monkey** has a long tail.
원숭이는 꼬리가 길다.

04 **month**   n 달   one of the twelve periods of time into which the year is divided
[mʌnθ]
November is the eleventh **month** of the year.
11월은 1년 중 11번째 달이다.

05 **morning**   n 아침, 오전   the early part of the day
[mɔ́ːrniŋ]
I saw her this **morning**.
나는 그녀를 오늘 아침에 봤어.

06 **mother**   n 어머니   a female parent of a child
[mʌ́ðəːr]
How old is your **mother**?
당신 어머니 연세가 어떻게 되세요?

07 **pants**   n 바지   a piece of clothing that covers each legs
[pænts]
Show me the black **pants**.
검정색 바지를 보여주세요.

08 **paper**   n 종이   the thin material that you write and draw on
[péipər]
I recycle **paper**.
나는 종이를 재활용합니다.

09 **park**   n 공원   a public land in a city where people go to walk
[paːrk]
Seoul has many beautiful **parks**.
서울에는 아름다운 공원이 많습니다.

---

key words
reach v 도달하다 / tail n 꼬리 / climb v (산을) 오르다 / material n 제재, 재료
write v 쓰다 / recycle v 재활용하다 / public a 공공의

🎧 Listen and repeat. Track 32

10	**pay** [pei]	**v** 지불하다	to give somebody money for work or services
			He will **pay** for this.
			이것은 그가 돈을 지불 할 것이다.

11	**pear** [pɛər]	**n** 배	a yellow fruit that is narrow at the top
			I like apples better than **pears**.
			나는 배보다 사과가 좋다.

12	**pencil** [pénsəl]	**n** 연필	an object that you write or draw with
			I like to draw with a **pencil**.
			나는 연필로 그림 그리는 걸 좋아한다.

13	**river** [rívə:r]	**n** 강	a large amount of liquid that goes into the sea
			This **river** is very deep.
			이 강은 굉장히 깊습니다.

14	**sell** [sel]	**v** 팔다	to give something to somebody in exchange for money
			The store **sells** vegetables.
			그 상점에서는 채소를 판다.

15	**send** [send]	**v** 보내다	to make something go or be taken to some place
			She is **sending** a letter.
			그녀는 편지를 보내고 있다.

16	**set** [set]	**v** 놓다, 넣다	to put something in a particular place
			He **set** a glass on the table.
			그가 유리잔을 테이블 위에 놓았다.

17	**sheep** [ʃi:p]	**n** 양	a farm animal covered with thick curly hair called wool
			He stays with the **sheep**.
			그는 양들과 지냅니다.

18	**ship** [ʃip]	**n** (큰)배	a large boat that carries people by sea
			We traveled by **ship**.
			우리는 배로 여행했습니다.

key words
narrow a 좁은 / than conj ~보다 / liquid n 액체 / exchange n 교환 / thick a 두꺼운
curly a 꼬불꼬불한 / carry v 운반하다 / travel v 여행하다

Unit 11

Exercise

A. Complete the sentence.

1. I saw her this _____.
   나는 그녀를 오늘 아침에 봤어.

2. I like apples better than _____.
   나는 배보다 사과가 좋다.

3. November is the eleventh _____ of the year.
   11월은 1년 중 11번째 달이다.

4. I like to draw with a _____.
   나는 연필로 그림 그리는 걸 좋아한다.

5. She is _____ a letter.
   그녀는 편지를 보내고 있다.

6. How old is your _____?
   당신 어머니 연세가 어떻게 되세요?

7. He _____ a glass on the table.
   그가 유리잔을 테이블 위에 놓았다.

8. She tried to catch the ball but she _____.
   그녀는 공을 잡으려고 했지만 놓쳤다.

9. We traveled by _____.
   우리는 배로 여행했습니다.

10. A _____ has a long tail.
    원숭이는 꼬리가 길다.

11. He will _____ for this.
    이것은 그가 돈을 지불 할 것이다.

12. Show me the black _____.
    검정색 바지를 보여주세요.

13. I recycle _____.
    나는 종이를 재활용합니다.

14. Seoul has many beautiful _____.
    서울에는 아름다운 공원이 많습니다.

15. This _____ is very deep.
    이 강은 굉장히 깊습니다.

16. The store _____ vegetables.
    그 상점에서는 채소를 판다.

17. I have some _____.
    나에게 돈이 조금 있습니다.

18. He stays with the _____.
    그는 양들과 지냅니다.

Hint

| miss | monkey | pay | set | morning | sell | mother | pants | river |
| money | park | month | pencil | send | pear | sheep | paper | ship |

Unit 11

Exercise

B. Fill in the word and meaning.

	Word	Meaning
01	monkey	
02	pants	
03	sell	
04	miss	
05	pencil	
06	mother	
07	pear	
08	send	
09	money	
10	sheep	
11	paper	
12	ship	
13	set	
14	park	
15	month	
16	river	
17	pay	
18	morning	

	Meaning	Word
01	놓치다	
02	돈	
03	원숭이	
04	달	
05	아침, 오전	
06	어머니	
07	바지	
08	종이	
09	공원	
10	지불하다	
11	배	
12	연필	
13	강	
14	팔다	
15	보내다	
16	놓다, 넣다	
17	양	
18	(큰)배	

🎧 **C. Listen, write the word and meaning.** Track 33

	Word	Meaning		Word	Meaning
01			10		
02			11		
03			12		
04			13		
05			14		
06			15		
07			16		
08			17		
09			18		

Unit 12

🎧 Listen and repeat. Track 34

01 sorry [sári] — **a** 미안한 — a way of apologizing to someone for something
I'm **sorry** that I broke the dish.
접시를 깨뜨려서 죄송합니다.

02 speak [spi:k] — **v** 말하다 — to have a conversation with somebody
She **speaks** very loudly.
그녀는 굉장히 큰 목소리로 말합니다.

03 spoon [spu:n] — **n** 숟가락 — a tool used for eating
Use your **spoon**, please.
숟가락을 사용하세요.

04 stand [stænd] — **v** 서다, 서 있다 — to be on someone's feet; to be upright
He was too weak to **stand**.
그는 몸이 너무 약해서 서 있을 수가 없었다.

05 star [sta:r] — **n** 별 — a large ball of burning gas in space
That **star** is really huge.
저 별은 정말 거대하다.

06 start [sta:rt] — **v** 시작하다 — to begin doing something
The vacation **starts** soon.
방학이 곧 시작될 것이다.

07 toe [tou] — **n** 발가락 — one of the five movable parts at the end of each foot
Did I step on your **toe**?
제가 당신 발가락을 밟았습니까?

08 together [təgéðəːr] — **ad** 함께 — with each other
We solved the puzzle **together**.
우리는 같이 퍼즐을 풀었습니다.

09 toilet [tɔ́ilit] — **n** 화장실 — where you get rid of waste matter from your body
Where can I find the **toilet**?
화장실이 어디 있습니까?

key words
apologize v 사과하다 / conversation n 대화 / loudly ad 큰소리로 / upright a 똑바로 선 / weak a 약한
burning a 불타는 / huge a 거대한 / movable a 움직일 수 있는 / rid v 제거하다 / waste a 폐물의, 내버려진

🎧 Listen and repeat. (Track 35)

10 tonight
[tənáit]
n 오늘 밤 / **ad** 오늘 밤에   the evening or night of today
I will go to bed early **tonight**.
오늘 밤에는 일찍 잘 것이다.

11 too
[tuː]
ad 너무   to say that something is more than is necessary
He is **too** young.
그는 너무 어리다.

12 tooth
[tuːθ]
n 이   one of the hard white objects in your mouth
The dentist pulled my **tooth**.
치과의사가 내 이빨을 뽑았다.

13 what
[hwat]
pron 무엇, 무슨   to ask for information about somebody or something
What are you doing here?
당신 여기서 뭐하십니까?

14 where
[hwɛəːr]
ad 어디에, 어디로   to ask questions about the place something is in
Where are my sneakers?
내 운동화는 어디 있습니까?

15 white
[hwait]
n 흰색 / **a** 흰색의   having the color of fresh snow
His hair is **white**.
그의 머리는 하얗습니다.

16 who
[huː]
pron 누구, 누가   to ask about the name or identity of people
Who is the most famous pianist?
가장 유명한 피아니스트는 누구니?

17 wide
[waid]
a 넓은   measuring a lot from one side to the other
It is a **wide** bed.
그것은 넓은 침대다.

18 wind
[wind]
n 바람   air that moves quickly as a result of natural forces
The **wind** is cold.
바람이 차다.

key words
necessary **a** 필요한 / dentist **n** 치과의사 / information **n** 정보 / sneaker **n** 운동화
identity **n** 신원, 동일함 / result **n** 결과 / natural **a** 자연의 / force **n** 힘

Exercise

A. Complete the sentence.

1. He was too weak to _____.
   그는 몸이 너무 약해서 서 있을 수가 없었다.

2. The vacation _____ soon.
   방학이 곧 시작될 것이다.

3. It is a _____ bed.
   그것은 넓은 침대다.

4. He is _____ young.
   그는 너무 어리다.

5. That _____ is really huge.
   저 별은 정말 거대하다.

6. The dentist pulled my _____.
   치과의사가 내 이빨을 뽑았다.

7. _____ is the most famous pianist?
   가장 유명한 피아니스트는 누구니?

8. The _____ is cold.
   바람이 차다.

9. I'm _____ that I broke the dish.
   접시를 깨뜨려서 죄송합니다.

10. I will go to bed early _____.
    오늘 밤에는 일찍 잘 것이다.

11. His hair is _____.
    그의 머리는 하얗습니다.

12. She _____ very loudly.
    그녀는 굉장히 큰 목소리로 말합니다.

13. _____ are you doing here?
    당신 여기서 뭐하십니까?

14. Use your _____, please.
    숟가락을 사용하세요.

15. We solved the puzzle _____.
    우리는 같이 퍼즐을 풀었습니다.

16. Where can I find the _____?
    화장실이 어디 있습니까?

17. _____ are my sneakers?
    내 운동화는 어디 있습니까?

18. Did I step on your _____?
    제가 당신 발을 밟았습니까?

Hint

| who | white | sorry | star | where | toe | together | too | spoon |
| tonight | wide | toilet | start | tooth | what | wind | stand | speak |

Unit 12

Exercise

B. Fill in the word and meaning.

	Word	Meaning
01	spoon	
02	tonight	
03	toe	
04	what	
05	sorry	
06	where	
07	too	
08	speak	
09	wide	
10	wind	
11	together	
12	who	
13	star	
14	toilet	
15	white	
16	start	
17	tooth	
18	stand	

	Meaning	Word
01	미안한	
02	말하다	
03	숟가락	
04	서다, 서 있다	
05	별	
06	시작하다	
07	발가락	
08	함께	
09	화장실	
10	오늘 밤, 오늘 밤에	
11	너무	
12	이	
13	무엇, 무슨	
14	어디에, 어디로	
15	흰색, 흰색의	
16	누구, 누가	
17	넓은	
18	바람	

C. Listen, write the word and meaning. (Track 36)

	Word	Meaning		Word	Meaning
01			10		
02			11		
03			12		
04			13		
05			14		
06			15		
07			16		
08			17		
09			18		

Review 6

A. Read and fill in the word and meaning.

word	definition	meaning
	the thin material that you write and draw on	
	the coins or bank notes to use to buy things	
	a female parent of a child	
	to fail to catch or reach something	
	an object that you write or draw with	
	one of the twelve periods of time into which the year is divided	
	a public land in a city where people go to walk	
	a piece of clothing that covers each legs	
	an animal with a long tail which climbs trees	
	a large boat that carries people by sea	
	the early part of the day	
	to make something go or be taken to some place	
	a yellow fruit that is narrow at the top	
	to give something to somebody in exchange for money	
	a farm animal covered with thick curly hair called wool	
	to give somebody money for work or services	
	to put something in a particular place	
	a large amount of liquid that goes into the sea	

Hint

miss   ship   mother   money   river   pay   pants   sell   morning
set   park   month   pencil   send   pear   sheep   paper   monkey

B. Read and fill in the word and meaning.

word	definition	meaning
	to have a conversation with somebody	
	to ask for information about somebody or something	
	having the color of fresh snow	
	a way of apologizing to someone for something	
	to ask questions about the place something is in	
	one of the hard white objects in your mouth	
	a tool used for eating	
	to begin doing something	
	to ask about the name or identity of people	
	to be on someone's feet; to be upright	
	air that moves quickly as a result of natural forces	
	a large ball of burning gas in space	
	measuring a lot from one side to the other	
	with each other	
	the evening or night of today	
	where you get rid of waste matter from your body	
	one of the five movable parts at the end of each foot	
	to say that something is more than is necessary	

Hint

| white | who | wide | star | where | toe | speak | start | together |
| spoon | sorry | toilet | what | tooth | too | wind | stand | tonight |

Review 6 65

Unit 13

🎧 Listen and repeat. Track 37

01 bad
[bæd]
a 나쁜   unpleasant; full of problems
It's **bad** behavior.
그건 나쁜 행동입니다.

02 ball
[bɔːl]
n 공   a round object used in games such as soccer and baseball
The man is kicking a **ball**.
남자가 공을 차고 있습니다.

03 balloon
[bəlúːn]
n 풍선   a rubber that becomes larger when you fill it with air
The children are running with the **balloons**.
아이들이 풍선을 들고 뛰고 있어요.

04 bank
[bæŋk]
n 은행   an institution where people can keep their money
We always keep money in the **bank**.
우리는 언제나 은행에 돈을 맡깁니다.

05 basket
[bǽskit]
n 바구니   a container for holding or carrying things
The **basket** is full of apples.
바구니에 사과가 가득합니다.

06 bean
[biːn]
n 콩   the seeds of a climbing plant
I like to eat **beans**.
나는 콩 먹는 것을 좋아합니다.

07 brother
[brʌ́ðər]
n 형제   a man who has the same mother and father
My **brother** broke a window yesterday.
내 형제가 어제 창문을 깨뜨렸습니다.

08 brown
[braun]
n 갈색 / **a** 갈색의   the color of earth
Brown is my favorite color.
내가 제일 좋아하는 색은 갈색입니다.

09 brush
[brʌʃ]
v 닦다 / **n** 빗, 솔   an object made of short stiff hairs
The door should be cleaned with a **brush**.
그 문은 솔을 가지고 닦아야 할 것이다.

---

key words
behavior **n** 행동 / kick **v** 차다 / rubber **n** 고무제품 / fill **v** 채우다 / institution **n** 시설, 기구 / favorite **a** 좋아하는 / stiff **a** 뻣뻣한

🎧 Listen and repeat. Track 38

10	**buy**	**v** 사다, 얻다 to obtain something by paying money for it
	[bai]	I will **buy** the blue raincoat. 나는 파란색 비옷을 살 것입니다.

11	**call**	**v** 전화를 걸다 / **n** 통화 to telephone somebody
	[kɔːl]	She **called** a computer repair shop. 그녀는 컴퓨터 수리점에 전화를 했다.

12	**cousin**	**n** 사촌 a child of your aunt or uncle
	[kʌzn]	That boy is my **cousin**. 저 소년은 내 사촌입니다.

13	**cry**	**v** 울다 to produce tears from eyes
	[krai]	It is no use **crying** over spilt milk. 엎질러진 우유를 두고 울어 봤자 소용없다.

14	**cut**	**v** 자르다, 베다 to divide something into pieces with a knife
	[kʌt]	He **cuts** a piece of paper. 그가 종이를 자릅니다.

15	**cute**	**a** 귀여운 very pretty or attractive
	[kjuːt]	This chick is **cute**. 이 병아리는 귀여워요.

16	**dance**	**v** 춤추다 to move body and feet following a rhythm
	[dæns]	He likes to **dance**. 그는 춤추는 걸 좋아합니다.

17	**dark**	**a** 어두운 / **n** 어둠 with no or very little light
	[daːrk]	It was a **dark** night with no moon. 달이 뜨지 않은 어두운 밤이었다.

18	**do**	**v** 하다 to take some action or perform an activity
	[duː]	What do you want to **do**? 너는 무엇을 하고 싶니?

key words

raincoat **n** 우비 / spill **v** 엎지르다 / divide **v** 쪼개다 / chick **n** 병아리 / rhythm **n** 리듬 / perform **v** 실행하다

Exercise

A. Complete the sentence.

1. It's _____ behavior.
   그건 나쁜 행동입니다.

2. The children are running with the _____.
   아이들이 풍선을 들고 뛰고 있어요.

3. My _____ broke a window yesterday.
   내 형제가 어제 창문을 깨뜨렸습니다.

4. _____ is my favorite color.
   내가 제일 좋아하는 색은 갈색입니다.

5. The man is kicking a _____.
   남자가 공을 차고 있습니다.

6. The door should be cleaned with a _____.
   그 문은 솔을 가지고 닦아야 할 것이다.

7. He likes to _____.
   그는 춤추는 걸 좋아합니다.

8. It was a _____ night with no moon.
   달이 뜨지 않은 어두운 밤이었다.

9. We always keep money in the _____.
   우리는 언제나 은행에 돈을 맡깁니다.

10. What do you want to _____?
    너는 무엇을 하고 싶니?

11. The _____ is full of apples.
    바구니에 사과가 가득합니다.

12. This chick is _____.
    이 병아리는 귀여워요.

13. I like to eat _____.
    나는 콩 먹는 것을 좋아합니다.

14. He _____ a piece of paper.
    그가 종이를 자릅니다.

15. I will _____ the blue raincoat.
    나는 파란색 비옷을 살 것입니다.

16. She _____ a computer repair shop.
    그녀는 컴퓨터 수리점에 전화를 했다.

17. That boy is my _____.
    저 소년은 내 사촌입니다.

18. It is no use _____ over spilt milk.
    엎질러진 우유를 두고 울어 봤자 소용없다.

Hint

| ball | bank | dance | bean | cute | do | brush | cut | balloon |
| basket | buy | call | brown | bad | cousin | dark | brother | cry |

Unit 13

Exercise

B. Fill in the word and meaning.

	Word	Meaning
01	brush	
02	balloon	
03	buy	
04	bean	
05	call	
06	bad	
07	cry	
08	cute	
09	brother	
10	brown	
11	dance	
12	ball	
13	dark	
14	do	
15	basket	
16	cut	
17	cousin	
18	bank	

	Meaning	Word
01	나쁜	
02	공	
03	풍선	
04	은행	
05	바구니	
06	콩	
07	형제	
08	갈색, 갈색의	
09	닦다, 빗, 솔	
10	사다, 얻다	
11	전화를 걸다, 통화	
12	사촌	
13	울다	
14	자르다, 베다	
15	귀여운	
16	춤추다	
17	어두운, 어둠	
18	하다	

C. Listen, write the word and meaning. (Track 39)

	Word	Meaning		Word	Meaning
01			10		
02			11		
03			12		
04			13		
05			14		
06			15		
07			16		
08			17		
09			18		

Unit 14

🎧 Listen and repeat. Track 40

01 enjoy — v 즐기다 — to find pleasure and satisfaction in doing something
[endʒɔ́i]
She is **enjoying** riding a horse.
그녀는 말 타는 것을 즐기고 있다.

02 evening — n 저녁 — the part of the day between the afternoon and the night
[íːvniŋ]
It is a quiet **evening**.
조용한 저녁입니다.

03 face — n 얼굴 — the front part of the head between the forehead and the chin
[feis]
Why don't you wash your **face**?
너는 왜 얼굴을 씻지 않니?

04 fat — a 살찐, 뚱뚱한 — weighing too much
[fæt]
The cat is very **fat**.
그 고양이는 살이 아주 쪘습니다.

05 father — n 아버지 — a male parent of a child
[fáːðər]
My **father** is a businessman.
우리 아빠는 사업가이다.

06 find — v 찾다, 알다 — to discover something or somebody
[faind]
He can't **find** his teddy bear.
그는 곰 인형을 찾을 수가 없습니다.

07 gray — n 회색 / a 회색의 — having the color of smoke or ashes
[grei]
My umbrella is **gray**.
내 우산은 회색입니다.

08 great — a 큰, 위대한 — very large, extremely good in ability
[greit]
The party was a **great** success.
파티는 대성공이었다.

09 green — n 녹색 / a 녹색의 — having the color of grass
[griːn]
The leaves in the tree are **green**.
나뭇잎들이 초록색입니다.

key words
satisfaction n 만족(감) / forehead n 이마 / chin n 아래턱 / ashes n 재 / extremely ad 극도로

🎧 Listen and repeat. (Track 41)

10 hair [hɛər]
n 머리카락   the fine threads that grow in a mass on head
The girl has straight **hair**.
그 소녀는 생머리이다.

11 hand [hænd]
n 손   the part of the body at the end of the arm
Let me look at your **hands**.
손을 보여 주십시오.

12 happy [hǽpi]
a 행복한   to have feelings of pleasure
They are both **happy**.
그 사람들은 둘 다 행복합니다.

13 king [kiŋ]
n 왕   a man who is the most important member of the royal family
I will be a good **king**.
나는 좋은 왕이 될 겁니다.

14 kitchen [kitʃin]
n 부엌   a room in which meals are cooked
Mother is in the **kitchen**.
엄마는 부엌에 계신다.

15 knee [ni:]
n 무릎   the place where your leg bends
I should kneel upon my **knees**.
나는 무릎을 꿇어야 한다.

16 knife [naif]
n 칼   a sharp blade with a handle
The **knife** is very sharp.
그 칼은 매우 날카롭다.

17 know [nou]
v 알고 있나   to have a fact or information correctly in your mind
I don't **know** his address.
나는 그 사람의 주소를 모릅니다.

18 lady [léidi]
n 숙녀   a woman who is polite and always behaves well
A **lady** stands in the hall.
한 숙녀가 복도에 서 있습니다.

key words
thread n 가는 줄 / straight a 곧은 / royal a 왕실의 / kneel v 무릎을 꿇다 / blade n 칼
handle v 다루다 / correctly ad 정확하게 / address n 주소 / hall n 복도

Unit 14   71

Exercise

A. Complete the sentence.

1. He can't _____ his teddy bear.
   그는 곰 인형을 찾을 수가 없습니다.

2. They are both _____.
   그 사람들은 둘 다 행복합니다.

3. The girl has straight _____.
   그 소녀는 생머리이다.

4. The _____ is very sharp.
   그 칼은 매우 날카롭다.

5. My _____ is a businessman.
   우리 아빠는 사업가이다.

6. I don't _____ his address.
   나는 그 사람의 주소를 모릅니다.

7. A _____ stands in the hall.
   한 숙녀가 복도에 서 있습니다.

8. She is _____ riding a horse.
   그녀는 말 타는 것을 즐기고 있다.

9. Let me look at your _____.
   손을 보여 주십시오.

10. I should kneel upon my _____.
    나는 무릎을 꿇어야 한다.

11. The cat is very _____.
    그 고양이는 살이 아주 쪘습니다.

12. It is a quiet _____.
    조용한 저녁입니다.

13. Why don't you wash your _____?
    너는 왜 얼굴을 씻지 않니?

14. The leaves in the tree are _____.
    나뭇잎들이 초록색입니다.

15. My umbrella is _____.
    내 우산은 회색입니다.

16. I will be a good _____.
    나는 좋은 왕이 될 겁니다.

17. The party was a _____ success.
    파티는 대성공이었다.

18. Mother is in the _____.
    엄마는 부엌에 계시다.

Hint

| gray | know | father | evening | face | king | find | green | fat |
| hair | enjoy | kitchen | great | happy | knife | lady | hand | knee |

Unit 14

Exercise

B. Fill in the word and meaning.

	Word	Meaning
01	face	
02	enjoy	
03	great	
04	evening	
05	hand	
06	kitchen	
07	fat	
08	knife	
09	know	
10	father	
11	lady	
12	king	
13	hair	
14	knee	
15	gray	
16	happy	
17	green	
18	find	

	Meaning	Word
01	즐기다	
02	저녁	
03	얼굴	
04	살찐, 뚱뚱한	
05	아버지	
06	찾다, 알다	
07	회색, 회색의	
08	큰, 위대한	
09	녹색, 녹색의	
10	머리카락	
11	손	
12	행복한	
13	왕	
14	부엌	
15	무릎	
16	칼	
17	알고 있다	
18	숙녀	

C. Listen, write the word and meaning. (Track 42)

	Word	Meaning		Word	Meaning
01			10		
02			11		
03			12		
04			13		
05			14		
06			15		
07			16		
08			17		
09			18		

Review 7

A. Read and fill in the word and meaning.

word	definition	meaning
	to obtain something by paying money for it	
	a child of your aunt or uncle	
	unpleasant; full of problems	
	to telephone somebody	
	to divide something into pieces with a knife	
	a round object used in games such as soccer and baseball	
	an institution where people can keep their money	
	to produce tears from eyes	
	a rubber that becomes larger when you fill it with air	
	very pretty or attractive	
	a man who has the same mother and father	
	an object made of short stiff hairs	
	with no or very little light	
	a container for holding or carrying things	
	to move body and feet following a rhythm	
	the seeds of a climbing plant	
	to take some action or perform an activity	
	the color of earth	

Hint
ball   bank   buy   bean   call   basket   cry   cut   balloon
do   dance   cute   brown   bad   cousin   dark   brush   brother

B. Read and fill in the word and meaning.

word	definition	meaning
	the part of the body at the end of the arm	
	a woman who is polite and always behaves well	
	to have feelings of pleasure	
	a room in which meals are cooked	
	to find pleasure and satisfaction in doing something	
	a man who is the most important member of the royal family	
	the part of the day between the afternoon and the night	
	the place where your leg bends	
	a male parent of a child	
	the fine threads that grow in a mass on head	
	weighing too much	
	having the color of grass	
	to discover something or somebody	
	the front part of the head between the forehead and the chin	
	a sharp blade with a handle	
	very large, extremely good in ability	
	to have a fact or information correctly in your mind	
	having the color of smoke or ashes	

Hint
fat   happy   evening   hand   face   king   knife   green   gray
knee   enjoy   kitchen   great   know   find   lady   father   hair

Review 7   75

Unit 15

🎧 Listen and repeat. (Track 43)

01 market n 시장 a place where goods are bought and sold
[má:rkit]
Where is the nearest **market**?
제일 가까운 시장이 어딘가요?

02 meat n 고기 flesh taken from a dead animal
[mi:t]
Grandmother likes **meat**.
할머니는 고기를 좋아하신다.

03 meet v 만나다 to come together by chance or promise
[mi:t]
Glad to **meet** you.
만나서 반가워요.

04 milk n 우유 the white liquid produced by female mammals
[milk]
Milk is delicious when it's cold.
우유는 차가울 때 맛있습니다.

05 minute n 분, 잠시 each of the 60 parts of an hour
[mínit]
We have five **minutes**.
우리에게는 5분이 남았어.

06 mirror n 거울 a flat piece of glass which reflects light
[mírər]
I am walking to the **mirror**.
나는 거울을 향해 걸어가고 있다.

07 open v 열다 to move so as to be no longer closed
[óupən]
Open the door, please.
문을 열어 주세요.

08 orange n 오렌지, 오렌지색 bright reddish-yellow in color
[ɔ́(:)rindʒ]
I like **orange** better than red.
나는 빨간색보다 오렌지색이 더 좋아요.

09 outside prep 바깥쪽에, 바깥쪽으로 in or to a place that is not in a room or building
[áutsáid]
Is it hot **outside**?
밖에 더워요?

---

key words
goods n 물건, 상품 / nearest a 가장 가까운 / flesh n 과육, 살 / chance n 기회 / promise n 약속
delicious a 맛있는 / reflect v 반사하다

🎧 Listen and repeat. Track 44

10 over
[óuvər]
prep ~의 위에, ~의 위로   resting on the surface of something
The birds fly **over** the clouds.
새들이 구름 위로 날아다닙니다.

11 ox
[aks]
n 수소   a male cow
The **ox** arrives at the field.
수소가 들판에 이르렀다.

12 page
[peidʒ]
n 쪽, 페이지   each side of the pieces of paper in a book
Open your book to **page** 27.
책의 27쪽을 펴십시오.

13 rain
[rein]
n 비   water that falls from the clouds in small drops
Rain began to fall.
비가 오기 시작했어요.

14 ready
[rédi]
a 준비가 된   to be properly prepared for something
I didn't have the time to get **ready**.
나는 준비할 시간이 없었다.

15 rice
[rais]
n 쌀, 밥, 벼   white or brown grains taken from a cereal plant
My mother is boiling **rice**.
엄마는 밥을 짓고 계시다.

16 rich
[ritʃ]
a 부유한   to have a lot of money
My uncle is very **rich**.
나의 삼촌은 매우 부유하다.

17 right
[rait]
n 오른쪽 / **a** 오른쪽의   the side of the body that faces east when a person faces north
Turn to the **right**.
오른쪽으로 도십시오.

18 ring
[riŋ]
n 반지 / **v** 울리다   jewelry that you wear on your finger, to make a sound
I want to have a gold **ring**.
나는 금반지를 갖고 싶다.

key words
field **n** 들판 / drop **n** 방울 / prepare **v** 준비하다 / grain **n** 곡식알
cereal **n** 곡류가 나는 식물 / jewelry **n** 보석류

Unit 15

Exercise

A. Complete the sentence.

1. Where is the nearest _____?
   제일 가까운 시장이 어딘가요?

2. I like _____ better than red.
   나는 빨간색보다 오렌지색이 더 좋아요.

3. _____ is delicious when it's cold.
   우유는 차가울 때 맛있습니다.

4. We have five _____.
   우리에게는 5분이 남았어.

5. Grandmother likes _____.
   할머니는 고기를 좋아하신다.

6. _____ the door, please.
   문을 열어 주세요.

7. Is it hot _____?
   밖에 더워요?

8. My uncle is very _____.
   나의 삼촌은 매우 부유하다.

9. The birds fly _____ the clouds.
   새들이 구름 위로 날아다닙니다.

10. The _____ arrives at the field.
    수소가 들판에 이르렀다.

11. Open your book to _____ 27.
    책의 27쪽을 펴십시오.

12. Glad to _____ you.
    만나서 반가워요.

13. _____ began to fall.
    비가 오기 시작했어요.

14. I am walking to the _____.
    나는 거울을 향해 걸어가고 있다.

15. I didn't have the time to get _____.
    나는 준비할 시간이 없었다.

16. I want to have a gold _____.
    나는 금반지를 갖고 싶다.

17. My mother is boiling _____.
    엄마는 밥을 짓고 계신다.

18. Turn to the _____.
    오른쪽으로 도십시오.

Hint

| meat | page | ring | meet | market | open | milk | outside | rich |
| ox | over | rain | minute | ready | mirror | rice | right | orange |

Exercise

B. Fill in the word and meaning.

	Word	Meaning
01	open	
02	over	
03	market	
04	page	
05	meat	
06	ready	
07	ring	
08	minute	
09	ox	
10	rice	
11	mirror	
12	outside	
13	right	
14	meet	
15	rich	
16	rain	
17	orange	
18	milk	

	Meaning	Word
01	시장	
02	고기	
03	만나다	
04	우유	
05	분, 잠시	
06	거울	
07	열다	
08	오렌지, 오렌지색	
09	바깥쪽에, 바깥쪽으로	
10	~의 위에, ~의 위로	
11	수소	
12	쪽, 페이지	
13	비	
14	준비가 된	
15	쌀, 밥, 벼	
16	부유한	
17	오른쪽, 오른쪽의	
18	반지, 울리다	

C. Listen, write the word and meaning. Track 45

	Word	Meaning		Word	Meaning
01			10		
02			11		
03			12		
04			13		
05			14		
06			15		
07			16		
08			17		
09			18		

Unit 16

🎧 Listen and repeat. Track 46

01 smile v 미소 짓다 to make the corners of mouth turn up and show teeth
[smail]
My teacher **smiled** at me.
선생님께서 나에게 미소를 지으셨다.

02 snow n 눈 soft white bits of frozen water that fall from the sky
[snou]
The **snow** is one meter deep.
눈이 1미터나 쌓였어요.

03 soap n 비누 something to use with water for washing yourself
[soup]
Wash your hands with **soap**.
비누로 손을 씻으세요.

04 soccer n 축구 a game played by two teams of 11 players using a round ball
[sákə:r]
He is an excellent **soccer** player.
그 사람은 뛰어난 축구 선수입니다.

05 socks n 양말 pieces of clothing which cover your foot
[saks]
Here's a pair of clean **socks**.
여기 깨끗한 양말 한 켤레가 있습니다.

06 song n 노래 a piece of music with words that you sing
[sɔ(:)ŋ]
I learned a new **song** today.
나는 오늘 새 노래를 배웠습니다.

07 there ad 거기에 in, at or to that place or position
[ðɛə:r]
We will go **there** by subway.
우리는 지하철로 그 곳에 갈 거에요.

08 think v 생각하다 to have a particular idea or opinion
[θiŋk]
I **think** he is right.
나는 그 사람이 옳다고 생각해요.

09 thumb n 엄지손가락 the short thick finger at the side of the hand
[θʌm]
I hurt my **thumb**.
엄지손가락을 다쳤어요.

---

key words
frozen a 언 / excellent a 뛰어난, 훌륭한 / pair n 한 쌍 / position n 위치, 방향
opinion n 의견, 견해 / thick a 두꺼운

🎧 Listen and repeat. Track 47

10 tie [tai]
v 묶다 / n 넥타이   to fasten something in position with rope, string, etc
This rope doesn't **tie** well.
이 끈은 잘 묶어지지 않습니다.

11 time [taim]
n 시간, 시각   what is measured in minutes, hours, days, and years
It's **time** to get up.
일어날 시간입니다.

12 tired [taiə:rd]
a 지친   feeling that you want to rest or sleep
I'm really **tired** today.
나는 오늘 너무 피곤합니다.

13 watch [watʃ]
v 보다 / n 시계   to look at somebody / something for a time
I **watched** a sad movie.
슬픈 영화를 보았어.

14 way [wei]
n 길, 방법   the route you take to reach somewhere
Please tell me the **way** to the library.
도서관으로 가는 길을 알려 주세요.

15 wear [wɛə:r]
v 입고(쓰고) 있다   to have clothes or shoes on your body
I want to **wear** the white dress.
그 흰옷을 입고 싶어요.

16 week [wi:k]
n 주   a period of seven days
I arrived here a **week** ago.
나는 여기 한 주전에 도착했습니다.

17 welcome [wélkəm]
n 환영 / v 환영하다   to greet somebody friendly when they arrive somewhere
Welcome to my house.
우리 집에 오신 것을 환영합니다.

18 well [wel]
ad 잘   in a good
I can speak English very **well**.
나는 영어를 매우 잘 합니다.

---

key words
fasten v 단단히 얽어매다 / string n 끈, 줄 / route n 길, 통로 / library n 도서관
greet v 인사하다, 환영하다 / friendly ad 친절히

Exercise

A. Complete the sentence.

1. The _____ is one meter deep.
   눈이 1미터나 쌓였어요.

2. Wash your hands with _____.
   비누로 손을 씻으세요.

3. He is an excellent _____ player.
   그 사람은 뛰어난 축구 선수입니다.

4. I can speak English very _____.
   나는 영어를 매우 잘 합니다.

5. My teacher _____ at me.
   선생님께서 나에게 미소를 지으셨다.

6. We will go _____ by subway.
   우리는 지하철로 그 곳에 갈 거에요.

7. I _____ he is right.
   나는 그 사람이 옳다고 생각해요.

8. I hurt my _____.
   엄지손가락을 다쳤어요.

9. This rope doesn't _____ well.
   이 끈은 잘 묶어지지 않습니다.

10. It's _____ to get up.
    일어날 시간입니다.

11. _____ to my house.
    우리 집에 오신 것을 환영합니다.

12. I arrived here a _____ ago.
    나는 여기 한 주전에 도착했습니다.

13. I'm really _____ today.
    나는 오늘 너무 피곤합니다.

14. Here's a pair of clean _____.
    여기 깨끗한 양말 한 켤레가 있습니다.

15. I _____ a sad movie.
    슬픈 영화를 보았어.

16. Please tell me the _____ to the library.
    도서관으로 가는 길을 알려 주세요.

17. I learned a new _____ today.
    나는 오늘 새 노래를 배웠습니다.

18. I want to _____ the white dress.
    그 흰옷을 입고 싶어요.

Hint

| there | watch | socks | well | week | snow | thumb | soap | tired |
| wear | soccer | time | welcome | smile | think | tie | way | song |

 Unit 16

Exercise

B. Fill in the word and meaning.

	Word	Meaning
01	socks	
02	think	
03	tie	
04	smile	
05	tired	
06	way	
07	snow	
08	welcome	
09	thumb	
10	week	
11	soap	
12	watch	
13	well	
14	soccer	
15	wear	
16	time	
17	there	
18	song	

	Meaning	Word
01	미소짓다	
02	눈	
03	비누	
04	축구	
05	양말	
06	노래	
07	거기에	
08	생각하다	
09	엄지손가락	
10	묶다, 넥타이	
11	시간, 시각	
12	지친	
13	보다, 시계	
14	길, 방법	
15	입고(쓰고) 있다	
16	주	
17	환영, 환영하다	
18	잘	

C. Listen, write the word and meaning. (Track 48)

	Word	Meaning		Word	Meaning
01			10		
02			11		
03			12		
04			13		
05			14		
06			15		
07			16		
08			17		
09			18		

Review 8

A. Read and fill in the word and meaning.

word	definition	meaning
open	to move so as to be no longer closed	
meet	to come together by chance or promise	
ox	a male cow	
market	a place where goods are bought and sold	
rain	water that falls from the clouds in small drops	
minute	each of the 60 parts of an hour	
page	each side of the pieces of paper in a book	
mirror	a flat piece of glass which reflects light	
meat	flesh taken from a dead animal	
over	resting on the surface of something	
right	the side of the body that faces east when a person faces north	
ring	jewelry that you wear on your finger, to make a sound	
milk	the white liquid produced by female mammals	
rich	to have a lot of money	
rice	white or brown grains taken from a cereal plant	
outside	in or to a place that is not in a room or building	
orange	bright reddish-yellow in color	
ready	to be properly prepared for something	

Hint

rain   right   ring   meet   rich   ready   ox   outside   market
milk   over   meat   page   open   mirror   rice   minute   orange

B. Read and fill in the word and meaning.

word	definition	meaning
	to fasten something in position with rope, string, etc	
	something to use with water for washing yourself	
	the route you take to reach somewhere	
	to make the corners of mouth turn up and show teeth	
	what is measured in minutes, hours, days, and years	
	the short thick finger at the side of the hand	
	soft white bits of frozen water that fall from the sky	
	to have a particular idea or opinion	
	to have clothes or shoes on your body	
	to look at somebody; something for a time	
	a game played by two teams of 11 players using a round ball	
	in a good	
	to greet somebody friendly when they arrive somewhere	
	a piece of music with words that you sing	
	feeling that you want to rest or sleep	
	a period of seven days	
	in, at or to that place or position	
	pieces of clothing which cover your foot	

Hint
tie   think   socks   well   week   snow   smile   soap   welcome
time   song   wear   way   thumb   watch   there   tired   soccer

Review 8

Unit 17

🎧 Listen and repeat. (Track 49)

01 baseball [béisbɔ̀:l]
n 야구, 야구공   a game using a bat and ball
He is on a **baseball** team.
그는 야구팀에 속해 있다.

02 beautiful [bjú:təfəl]
a 아름다운, 예쁜   pleasing to the senses; having beauty
I hear a **beautiful** voice.
아름다운 목소리가 들려요.

03 beef [bi:f]
n 쇠고기   meat that comes from a cow
This **beef** is very tough.
이 쇠고기는 너무 질기다.

04 begin [bigín]
v 시작하다   to start doing something
School **begins** at 9:00 am.
학교는 오전 9시에 시작합니다.

05 behind [biháind]
prep ~의 뒤에   at or towards the back of somebody / something
There is a fox **behind** the rock.
바위 뒤에 여우 한 마리가 있다.

06 belong [bilɔ́(:)ŋ]
v ~에 속하다   to be a member of a group
Do you **belong** to the tennis club?
너는 테니스 클럽에 소속되어 있니?

07 catch [kætʃ]
v 잡다   to hold a moving object, especially in your hand
He **catches** some fish.
그는 몇 마리의 물고기들을 잡는다.

08 chair [tʃɛər]
n 의자   a furniture for 1 person to sit on
He sat in a low **chair**.
그는 낮은 의자에 앉아 있었다.

09 chalk [tʃɔ:k]
n 분필   a type of white stone for writing or drawing
Bring me a piece of **chalk**.
분필 한 개를 갖다 주세요.

---

key words
voice n 목소리 / tough a 강인한, 질긴 / member n 회원 / especially ad 특히 / furniture n 가구

🎧 Listen and repeat. Track 50

10 chest [tʃest]
n 가슴   the top part of the front of your body where your heart is
I hear my heart beating in the **chest**.
내 가슴에서 심장 뛰는 소리가 들려요.

11 chicken [tʃíkin]
n 닭, 닭고기   a bird which are kept on a farm for their eggs and for their meat
The **chickens** make a lot of noise.
닭들이 너무나 시끄러워요.

12 child [tʃaild]
n 어린이, 아이   a human being who is not yet an adult
I'm looking for a **child**.
나는 아이를 한 명 찾고 있어요.

13 color [kʌ́lər]
n 색, 빛깔   the fact that something is red, green, yellow, etc
Look at the **color** of his umbrella.
그의 우산 색 좀 보세요.

14 come [kʌm]
v 오다   to move to or towards a person or place
I will **come** back next Friday.
다음 주 금요일에 돌아올게요.

15 cook [kuk]
n 요리사 / v 요리하다   to prepare food by heating it
Hanna learned how to **cook** spaghetti from Jane.
Hanna는 Jane으로부터 스파게티를 요리하는 법을 배웠다.

16 cookie [kúki]
n 쿠키   a small flat sweet cake
I had a **cookie**.
나는 쿠키 한 개를 먹었어요.

17 count [kaunt]
v 세다, 계산하다   to say numbers in the correct order
Close your eyes and **count** up to 20.
눈을 감고 20까지 세어 보세요.

18 country [kʌ́ntri]
n 나라, 시골   an area of land that has own government and laws
Russia is a big **country**.
러시아는 큰 나라이다.

---

key words
front n 정면 / beat v (심장)뛰다 / heat v 가열하다 / flat a 평평한, 납작한 / correct a 옳은, 정확한
order n 순서, 차례 / area n 지역, 구역 / government n 정부

Exercise

A. Complete the sentence.

1. I hear a _____ voice.
   아름다운 목소리가 들려요.
2. This _____ is very tough.
   이 쇠고기는 너무 질기다.
3. Do you _____ to the tennis club?
   너는 테니스 클럽에 소속되어 있니?
4. He _____ some fish.
   그는 몇 마리의 물고기들을 잡는다.
5. Russia is a big _____.
   러시아는 큰 나라이다.
6. He sat in a low _____.
   그는 낮은 의자에 앉아 있었다.
7. I hear my heart beating in the _____.
   내 가슴에서 심장 뛰는 소리가 들려요.
8. School _____ at 9:00 am.
   학교는 오전 9시에 시작합니다.
9. The _____ make a lot of noise.
   닭들이 너무 시끄러워요.
10. He is on a _____ team.
    그는 야구팀에 속해 있다.
11. I'm looking for a _____.
    나는 아이를 한명 찾고 있어요.
12. Close your eyes and _____ up to 20.
    눈을 감고 20까지 세어 보세요.
13. Look at the _____ of his umbrella.
    그의 우산 색 좀 보세요.
14. I will _____ back next Friday.
    다음 주 금요일에 돌아올게요.
15. There is a fox _____ the rock.
    바위 뒤에 여우 한 마리가 있다.
16. I had a _____.
    나는 쿠키 한 개를 먹었어요.
17. Bring me a piece of _____.
    분필 한 개를 갖다 주세요.
18. Hanna learned how to _____ spaghetti from Jane.
    Hanna는 Jane으로부터 스파게티를 요리하는 법을 배웠다.

Hint

| chicken | count | begin | cook | chair | belong | catch | beef | child |
| chalk | chest | beautiful | color | come | behind | cookie | baseball | country |

Exercise

B. Fill in the word and meaning.

	Word	Meaning
01	catch	
02	behind	
03	chair	
04	baseball	
05	cookie	
06	chicken	
07	beef	
08	come	
09	color	
10	beautiful	
11	count	
12	chest	
13	country	
14	begin	
15	child	
16	cook	
17	chalk	
18	belong	

	Meaning	Word
01	야구, 야구공	
02	아름다운, 예쁜	
03	쇠고기	
04	시작하다	
05	~의 뒤에	
06	~에 속하다	
07	잡다	
08	의자	
09	분필	
10	가슴	
11	닭, 닭고기	
12	어린이, 아이	
13	색, 빛깔	
14	오다	
15	요리사, 요리하다	
16	쿠키	
17	세다, 계산하다	
18	나라, 시골	

C. Listen, write the word and meaning. Track 51

	Word	Meaning		Word	Meaning
01			10		
02			11		
03			12		
04			13		
05			14		
06			15		
07			16		
08			17		
09			18		

Unit 18

🎧 Listen and repeat. Track 52

01 doll n 인형   a child's toy which looks like a baby
[dal]
I want to have a **doll** for my birthday present.
나는 생일선물로 인형이 갖고 싶어요.

02 easy a 쉬운   do something without difficulty or effort
[íːzi]
The work is **easy** for me.
저에게 그 일은 쉬워요.

03 eat v 먹다   put something into your mouth
[iːt]
Did you ever **eat** kimchi?
너는 김치를 먹어본 적이 있니?

04 egg n 달걀   a small oval object with a thin hard shell produced by a female bird
[eg]
Can you buy me several **eggs**?
달걀 몇 개만 사다 줄래?

05 elephant n 코끼리   a large animal with grey skin, a long nose and large ears
[éləfənt]
An **elephant** is very big.
코끼리는 정말 커요.

06 end n 끝 / v 끝나다   the furthest of the last part of something
[end]
He lives at the **end** of the street.
그는 그 거리의 끝에 산다.

07 glad a 기쁜   be happy and pleased about something
[glæd]
I'm so **glad** to meet you.
당신을 만나게 되어 너무 기쁩니다.

08 glass n 유리(잔)   a hard transparent substance such as windows
[glæs]
He broke the **glass** of the window.
그가 유리 창문을 깨뜨렸다.

09 goat n 염소   an animal with horns and a hairy coat
[gout]
The mother **goat** came back home.
엄마 염소가 집으로 돌아왔다.

---

key words
difficulty n 어려움 / effort n 노력 / oval a 타원형의 / shell n 껍질 / several a 몇 개의
transparent a 투명한 / horn n 뿔 / hairy a 털 많은

🎧 Listen and repeat. (Track 53)

10 good [gud]
a 좋은, 즐거운 of a high quality, pleasant or enjoyable
A **good** beginning makes a good ending.
시작이 좋으면 끝도 좋다.

11 grandfather [grǽndfὰːðər]
n 할아버지 the father of your father or mother
This is my **grandfather**.
이 사람은 나의 할아버지예요.

12 grandmother [grǽndmʌ̀ðər]
n 할머니 the mother of your father or mother
His **grandmother** is very healthy.
그의 할머니께서는 매우 건강하십니다.

13 hospital [háspitl]
n 병원 a place where sick people are looked after by doctors
Jane was in the **hospital** for one week.
제인은 일주일 동안 병원에 입원했다.

14 hot [hat]
a 더운 having a high temperature
It's **hot** and dry today.
오늘은 덥고 건조하다.

15 hour [áuər]
n 시각, 한 시간 a period of 60 minutes
I jog for an **hour** in the morning.
나는 아침에 1시간 동안 조깅을 한다.

16 jump [dʒʌmp]
v 뛰다 away from a surface by pushing yourself with legs and feet
We **jumped** together.
우리는 함께 뛰었다.

17 just [dʒʌst]
ad 바로, 꼭, 막 at the same moment, a very short time before
I'm leaving **just** now.
나는 막 나가는 길이다.

18 kind [kaind]
a 친절한 / n 종류 caring about others; gentle and friendly, a particular type
It is very **kind** of you.
당신은 정말 친절하시군요.

---

key words
quality n 품질 / temperature n 온도 / jog v 조깅하다 / away ad 멀리 / surface n 지면 / moment a 순간

Exercise

A. Complete the sentence.

1. I'm leaving _____ now.
   나는 막 나가는 길이다.

2. The work is _____ for me.
   저에게 그 일은 쉬워요.

3. It is very _____ of you.
   당신은 정말 친절하시군요.

4. Did you ever _____ kimchi?
   너는 김치를 먹어본 적이 있니?

5. Can you buy me several _____?
   달걀 몇 개만 사다 줄래?

6. His _____ is very healthy.
   그의 할머니께서는 매우 건강하십니다.

7. An _____ is very big.
   코끼리는 정말 커요.

8. He lives at the _____ of the street.
   그는 그 거리의 끝에 산다.

9. It's _____ and dry today.
   오늘은 덥고 건조하다.

10. I'm so _____ to meet you.
    당신을 만나게 되어 너무 기쁩니다.

11. I jog for an _____ in the morning.
    나는 아침에 1시간 동안 조깅을 한다.

12. I want to have a _____ for my birthday present.
    나는 생일선물로 인형이 갖고 싶어요.

13. He broke the _____ of the window.
    그가 유리 창문을 깨뜨렸다.

14. Jane was in the _____ for one week.
    제인은 일주일 동안 병원에 입원했다.

15. The mother _____ came back home.
    엄마 염소가 집으로 돌아왔다.

16. We _____ together.
    우리는 함께 뛰었다.

17. A _____ beginning makes a good ending.
    시작이 좋으면 끝도 좋다.

18. This is my _____.
    이 사람은 나의 할아버지에요.

Hint

| eat | grandfather | easy | glass | elephant | glad | just | goat | hot |
| good | grandmother | doll | end | hour | jump | hospital | kind | egg |

Exercise

B. Fill in the word and meaning.

	Word	Meaning
01	egg	
02	grandfather	
03	hospital	
04	easy	
05	kind	
06	just	
07	elephant	
08	jump	
09	glad	
10	grandmother	
11	goat	
12	doll	
13	glass	
14	hour	
15	end	
16	hot	
17	eat	
18	good	

	Meaning	Word
01	인형	
02	쉬운	
03	먹다	
04	달걀	
05	코끼리	
06	끝, 끝나다	
07	기쁜	
08	유리(잔)	
09	염소	
10	좋은, 즐거운	
11	할아버지	
12	할머니	
13	병원	
14	더운	
15	시각, 한 시간	
16	뛰다	
17	바로, 꼭, 막	
18	친절한, 종류	

🎧 C. Listen, write the word and meaning. (Track 54)

	Word	Meaning		Word	Meaning
01			10		
02			11		
03			12		
04			13		
05			14		
06			15		
07			16		
08			17		
09			18		

Unit 18

Review 9

A. Read and fill in the word and meaning.

word	definition	meaning
	a type of white stone for writing or drawing	
	a game using a bat and ball	
	a furniture for 1 person to sit on	
	the fact that something is red, green, yellow, etc	
	pleasing to the senses; having beauty	
	to hold a moving object, especially in your hand	
	to move to or towards a person or place	
	meat that comes from a cow	
	an area of land that has own government and laws	
	a human being who is not yet an adult	
	to start doing something	
	the top part of the front of your body where your heart is	
	at or towards the back of somebody/something	
	to say numbers in the correct order	
	a small flat sweet cake	
	to be a member of a group	
	a bird which are kept on a farm for their eggs and for their meat	
	to prepare food by heating it	

Hint

| child | begin | count | come | cookie | belong | catch | beautiful | chicken |
| chest | chalk | beef | color | cook | behind | chair | baseball | country |

B. Read and fill in the word and meaning.

word	definition	meaning
	of a high quality, pleasant or enjoyable	
	an animal with horns and a hairy coat	
	a place where sick people are looked after by doctors	
	do something without difficulty or effort	
	the father of your father or mother	
	put something into your mouth	
	the mother of your father or mother	
	a small oval object with a thin hard shell produced by a female bird	
	a child's toy which looks like a baby	
	caring about others; gentle and friendly, a particular type	
	a hard transparent substance such as windows	
	at the same moment, a very short time before	
	be happy and pleased about something	
	a period of 60 minutes	
	a large animal with grey skin, a long nose and large ears	
	away from a surface by pushing yourself with legs and feet	
	the furthest of the last part of something	
	having a high temperature	

Hint
hour   hospital   easy   doll   grandmother   egg   kind   goat   hot
good   elephant   glass   end   grandfather   jump   eat   just   glad

Review 9

Unit 19

🎧 Listen and repeat. Track 55

01 low [lou]
a 낮은 not high or tall; not far above the ground
He sat in a **low** chair.
그는 낮은 의자에 앉았다.

02 lunch [lʌntʃ]
n 점심 식사 the meal that you have in the middle of the day
They had **lunch** together at the restaurant.
그들은 식당에서 함께 점심을 먹었다.

03 make [meik]
v 만들다 to create something by combining materials
I'll **make** glasses for you.
제가 당신의 안경을 만들어 드릴게요.

04 man [mæn]
n 남자, 사람 an adult male human being
The **man** is cleaning his car.
남자가 차를 청소하고 있다.

05 many [méni]
a (수가) 많은 a large number of people or things
How **many** people are there?
거기에 얼마나 많은 사람이 있니?

06 map [mæp]
n 지도 a drawing of the earth's surface
He is studying the **map**.
그는 그 지도를 살펴보고 있어요.

07 noon [nu:n]
n 정오, 한낮 12 o'clock in the middle of the day
I hope to see you at **noon**.
정오에 만나면 좋겠습니다.

08 nose [nouz]
n 코 the part of face which sticks out above mouth
I hurt my **nose** and lips.
나는 코와 입술을 다쳤어.

09 number [nʌ́mbəːr]
n 번호, 수 a word such as two or nine
The total **number** of the apples was 24.
그 사과의 총합은 24개였다.

key words
tall **a** 높은 / middle **n** 중간 / create **v** 창조하다 / combine **v** 결합하다 / material **n** 재료
hope **v** 바라다 / stick **v** 달라 붙다 / adult **n** 성인

🎧 Listen and repeat. Track 56

10 often [ɔ́(ː)ftən]
ad 종종, 자주　many times, in many cases
I **often** see him.
나는 그 사람을 자주 만나요.

11 old [ould]
a 늙은, ~살의　having lived for a long time
The submarine is **old** and slow.
그 잠수함은 낡고 속도가 느려요.

12 once [wʌns]
ad 한 번　one occasion only; one time
I visit my grandfather **once** a week.
나는 일주일에 한 번씩 할아버지 댁에 간다.

13 puppy [pʌ́pi]
n 강아지　a young dog
Do you want a **puppy**?
강아지가 갖고 싶니?

14 purple [pə́ːrpəl]
n 보라색 / a 보라색의　a reddish-blue color
He painted the chair **purple**.
그는 의자를 보라색으로 칠했어요.

15 push [puʃ]
v 밀다　to use force to make something move away from you
Push the door inside.
문을 안쪽으로 미세요.

16 put [put]
v 놓다, 넣다　to move something into a particular place
He **put** the box on the shelf.
그는 상자를 선반 위에 놓았습니다.

17 queen [kwiːn]
n 여왕, 왕비　the female ruler of an independent state, the wife of a king
I saw **Queen** Elizabeth.
나는 엘리자베스 여왕을 보았다.

18 quiet [kwáiət]
a 조용한　making very little noise
Please be **quiet** because I'm reading.
독서를 하고 있으니 제발 조용히 해주세요.

key words
submarine n 잠수함 / occasion n 경우, 기회 / shelf n 선반 / ruler n 통치자 / independent a 독립한

Unit 19　97

Exercise

A. Complete the sentence.

1. They had _____ together at the restaurant.
   그들은 식당에서 함께 점심을 먹었다.

2. He sat in a _____ chair.
   그는 낮은 의자에 앉았다.

3. The _____ is cleaning his car.
   남자가 차를 청소하고 있다.

4. _____ the door inside.
   문을 안쪽으로 미세요.

5. I saw _____ Elizabeth.
   나는 엘리자베스 여왕을 보았다.

6. He is studying the _____.
   그는 그 지도를 살펴보고 있어요.

7. I hope to see you at _____.
   정오에 만나면 좋겠습니다.

8. Please be _____ because I'm reading.
   독서를 하고 있으니 제발 조용히 해주세요.

9. I hurt my _____ and lips.
   나는 코와 입을 다쳤어.

10. How _____ people are there?
    거기에 얼마나 많은 사람이 있니?

11. The total _____ of the apples was 24.
    그 사과의 총합은 24개였다.

12. I _____ see him.
    나는 그 사람을 자주 만나요.

13. I visit my grandfather _____ a week.
    나는 일주일에 한 번씩 할아버지 댁에 간다.

14. Do you want a _____?
    강아지가 갖고 싶니?

15. The submarine is _____ and slow.
    그 잠수함은 낡고 속도가 느려요.

16. I'll _____ glasses for you.
    제가 당신의 안경을 만들어 드릴게요.

17. He painted the chair _____.
    그는 의자를 보라색으로 칠했어요.

18. He _____ the box on the shelf.
    그는 상자를 선반 위에 놓았습니다.

Hint

| queen | lunch | make | put | man | nose | quiet | map | often |
| number | push | old | once | low | many | noon | purple | puppy |

Exercise

B. Fill in the word and meaning.

	Word	Meaning
01	lunch	
02	many	
03	noon	
04	often	
05	low	
06	once	
07	push	
08	nose	
09	quiet	
10	number	
11	make	
12	purple	
13	queen	
14	map	
15	put	
16	puppy	
17	old	
18	man	

	Meaning	Word
01	낮은	
02	점심 식사	
03	만들다	
04	남자, 사람	
05	(수가)많은	
06	지도	
07	정오, 한낮	
08	코	
09	번호, 수	
10	종종, 자주	
11	늙은, ~살의	
12	한 번	
13	강아지	
14	보라색, 보라색의	
15	밀다	
16	놓다, 넣다	
17	여왕, 왕비	
18	조용한	

C. Listen, write the word and meaning. (Track 57)

	Word	Meaning		Word	Meaning
01			10		
02			11		
03			12		
04			13		
05			14		
06			15		
07			16		
08			17		
09			18		

Unit 20

🎧 Listen and repeat. Track 58

01 **sing**   v 노래하다   to make musical sounds with your voice
[siŋ]
We **sing** together when we are free.
우리는 자유 시간에 함께 노래를 불러.

02 **sister**   n 여자형제, 자매   a woman who has the same parents as you
[sístəːr]
My **sister** is pretty and smart.
우리 누나는 예쁘고 똑똑해요.

03 **skirt**   n 스커트, 치마   a piece of clothing worn by women and girls
[skəːrt]
She wears only **skirts**.
그녀는 치마만 입어요.

04 **sky**   n 하늘   the space that you can see when you look up from the earth
[skai]
Look at the beautiful birds in the **sky**.
하늘의 아름다운 새들을 보아라.

05 **slow**   a 느린   moving without much speed, not fast
[slou]
The turtle is too **slow**.
거북이는 너무 느려요.

06 **small**   a 작은   not large in size, number and degree; between tiny and large
[smɔːl]
This is just a **small** stone.
이건 단지 조그마한 돌이잖아.

07 **teach**   v 가르치다   to give lessons to students in a school, college, etc.
[tiːtʃ]
My father **teaches** English.
내 아버지는 영어를 가르치십니다.

08 **telephone**   n 전화기   a system for talking to somebody over long distance
[téləfoun]
The **telephone** is on the table.
전화가 탁자 위에 있어요.

09 **television**   n 텔레비전   an equipment which you can watch moving pictures
[téləviʒən]
I like watching **television** after school.
나는 방과 후에 텔레비전 보는 것을 좋아한다.

---

key words
musical a 음악의 / same a 같은 / space n 공간 / degree n 등급, 단계 / tiny a 작은
lesson n 학과, 수업 / distance n 거리 / equipment n 장비

🎧 Listen and repeat. (Track 59)

10 tell v 말하다   to give information to somebody by speaking
[tel]
Tell me the truth.
내게 진실을 말해줘요.

11 tennis n 테니스   the game using rackets and a ball
[ténis]
Let's play **tennis** together.
우리 같이 테니스를 칩시다.

12 then ad 그 때에   used to refer to a particular time in the past and future
[ðen]
I'll see you **then**.
그때 보도록 해요.

13 very ad 대단히, 몹시   to give emphasis to an adjective or adverb
[véri]
I like her **very** much.
나는 그녀를 대단히 좋아해요.

14 visit v 방문하다   to go to see someone and spend time with him / her
[vízit]
The President of Russia will **visit** Korea.
러시아 대통령이 한국을 방문할 것이다.

15 wait v 기다리다   to spend some time doing very little
[weit]
I will **wait** at the bus stop.
내가 버스 정류장에서 기다릴게요.

16 walk v 걷다   to move or go somewhere by your foot
[wɔːk]
I **walk** to work every day.
나는 매일 걸어서 일하러 간다.

17 want v 원하다   to have a desire or a wish for something
[wɔ(ː)nt]
I **want** to join the band.
나는 그 밴드에 가입하고 싶다.

18 wash v 씻다   to make something / somebody clean using water
[waʃ]
Wash your hands first.
먼저 손을 씻으세요.

key words
refer v 언급하다 / past n 과거 / future n 미래 / emphasis n 강조, 윤곽 / adjective n 형용사
adverb n 부사 / desire n 소망, 욕망

Exercise

A. Complete the sentence.

1. She wears only _____.
   그녀는 치마만 입어요.

2. Look at the beautiful birds in the _____.
   하늘의 아름다운 새들을 보아라.

3. This is just a _____ stone.
   이건 단지 조그마한 돌이잖아.

4. My father _____ English.
   내 아버지는 영어를 가르치십니다.

5. The _____ is on the table.
   전화가 탁자 위에 있어요.

6. The turtle is too _____.
   거북이는 너무 느려요.

7. My _____ is pretty and smart.
   우리 누나는 예쁘고 똑똑해요.

8. _____ me the truth.
   내게 진실을 말해줘요.

9. We _____ together when we are free.
   우리는 자유 시간에 함께 노래를 불러.

10. Let's play _____ together.
    우리 같이 테니스를 칩시다.

11. I _____ to join the band.
    나는 그 밴드에 가입하고 싶다.

12. I like watching _____ after school.
    나는 방과 후에 텔레비전 보는 것을 좋아한다.

13. I'll see you _____.
    그때 보도록 해요.

14. I like her _____ much.
    나는 그녀를 대단히 좋아해요.

15. _____ your hands first.
    먼저 손을 씻으세요.

16. The President of Russia will _____ Korea.
    러시아 대통령이 한국을 방문할 것이다.

17. I will _____ at the bus stop.
    내가 버스 정류장에서 기다릴게요.

18. I _____ to work every day.
    나는 매일 걸어서 일하러 간다.

Hint

| sing | tennis | skirt | wait | teach | slow | very | telephone | sky |
| wash | tell | sister | visit | television | then | walk | want | small |

Unit 20

Exercise

B. Fill in the word and meaning.

	Word	Meaning
01	slow	
02	telephone	
03	visit	
04	sing	
05	wait	
06	television	
07	wash	
08	want	
09	skirt	
10	teach	
11	tennis	
12	sky	
13	walk	
14	then	
15	small	
16	very	
17	tell	
18	sister	

	Meaning	Word
01	노래하다	
02	여자형제, 자매	
03	스커트, 치마	
04	하늘	
05	느린	
06	작은	
07	가르치다	
08	전화기	
09	텔레비전	
10	말하다	
11	테니스	
12	그 때에	
13	대단히, 몹시	
14	방문하다	
15	기다리다	
16	걷다	
17	원하다	
18	씻다	

C. Listen, write the word and meaning. (Track 60)

	Word	Meaning		Word	Meaning
01			10		
02			11		
03			12		
04			13		
05			14		
06			15		
07			16		
08			17		
09			18		

Review 10

A. Read and fill in the word and meaning.

word	definition	meaning
	12 o' clock in the middle of the day	
	making very little noise	
	not high or tall; not far above the ground	
	the part of face which sticks out above mouth	
	the meal that you have in the middle of the day	
	a drawing of the earth's surface	
	one occasion only; one time	
	a large number of people or things	
	a young dog	
	an adult male human being	
	a reddish-blue color	
	to create something by combining materials	
	the female ruler of an independent state, the wife of a king	
	to move something into a particular place	
	many times, in many cases	
	to use force to make something move away from you	
	a word such as two or nine	
	having lived for a long time	

Hint

| map | puppy | make | low | man | push | once | purple | number |
| nose | often | many | put | old | quiet | noon | lunch | queen |

B. Read and fill in the word and meaning.

word	definition	meaning
	to make musical sounds with your voice	
	to give information to somebody by speaking	
	to have a desire or a wish for something	
	the game using rackets and a ball	
	a woman who has the same parents as you	
	used to refer to a particular time in the past and future	
	moving without much speed, not fast	
	a piece of clothing worn by women and girls	
	an equipment which you can watch moving pictures	
	to move or go somewhere by your foot	
	the space that you can see when you look up from the earth	
	to give emphasis to an adjective or adverb	
	a system for talking to somebody over long distance	
	to spend some time doing very little	
	not large in size, number and degree; between tiny and large	
	to go to see someone and spend time with him / her	
	to give lessons to students in a school, college, etc.	
	to make something / somebody clean using water	

Hint
sing   tennis   skirt   wait   teach   slow   very   telephone   sky
wash   tell   sister   visit   television   then   walk   want   small

Unit 21

🎧 Listen and repeat. Track 61

01 absent [ǽbsənt]
a 결석의, 부재의   not in one's expected place
Why were you **absent** from school?
너는 왜 학교에 결석했니?

02 accept [æksépt]
v 받아들이다   to agree to take something
Please **accept** this small gift.
이 작은 선물을 받아주세요.

03 action [ǽkʃən]
n 행동, 활동   doing things for a particular purpose
I put my idea into **action**.
나는 나의 생각을 행동으로 옮겼다.

04 any [éni]
a 얼마간의   some of a particular thing
Do you have **any** butter?
약간의 버터가 있나요?

05 bath [bæθ]
n 목욕   an act of washing the body
You should take a **bath**.
목욕을 꼭 하세요.

06 beach [bi:tʃ]
n 해변, 바닷가   an area of sand or small stones beside the sea
I want to see a beautiful **beach**.
아름다운 해변이 보고 싶어요.

07 bill [bil]
n 계산서, 지폐   a piece of paper showing how much money you owe
Can I have the **bill**, please?
계산서 좀 갖다 주세요.

08 birth [bə:rθ]
n 출생, 탄생   being born; coming out of a mother's body
What's your date of **birth**?
너의 생일은 언제니?

09 butter [bʌ́tər]
n 버터   a soft yellow fat made from cream
Put some **butter** in the pan.
냄비에 버터를 넣으세요.

---

key words
expect v 기대하다 / agree v 동의하다 / purpose n 목적, 의지
sand n 모래 / beside prep ~ 옆에 / fat n 지방(질)

🎧 Listen and repeat. (Track 62)

10 button
[bʌ́tn]
n 단추, 버튼   a small piece of plastic used for fastening your clothes
One **button** on my shirt has come off.
셔츠의 단추 하나가 떨어졌어.

11 cheap
[tʃi:p]
a 값이 싼   low in price; inexpensive
This book is **cheap** so I can buy it.
이 책은 값이 싸서 살 수 있어.

12 check
[tʃek]
v 체크하다, 대조하다   to examine or test to make sure something
He **checked** my teeth.
그는 내 치아를 검사했다.

13 clothes
[klouðz]
n 옷, 의복   the things that you wear
She was wearing new **clothes** and new shoes.
그녀는 새 옷을 입고 새 신발을 신고 있다.

14 club
[klʌb]
n 곤봉, 동호회   a heavy stick, a group of people who share an interest
Let's join the science **club** together.
같이 과학 동호회에 가입하자.

15 corner
[kɔ́:rnər]
n 구석, 길모퉁이   a place where lines, edges or roads meet
There is a small table in the **corner**.
구석에 작은 탁자가 있다.

16 crane
[krein]
v 두루미, 기중기   a large machine with a long metal arm used for moving or lifting
I saw a bridge **crane** near the school.
나는 학교 근처에서 다리 모양의 기중기를 보았다.

17 dead
[ded]
a 죽은   no longer living; not alive
My dog is **dead** because he was old.
나의 개는 나이 들어서 죽었다.

18 dear
[diər]
a 귀여운, 친애하는   loved by or important to somebody
Dear Kate, I got your letter last Sunday.
친애하는 케이트, 지난 일요일에 너의 편지를 받았어.

---

key words
fasten **v** 채우다 / inexpensive **a** 비싸지 않은 / examine **v** 조사하다
share **v** 나누다, 공유하다 / edge **n** 가장자리 / metal **a** 금속의

Unit 21   **107**

Exercise

A. Complete the sentence.

1. He _____ my teeth.
   그는 내 치아를 검사했다.

2. Please _____ this small gift.
   이 작은 선물을 받아주세요.

3. Let's join the science _____ together.
   같이 과학 동호회에 가입하자.

4. Why were you _____ from school?
   너는 왜 학교에 결석했니?

5. I saw a bridge _____ near the school.
   나는 학교 근처에서 다리 모양의 기중기를 보았다.

6. Do you have _____ butter?
   약간의 버터가 있나요?

7. I want to see a beautiful _____.
   아름다운 해변이 보고 싶어요.

8. _____ Kate, I got your letter last Sunday.
   친애하는 케이트, 지난 일요일에 너의 편지를 받았어.

9. What's your date of _____?
   너의 생일은 언제니?

10. Put some _____ in the pan.
    냄비에 버터를 넣으세요.

11. I put my idea into _____.
    나의 생각을 행동으로 옮겼다.

12. One _____ on my shirt has come off.
    셔츠의 단추 하나가 떨어졌어.

13. This book is _____ so I can buy it.
    이 책은 값이 싸서 살 수 있어.

14. She was wearing new _____ and new shoes.
    그녀는 새 옷을 입고 새 신발을 신고 있다.

15. There is a small table in the _____.
    구석에 작은 탁자가 있다.

16. You should take a _____.
    목욕을 꼭 하세요.

17. My dog is _____ because he was old.
    나의 개는 나이 들어서 죽었다.

18. Can I have the _____, please?
    계산서 좀 갖다 주세요.

Hint

| bill | corner | birth | accept | beach | action | bath | butter | dead |
| club | button | any | cheap | absent | crane | dear | check | clothes |

Unit 21

Exercise

B. Fill in the word and meaning.

	Word	Meaning
01	accept	
02	bath	
03	cheap	
04	absent	
05	button	
06	crane	
07	any	
08	clothes	
09	dead	
10	action	
11	bill	
12	club	
13	butter	
14	corner	
15	birth	
16	dear	
17	check	
18	beach	

	Meaning	Word
01	결석의, 부재의	
02	받아들이다	
03	행동, 활동	
04	얼마간의	
05	목욕	
06	해변, 바닷가	
07	계산서, 지폐	
08	출생, 탄생	
09	버터	
10	단추, 버튼	
11	값이 싼	
12	체크하다, 대조하다	
13	옷, 의복	
14	곤봉, 동호회	
15	구석, 길모퉁이	
16	두루미, 기중기	
17	죽은	
18	귀여운, 친애하는	

C. Listen, write the word and meaning. Track 63

	Word	Meaning		Word	Meaning
01			10		
02			11		
03			12		
04			13		
05			14		
06			15		
07			16		
08			17		
09			18		

Unit 22

🎧 Listen and repeat. Track 64

01 dollar [dálər]
n 달러   the standard unit of money in some countries
One **dollar** is one hundred cents.
1달러는 100센트이다.

02 dream [dri:m]
n 꿈   a event which happen in your mind when you are sleep
I had a strange **dream**.
나는 이상한 꿈을 꾸었다.

03 engine [éndʒən]
n 엔진, 기관   the part of a vehicle that produces power
The **engine** of my car is out of order.
내 자동차의 엔진이 고장 났어.

04 enjoyment [endʒɔ́imənt]
n 즐거움, 기쁨   pleasure or a thing which gives pleasure
She gets a lot of **enjoyment** from teaching.
그녀는 가르치는 일에 큰 기쁨을 느낀다.

05 family [fǽməli]
n 가족   a group consisting of a set of parents and children
I miss all my **family**.
나는 가족 모두가 보고 싶다.

06 far [fa:r]
ad 멀리   distant; a long way away
It is very **far** from my home to school.
집에서 학교까지 거리가 너무 멀다.

07 fire [faiər]
n 불, 화재   burning and flames
The **fire** broke out in my store.
화재가 내 가게에서 발생했다.

08 fix [fiks]
v 고치다, 붙이다   to repair something, to put something firmly
She will **fix** the poster to a wall.
그녀는 벽에 포스터를 붙일 것이다.

09 glove [glʌv]
n 장갑, 글러브   a piece of clothing that covers your hand and fingers
I need a new pair of **gloves**.
나는 새 장갑이 필요해요.

key words
standard a 표준의 / unit n 단위 / vehicle n 탈 것 / distant a 먼, 떨어진 / burn v 불타다
flame n 불꽃 / repair v 수리하다 / firmly ad 굳게, 단단히 / poster n 포스터, 벽보

🎧 Listen and repeat. Track 65

10 go
[gou]
v 가다 — to move or travel from one place to another
She always **goes** home by bus.
그녀는 항상 버스로 집에 간다.

11 handle
[hǽndl]
n 손잡이 — the part of a door by which it is held to be moved
She turned the **handle** of the door.
그녀가 문의 손잡이를 돌렸다.

12 hear
[hiər]
v 듣다 — to receive sounds with your ears
I can't **hear** very well.
잘 들리지가 않아요.

13 holiday
[hálədèi]
n 휴가, 휴일 — a period of recreational time spent away from work
I am waiting for this **holiday**.
나는 이번 휴가를 기다리고 있다.

14 huge
[hju:dʒ]
a 거대한 — very big
The film was a **huge** success.
그 영화는 크게 성공했다.

15 husband
[hʌ́zbənd]
n 남편 — a man that a woman is married to
Her **husband** is a very nice guy.
그녀의 남편은 정말 멋진 남자이다.

16 jealous
[dʒéləs]
a 질투하는 — feeling upset because you want to be like somebody
She is a very **jealous** girl.
그녀는 매우 질투심이 많아.

17 keep
[kip]
v 기르다, 유지하다 — to continue or be frequently doing something
It is hard to **keep** my weight.
내 몸무게를 그대로 유지하기가 힘들다.

18 kid
[kid]
n 아이 — a human being who is not yet an adult
Several **kids** are playing in the playground.
몇 명의 아이들이 놀이터에서 놀고 있다.

---

key words
receive **v** 받다 / recreational **a** 휴양의 / upset **n** 마음이 동요한
frequently **ad** 종종, 자주 / adult **a** 어른의 / playground **n** 놀이터, 운동장

Unit 22 111

Exercise

A. Complete the sentence.

1. I had a strange _____.
   나는 이상한 꿈을 꾸었다.

2. She gets a lot of _____ from teaching.
   그는 음악 듣는 것을 즐긴다.

3. One _____ is one hundred cents.
   1달러는 100센트이다.

4. The _____ of my car is out of order.
   내 자동차의 엔진이 고장 났어.

5. I miss all my _____.
   나는 가족 모두가 보고 싶다.

6. The _____ broke out in my store.
   화재가 내 가게에서 발생했다.

7. She will _____ the poster to a wall.
   그녀는 벽에 포스터를 붙일 것이다.

8. I can't _____ very well.
   잘 들리지가 않아요.

9. She is a very _____ girl.
   그녀는 매우 질투심이 많아.

10. Several _____ are playing in the playground.
    몇 명의 아이들이 놀이터에서 놀고 있다.

11. She always _____ home by bus.
    그녀는 항상 버스로 집에 간다.

12. She turned the _____ of the door.
    그녀가 문의 손잡이를 돌렸다.

13. I am waiting for this _____.
    나는 이번 휴가를 기다리고 있다.

14. The film was a _____ success.
    그 영화는 크게 성공했다.

15. Her _____ is a very nice guy.
    그녀의 남편은 정말 멋진 남자이다.

16. It is very _____ from my home to school.
    집에서 학교까지 거리가 너무 멀다.

17. It is hard to _____ my weight.
    내 몸무게를 그대로 유지하기가 힘들다.

18. I need a new pair of _____.
    나는 새 장갑이 필요해요.

Hint

| dollar | family | husband | fire | dream | engine | kid | far | glove |
| handle | go | hear | fix | huge | jealous | keep | holiday | enjoyment |

Exercise

B. Fill in the word and meaning.

	Word	Meaning
01	engine	
02	dream	
03	glove	
04	handle	
05	dollar	
06	family	
07	holiday	
08	keep	
09	jealous	
10	fire	
11	kid	
12	huge	
13	fix	
14	husband	
15	hear	
16	far	
17	go	
18	enjoyment	

	Meaning	Word
01	달러	
02	꿈	
03	엔진, 기관	
04	즐거움, 기쁨	
05	가족	
06	멀리	
07	불, 화재	
08	고치다, 붙이다	
09	장갑, 글러브	
10	가다	
11	손잡이	
12	듣다	
13	휴가, 휴일	
14	거대한	
15	남편	
16	질투하는	
17	기르다, 유지하다	
18	아이	

C. Listen, write the word and meaning. (Track 66)

	Word	Meaning		Word	Meaning
01			10		
02			11		
03			12		
04			13		
05			14		
06			15		
07			16		
08			17		
09			18		

Review 11

A. Read and fill in the word and meaning.

word	definition	meaning
	an area of sand or small stones beside the sea	
	a large machine with a long metal arm used for moving or lifting	
	doing things for a particular purpose	
	to examine or test to make sure something	
	low in price; inexpensive	
	some of a particular thing	
	a soft yellow fat made from cream	
	a heavy stick, a group of people who share an interest	
	to agree to take something	
	a place where lines, edges or roads meet	
	an act of washing the body in a bath	
	the things that you wear	
	a small piece of plastic used for fastening your clothes	
	not in one's expected place	
	being born; coming out of a mother's body	
	loved by or important to somebody	
	a piece of paper showing how much money you owe	
	no longer living; not alive	

Hint

| dear | corner | bath | dead | beach | button | birth | absent | accept |
| club | action | any | cheap | butter | crane | bill | clothes | check |

B. Read and fill in the word and meaning.

word	definition	meaning
	distant; a long way away	
	to repair something, to put something firmly	
	a group consisting of a set of parents and children	
	very big	
	burning and flames	
	a piece of clothing that covers your hand and fingers	
	pleasure or a thing which gives pleasure	
	a man that a woman is married to	
	to move or travel from one place to another	
	the part of a vehicle that produces power	
	to continue or be frequently doing something	
	feeling upset because you want to be like somebody	
	a human being who is not yet an adult	
	the part of a door by which it is held to be moved	
	a event which happen in your mind when you are sleep	
	to receive sounds with your ears	
	a period of recreational time spent away from work	
	the standard unit of money in some countries	

Hint

dollar   huge   kid   go   dream   holiday   far   husband   glove
family   hear   fire   fix   handle   jealous   keep   engine   enjoyment

Unit 23

🎧 Listen and repeat. (Track 67)

01 leave   v 떠나다   to go away from someone or somewhere
[li:v]
I want to **leave** this company.
나는 이 회사를 떠나고 싶어요.

02 letter   n 편지, 글자   a written or printed message that you send
[létə:r]
I am writing a thank-you **letter** to my teacher.
나는 선생님께 감사편지를 쓰고 있어.

03 luck   n 운, 행운   having good fortune
[lʌk]
This ring will bring me **luck**.
이 반지는 나에게 행운을 가져다 줄 거에요.

04 mad   a 화난, 미친   having a mind that does not work normally
[mæd]
You must be **mad** to sleep all day.
하루 종일 자다니 정말 미쳤구나.

05 note   n 기록, 노트   a brief written record
[nout]
Keep a **note** of who has paid and who hasn't.
누가 돈을 지불했고 안 했는지 기록해 두세요.

06 number   n 번호, 숫자   a word or symbol that indicates a quantity
[nʌ́mbə:r]
Choose a **number** between ten and twenty.
10에서 20까지 중 숫자를 하나 고르세요.

07 peel   v 껍질을 벗기다   to take the skin off a fruit or vegetable
[pi:l]
Could you **peel** the potatoes, please?
감자 껍질 좀 벗겨 주실래요?

08 pen   n 펜, 우리   an object that you use for writing in ink
[pen]
He gave me a great fountain **pen** for my birthday present.
그는 나에게 생일선물로 근사한 만년필을 주었다.

09 please   ad 제발, 부디   used as a polite way of asking for something
[pli:z]
Please forgive me.
부디 저를 용서해 주세요.

---

key words

company n 회사 / fortune n 운 / normally ad 정상적으로 / brief a 간결한 / symbol n 기호 / quantity n 양, 수량 / skin n 껍질 / fountain pen n 만년필 / forgive v 용서하다

🎧 Listen and repeat. Track 68

10 police [pəlíːs]
n 경찰   the official organization to prevent and solve crime
He saw a **police** car and ran away.
그는 경찰차를 보고는 도망갔다.

11 purse [pəːrs]
n 지갑   a small bag for carrying coins and paper money
The woman who has a heavy **purse** seems to be rich.
두둑한 지갑을 가진 그 여자는 부유해 보인다.

12 puzzle [pʌzl]
n 퍼즐, 수수께끼   something that is difficult to understand; a mystery
Let's solve the **puzzle** together.
함께 수수께끼를 풀어보자.

13 rest [rest]
n 휴식   to relay or sleep after a period of activity
He has worked for a week without **rest**.
그는 일주일 동안 휴식 없이 일해 왔다.

14 restaurant [réstərənt]
n 음식점, 레스토랑   a place where you can eat a meal
I had dinner with family in a Chinese **restaurant**.
중국 음식점에서 가족과 함께 저녁을 먹었다.

15 safe [seif]
a 안전한   free from danger
You need to go somewhere **safe**.
당신은 안전한 곳으로 가야 해요.

16 salt [sɔːlt]
n 소금   a common white substance that is found in sea water
To eat a lot of **salt** is not healthy.
소금을 많이 먹는 것은 건강에 좋지 않다.

17 sheep [ʃiːp]
n 양   a farm animal covered with thick curly hair called wool
Don't let that dog loose among the **sheep**.
그 개를 양들 사이에 풀어 놓지 마세요.

18 sheet [ʃiːt]
n 시트, 커버   a large piece of material used on a bed
My mother bought a new **sheet** for the bed.
엄마가 새 침대 시트를 사셨다.

key words
organization **n** 조직, 기구 / crime **n** 죄 / mystery **n** 신비, 수수께끼
relay **v** 새 사람(것)으로 바꾸게 하다 / danger **n** 위험 / farm **n** 농장 / loose **v** 풀어주다

Unit 23

Exercise

A. Complete the sentence.

1. This ring will bring me _____.
   이 반지는 나에게 행운을 가져다 줄 거에요.

2. Keep a _____ of who has paid and who hasn't.
   누가 돈을 지불했고 안 했는지 기록해 두세요.

3. Choose a _____ between ten and twenty.
   10에서 20까지 중 숫자를 하나 고르세요.

4. You must be _____ to sleep all day.
   하루 종일 자다니 정말 미쳤구나.

5. To eat a lot of _____ is not healthy.
   소금을 많이 먹는 것은 건강에 좋지 않다.

6. He gave me a great fountain _____ for my birthday present.
   그는 나에게 생일선물로 근사한 만년필을 주었다.

7. _____ forgive me.
   부디 저를 용서해 주세요.

8. I want to _____ this company.
   나는 이 회사를 떠나고 싶어요.

9. He saw a _____ car and ran away.
   그는 경찰차를 보고는 도망갔다.

10. The woman who has a heavy _____ seems to be rich.
    두둑한 지갑을 가진 그 여자는 부유해 보인다.

11. He has worked for a week without _____.
    그는 일주일 동안 휴식 없이 일해 왔다.

12. I am writing a thank-you _____ to my teacher.
    나는 선생님께 감사편지를 쓰고 있어.

13. I had dinner with family in a Chinese _____.
    중국 음식점에서 가족과 함께 저녁을 먹었다.

14. You need to go somewhere _____.
    당신은 안전한 곳으로 가야 해요.

15. Let's solve the _____ together.
    함께 수수께끼를 풀어보자.

16. Don't let that dog loose among the _____.
    그 개를 양들 사이에 풀어 놓지 마세요.

17. Could you _____ the potatoes, please?
    감자 껍질 좀 벗겨 주실래요?

18. My mother bought a new _____ for the bed.
    엄마가 새 침대 시트를 사셨다.

Hint

| leave | mad | puzzle | note | sheet | number | peel | sheep | please |
| purse | luck | rest | police | salt | restaurant | pen | safe | letter |

Exercise

B. Fill in the word and meaning.

	Word	Meaning
01	please	
02	mad	
03	letter	
04	leave	
05	rest	
06	purse	
07	luck	
08	number	
09	puzzle	
10	sheep	
11	safe	
12	pen	
13	sheet	
14	police	
15	salt	
16	restaurant	
17	peel	
18	note	

	Meaning	Word
01	떠나다	
02	편지, 글자	
03	운, 행운	
04	화난, 미친	
05	기록, 노트	
06	번호, 숫자	
07	껍질을 벗기다	
08	펜, 우리	
09	제발, 부디	
10	경찰	
11	지갑	
12	퍼즐, 수수께끼	
13	휴식	
14	음식점, 레스토랑	
15	안전한	
16	소금	
17	양	
18	시트, 커버	

C. Listen, write the word and meaning. (Track 69)

	Word	Meaning		Word	Meaning
01			10		
02			11		
03			12		
04			13		
05			14		
06			15		
07			16		
08			17		
09			18		

Unit 23

Unit 24

🎧 Listen and repeat. Track 70

01 **sleep** — v 잠자다 — to rest with your eyes closed
[sli:p]
I couldn't get to **sleep** last night.
나는 지난밤에 잠을 잘 수가 없었어.

02 **slide** — v (미끄럼틀을) 타다 — to move smoothly along a surface
[slaid]
You have to **slide** one by one.
한 명씩 차례대로 미끄럼틀을 타야 해요.

03 **south** — n 남쪽 / ad 남쪽으로 — the direction on your right when you watch the sun rise
[sauθ]
Which way is **south**?
어느 방향이 남쪽인가요?

04 **spell** — v 철자를 쓰다 — to write the letters of a word
[spel]
She could **spell** very well.
그녀는 철자 쓰기를 매우 잘해요.

05 **stick** — n 막대기, 지팡이 — a thin branch which has fallen off a tree
[stik]
The lion jumps over a **stick**.
사자가 막대기를 뛰어 넘는다.

06 **stone** — n 돌 — a hard solid substance that is found in the ground
[stoun]
The house was built of grey **stone**.
그 집은 회색 돌로 지어졌다.

07 **supper** — n 저녁 식사 — the main meal eaten in the early part of the evening
[sʌ́pər]
After **supper**, he sat on the porch waiting.
저녁 식사 후에 그는 현관에서 앉아서 기다렸다.

08 **sure** — a 확신한 — having no doubt; certain
[ʃuər]
I'm not **sure** what to do next.
다음으로 무엇을 해야 할 지 확실치 않다.

09 **test** — n 시험 — a short exam to measure one's knowledge or skill
[test]
We have a math **test** every Friday.
우리는 매주 금요일 수학 시험을 봅니다.

---

key words
smoothly ad 매끄럽게 / branch n 가지 / solid a 고체의
porch n 현관 / doubt n 의심, 불확실함 / knowledge n 지식 / math n 수학

🎧 Listen and repeat. (Track 71)

10 than [ðæn]
conj ~보다   used when you are comparing two things
He is taller **than** me.
그는 나보다 키가 크다.

11 together [təgéðəːr]
ad 함께, 같이   with or near each other
I think all the family should do the housework **together**.
집안 일은 가족 모두가 같이 해야 한다고 생각한다.

12 tomato [təméitou]
n 토마토   a soft red fruit that is often eaten being cooked
Cut up a **tomato** into small slices.
토마토를 작은 조각으로 얇게 썰으세요.

13 understand [ʌ̀ndərstǽnd]
v 이해하다   to know or realize the meaning or the reason
She learns all the parts and then **understands** the whole.
그녀는 모든 부분을 다 배운 후 전체를 이해한다.

14 until [əntíl]
conj ~할 때까지   up to the time
The restaurant is open **until** 10:00pm.
그 식당은 밤 10시까지 문을 열어요.

15 vegetable [védʒətəbəl]
n 야채   a plant or part of a plant that we eat
I prefer meat to **vegetables**.
나는 야채보다 고기를 더 좋아한다.

16 video [vídiòu]
n 비디오   the system showing moving pictures using a machine
We recorded the wedding on **video**.
우리는 결혼식 비디오를 찍었다.

17 visit [vízit]
v 방문하다   to go to see a person for a period of time
She's going to **visit** her parents.
그녀는 부모님을 방문하러 갈 예정이다.

18 wake [weik]
v 일어나다   to stop sleeping
Suddenly he **woke** from sleep.
갑자기 그는 잠에서 일어났다.

key words
compare **v** 비교하다 / slice **n** 조각 / realize **v** 깨닫다 / reason **n** 이유, 까닭 / record **v** 기록하다

Exercise

A. Complete the sentence.

1. The restaurant is open _____ 10:00pm.
   그 식당은 밤 10시까지 문을 열어요.

2. She could _____ very well.
   그녀는 철자 쓰기를 매우 잘해요.

3. I couldn't get to _____ last night.
   나는 지난밤에 잠을 잘 수가 없었어.

4. We recorded the wedding on _____.
   우리는 결혼식 비디오를 찍었다.

5. Which way is _____?
   어느 방향이 남쪽인가요?

6. The lion jumps over a _____.
   사자가 막대기를 뛰어 넘는다.

7. I think all the family should do the housework _____.
   집안 일은 가족 모두가 같이 해야 한다고 생각한다.

8. After _____, he sat on the porch waiting.
   저녁 식사 후에 그는 현관에서 앉아서 기다렸다.

9. She's going to _____ her parents.
   그녀는 부모님을 방문하러 갈 예정이다.

10. I'm not _____ what to do next.
    다음으로 무엇을 해야 할 지 확실치 않다.

11. We have a math _____ every Friday.
    우리는 매주 금요일 수학 시험을 봅니다.

12. The house was built of grey _____.
    그 집은 회색 돌로 지어졌다.

13. He is taller _____ me.
    그는 나보다 키가 크다.

14. You have to _____ one by one.
    한 명씩 차례대로 미끄럼틀을 타야 해요.

15. Cut up a _____ into small slices.
    토마토를 작은 조각으로 얇게 썰어라.

16. She learns all the parts and then _____ the whole.
    그녀는 모든 부분을 다 배운 후 전체를 이해한다.

17. I prefer meat to _____.
    나는 야채보다 고기를 더 좋아한다.

18. Suddenly he _____ from sleep.
    갑자기 그는 잠에서 일어났다.

Hint

| slide | understand | spell | visit | stick | south | wake | sure | test |
| stone | than | | vegetable | sleep | together | supper | until | video | tomato |

Exercise

B. Fill in the word and meaning.

	Word	Meaning
01	supper	
02	test	
03	sleep	
04	until	
05	slide	
06	visit	
07	than	
08	stick	
09	wake	
10	video	
11	spell	
12	tomato	
13	sure	
14	vegetable	
15	stone	
16	understand	
17	together	
18	south	

	Meaning	Word
01	잠자다	
02	(미끄럼틀을) 타다	
03	남쪽, 남쪽으로	
04	철자를 쓰다	
05	막대기, 지팡이	
06	돌	
07	저녁 식사	
08	확신한	
09	시험	
10	~보다	
11	함께, 같이	
12	토마토	
13	이해하다	
14	~할 때까지	
15	야채	
16	비디오	
17	방문하다	
18	일어나다	

C. Listen, write the word and meaning. (Track 72)

	Word	Meaning		Word	Meaning
01			10		
02			11		
03			12		
04			13		
05			14		
06			15		
07			16		
08			17		
09			18		

Review 12

A. Read and fill in the word and meaning.

word	definition	meaning
	a word or symbol that indicates a quantity	
	to relay or sleep after a period of activity	
	free from danger	
	a small bag for carrying coins and paper money	
	a written or printed message that you send	
	to take the skin off a fruit or vegetable	
	having a mind that does not work normally	
	a farm animal covered with thick curly hair called wool	
	a common white substance that is found in sea water	
	having good fortune	
	a brief written record	
	a place where you can eat a meal	
	an object that you use for writing in ink	
	a large piece of material used on a bed	
	used as a polite way of asking for something	
	the official organization to prevent and solve crime	
	to go away from someone or somewhere	
	something that is difficult to understand; a mystery	

Hint

| number | mad | sheet | note | puzzle | police | sheep | luck | please |
| purse | peel | rest | leave | salt | letter | pen | safe | restaurant |

B. Read and fill in the word and meaning.

word	definition	meaning
	to move smoothly along a surface	
	used when you are comparing two things	
	a soft red fruit that is often eaten being cooked	
	the direction on your right when you watch the sun rise	
	with or near each other	
	to rest with your eyes closed	
	a short exam to measure one's knowledge or skill	
	to go to see a person for a period of time	
	to write the letters of a word	
	having no doubt; certain	
	to stop sleeping	
	the system showing moving pictures using a machine	
	a hard solid substance that is found in the ground	
	to know or realize the meaning or the reason	
	a plant or part of a plant that we eat	
	the main meal eaten in the early part of the evening	
	a thin branch which has fallen off a tree	
	up to the time	

Hint

slide   test   spell   visit   supper   tomato   video   sure   understand
until   than   south   sleep   together   stick   stone   wake   vegetable

Unit 25

🎧 **Listen and repeat.** Track 73

01 age [eidʒ] — **n** 나이, 연령 — the length of time that somebody has lived
He needs a friend of his own **age**.
그는 또래의 친구가 필요하다.

02 ago [əgóu] — **ad** ~전에 — in the past; back in time from now
My sister stopped playing the piano two years **ago**.
언니는 2년 전에 피아노 치는 것을 그만두었다.

03 apartment [əpá:rtmənt] — **n** 아파트 — a set of rooms for living in
What do you think of my new **apartment**?
내 새 아파트가 어떤 것 같아요?

04 as [æz] — **prep** ~로서 — used for talking about something / somebody's job or role
I respect him **as** my teacher.
나는 나의 선생님으로서 그를 존경한다.

05 beat [bi:t] — **v** 때리다, 부딪치다 — to hit many times, usually very hard
The rain is **beating** on the window.
빗방울이 창문에 부딪치고 있다.

06 beggar [bégər] — **n** 거지 — a person who lives by asking people for money, food
Even the **beggar** envies another **beggar**.
거지 조차 다른 거지를 샘낸다.

07 birthday [bá:rθdèi] — **n** 생일 — the day in each year when you were born
Thank you for my **birthday** present.
생일 선물 고마워요.

08 block [blak] — **n** 블록, 한 구획 — a group of buildings which has streets on all four sides
The restaurant is three **blocks** away.
그 식당은 세 블록 떨어져 있다.

09 cake [keik] — **n** 케이크 — a sweet food made by mixing flour and eggs and baking the mixture
Would you like some more **cake**?
케이크 더 드실래요?

key words
length **n** 길이 / role **n** 역할 / respect **v** 존경하다 / envy **v** 부러워하다
bear **v** 낳다 / mix **v** 섞다 / bake **v** 굽다

🎧 Listen and repeat. Track 74

10 camera   n 카메라   an equipment that you use for taking photographs
[kǽmərə]
The man is wrapping the **camera**.
남자가 카메라를 포장하고 있다.

11 cheese   n 치즈   a type of food made from milk
[tʃiːz]
There is a piece of **cheese** cake in the kitchen.
부엌에 치즈 케이크가 있어.

12 chess   n 체스   a game played on a board with 64 black and white squares
[tʃes]
I played **chess** with my sister.
나는 누나와 체스를 두었습니다.

13 cock   n 수탉   an adult male chicken
[kak]
His nickname is a game **cock**.
그의 별명은 싸움닭이다.

14 coffee   n 커피   the cooked beans of tropical tree
[kɔ́ːfi]
I'll have tea instead of **coffee**, please.
커피 대신에 차를 마실 게요.

15 courage   n 용기, 담력   the ability to control fear in a dangerous situation
[kə́ːridʒ]
He showed real **courage** going into the burning building.
그는 불타는 건물 속으로 뛰어드는 진짜 용기를 보여 주었다.

16 cover   v 덮다, 씌우다   to put something to hide or protect it
[kʌ́vər]
I **covered** the floor with newspaper before I started painting.
나는 페인트칠을 시작하기 전에 신문지로 바닥을 덮었다.

17 deep   a 깊은   going a long way down from the surface
[diːp]
This coat has **deep** pockets.
이 코트는 주머니가 깊다.

18 deer   n 사슴   a large wild grass-eating animal
[diər]
The **deer** ran off in alarm.
사슴은 놀라서 달아났다.

---

key words
equipment n 장비 / wrap v 포장하다 / square n 정사각형 / tropical a 열대(지방)의
instead ad 대신에 / hide v 숨기다, 덮다 / alarm n 놀람

Exercise

A. Complete the sentence.

1. He needs a friend of his own _____.
   그는 또래의 친구가 필요하다.
2. The _____ ran off in alarm.
   사슴은 놀라서 달아났다.
3. Would you like some more _____?
   케이크 더 드실래요?
4. What do you think of my new _____?
   내 새 아파트가 어떤 것 같아요?
5. The rain is _____ on the window.
   빗방울이 창문에 부딪치고 있다.
6. The restaurant is three _____ away.
   그 식당은 세 블록 떨어져 있다.
7. The man is wrapping the _____.
   남자가 카메라를 포장하고 있다.
8. He showed real _____ going into the burning building.
   그는 불타는 건물 속으로 뛰어드는 진짜 용기를 보여 주었다.
9. There is a piece of _____ cake in the kitchen.
   부엌에 치즈 케이크가 있어.
10. I respect him _____ my teacher.
    나는 나의 선생님으로서 그를 존경한다.
11. I played _____ with my sister.
    나는 누나와 체스를 두었습니다.
12. Thank you for my _____ present.
    생일 선물 고마워요.
13. His nickname is a game _____.
    그의 별명은 싸움닭이다.
14. Even the _____ envies another _____.
    거지 조차 다른 거지를 샘낸다.
15. I _____ the floor with newspaper before I started painting.
    나는 페인트칠을 시작하기 전에 신문지로 바닥을 덮었다.
16. My sister stopped playing the piano two years _____.
    나의 언니는 2년 전에 피아노 치는 것을 그만두었다.
17. I'll have tea instead of _____, please.
    커피 대신에 차를 마실 게요.
18. This coat has _____ pockets.
    이 코트는 주머니가 깊다.

Hint

| birthday | age | cake | block | camera | ago | courage | beat | chess |
| apartment | cock | coffee | beggar | cover | deep | cheese | as | deer |

Exercise

B. Fill in the word and meaning.

	Word	Meaning
01	beggar	
02	age	
03	birthday	
04	ago	
05	cock	
06	beat	
07	coffee	
08	deep	
09	camera	
10	as	
11	courage	
12	cover	
13	cheese	
14	deer	
15	chess	
16	block	
17	cake	
18	apartment	

	Meaning	Word
01	나이, 연령	
02	~전에	
03	아파트	
04	~로서	
05	때리다, 부딪치다	
06	거지	
07	생일	
08	블록, 한 구획	
09	케이크	
10	카메라	
11	치즈	
12	체스	
13	수탉	
14	커피	
15	용기, 담력	
16	덮다, 씌우다	
17	깊은	
18	사슴	

C. Listen, write the word and meaning. Track 75

	Word	Meaning		Word	Meaning
01			10		
02			11		
03			12		
04			13		
05			14		
06			15		
07			16		
08			17		
09			18		

Unit 25

Unit 26

🎧 Listen and repeat. Track 76

01 dress
[dres]
n 드레스, 의복   a piece of clothing worn by a woman or girl
She was wearing a black **dress**.
그녀는 검정색 드레스를 입고 있었다.

02 drink
[driŋk]
v 마시다   to take liquid into your body through your mouth
Would you like something cold to **drink**?
차가운 것 좀 마실래요?

03 every
[évriː]
a ~마다, 모두   all of the people or things in a group
She knows **every** student in the school.
그녀는 학교의 모든 학생들을 알고 있다.

04 exam
[igzǽm]
n 시험   a practical test of what you know or you can do
It was unlucky that he failed the **exam**.
유감스럽게도 그는 시험에 떨어졌다.

05 farm
[faːrm]
n 농장   a land with fields used for growing crops and keeping animals
My grandfather works on a **farm**.
나의 할아버지는 농장에서 일하신다.

06 fast
[fæst]
a 빠른 / **ad** 빨리   able to move or act at great speed
The taxi driver drove the car too **fast**.
택시 운전기사는 차를 너무 빨리 몰았다.

07 flag
[flæg]
n 깃발   a piece of cloth with a picture on it, tied to a pole
That's the **flag** of Korea, isn't it?
저것이 한국의 국기지, 그렇지 않니?

08 floor
[flɔːr]
n 마루, 바닥   the flat surface that you walk on indoors
They are mopping the **floor**.
그들은 대걸레로 바닥을 청소하고 있다.

09 gold
[gould]
n 금   a precious yellow metal
Is your ring made of **gold**?
너의 반지는 금으로 만들어졌니?

---

key words
unlucky **a** 운이 없는 / crop **n** 농작물 / speed **n** 속도 / pole **n** 막대기, 장대
mop **v** 대걸레로 닦다 / precious **a** 비싼, 귀중한

🎧 Listen and repeat. Track 77

10 grandparent [grǽndpɛ̀ərənt]
n 조부모   the mother or father of one of your parents
My **grandparents** want to live in the country.
나의 조부모님은 시골에서 살 길 원하신다.

11 heart [hɑːrt]
n 심장, 가슴   the organ inside your chest that sends blood
When you exercise, your **heart** beats faster.
운동을 할 때 너의 심장은 더 빨리 뛴다.

12 helicopter [hélikàptər]
n 헬리콥터   a small aircraft that can go straight up into the air
Would you like to go on a **helicopter** ride?
헬리콥터를 타러 가고 싶나요?

13 hose [houz]
n 호스   a long rubber or plastic tube
He learned how to turn the **hose** on.
그는 호스를 켜는 방법을 배웠다.

14 hospital [háspitl]
n 병원   a place where sick people are looked after by doctors
At last I got to be treated at the **hospital**.
결국 나는 병원에서 치료를 받게 되었다.

15 kill [kil]
v 죽이다   to make somebody die
Men also **killed** so many animals.
사람도 역시 많은 동물을 죽였어.

16 knock [nak]
n 노크, 두드림   to make a noise by hitting something with your hand
I heard a loud **knock** at the door but I couldn't answer.
나는 문을 두드리는 큰 소리를 들었지만, 대답 할 수 없었다.

17 library [láibrèri]
n 도서관   a room that has a collection of books
There is a new **library** near the bank.
은행 근처에 새 도서관이 있어요.

18 life [laif]
n 생명, 생물   living things
Is there any **life** on Mars?
화성에는 어떤 생물이 있나요?

---

key words
organ n 기관 / blood n 피 / aircraft n 항공기 / treat v 치료하다 / Mars n 화성

Exercise

A. Complete the sentence.

1. The taxi driver drove the car too _____.
   택시 운전기사는 차를 너무 빨리 몰았다.

2. Would you like something cold to _____?
   차가운 것 좀 마실래요?

3. She knows _____ student in the school.
   그녀는 학교의 모든 학생들을 알고 있다.

4. My grandfather works on a _____.
   나의 할아버지는 농장에서 일하신다.

5. That's the _____ of Korea, isn't it?
   저것이 한국의 국기지, 그렇지 않니?

6. At last I got to be treated at the _____.
   결국 나는 병원에서 치료를 받게 되었다.

7. There is a new _____ near the bank.
   은행 근처에 새 도서관이 있어요.

8. They are mopping the _____.
   그들은 대걸레로 바닥을 청소하고 있다.

9. She was wearing a black _____.
   그녀는 검정색 드레스를 입고 있었다.

10. My _____ want to live in the country.
    나의 조부모님은 시골에서 살 길 원하신다.

11. When you exercise, your _____ beats faster.
    운동을 할 때 너의 심장은 더 빨리 뛴다.

12. Is your ring made of _____?
    너의 반지는 금으로 만들어졌니?

13. Would you like to go on a _____ ride?
    헬리콥터를 타러 가고 싶나요?

14. Men also _____ so many animals.
    사람도 역시 많은 동물을 죽였어.

15. It was unlucky that he failed the _____.
    유감스럽게도 그는 시험에 떨어졌다.

16. I heard a loud _____ at the door but I couldn't answer.
    나는 문을 두드리는 큰 소리를 들었지만 대답 할 수 없었다.

17. He learned how to turn the _____ on.
    그는 호스를 켜는 방법을 배웠다.

18. Is there any _____ on Mars?
    화성에는 어떤 생물이 있나요?

Hint

| dress | library | floor | knock | hospital | exam | farm | flag | every |
| helicopter | hose | grandparent | life | drink | heart | kill | fast | gold |

Exercise

B. Fill in the word and meaning.

	Word	Meaning
01	drink	
02	flag	
03	grandparent	
04	kill	
05	heart	
06	dress	
07	knock	
08	exam	
09	floor	
10	hospital	
11	every	
12	helicopter	
13	library	
14	gold	
15	farm	
16	life	
17	hose	
18	fast	

	Meaning	Word
01	드레스, 의복	
02	마시다	
03	~마다, 모두	
04	시험	
05	농장	
06	빠른, 빨리	
07	깃발	
08	마루, 바닥	
09	금	
10	조부모	
11	심장, 가슴	
12	헬리콥터	
13	호스	
14	병원	
15	죽이다	
16	노크, 두드림	
17	도서관	
18	생명, 생물	

C. Listen, write the word and meaning. (Track 78)

	Word	Meaning		Word	Meaning
01			10		
02			11		
03			12		
04			13		
05			14		
06			15		
07			16		
08			17		
09			18		

Review 13

A. Read and fill in the word and meaning.

word	definition	meaning
	a set of rooms for living in	
	a person who lives by asking people for money, food	
	a group of buildings which has streets on all four sides	
	in the past; back in time from now	
	the day in each year when you were born	
	an adult male chicken	
	the length of time that somebody has lived	
	the cooked beans of tropical tree	
	to hit many times, usually very hard	
	a game played on a board with 64 black and white squares	
	used for talking about something / somebody's job or role	
	to put something to hide or protect it	
	a type of food made from milk	
	going a long way down from the surface	
	a sweet food made by mixing flour and eggs and baking the mixture	
	a large wild grass-eating animal	
	an equipment that you use for taking photographs	
	the ability to control fear in a dangerous situation	

Hint

| chess | age | ago | cover | camera | cake | courage | beat | beggar |
| deer | as | coffee | block | birthday | deep | cheese | cock | apartment |

B. Read and fill in the word and meaning.

word	definition	meaning
	the organ inside your chest that sends blood	
	able to move or act at great speed	
	to make somebody die	
	the flat surface that you walk on indoors	
	a piece of clothing worn by a woman or girl	
	a small aircraft that can go straight up into the air	
	a land with fields used for growing crops and keeping animals	
	a long rubber or plastic tube	
	a precious yellow metal	
	a piece of cloth with a picture on it, tied to a pole	
	a place where sick people are looked after by doctors	
	the mother or father of one of your parents	
	living things	
	all of the people or things in a group	
	a room that has a collection of books	
	to take liquid into your body through your mouth	
	to make a noise by hitting something with your hand	
	a practical test of what you know or you can do	

Hint

dress drink floor kill hospital hose farm flag grandparent
gold exam every fast library heart knock life helicopter

Unit 27

🎧 Listen and repeat. Track 79

01 market
[máːrkit]
n 시장   a place where people buy and sell things
This city is famous for a big fish **market**.
이 도시는 큰 생선시장으로 유명하다.

02 may
[mei]
aux ~해도 좋다   used for saying that something is possible
May I use your bathroom?
내가 너의 욕실을 사용해도 되니?

03 move
[muːv]
v 움직이다, 옮기다   to change position or to put in a different place
Please **move** the desk and chair.
책상과 의자를 옮겨 주세요.

04 near
[niər]
prep ~의 가까이에   not far away in time or distance
There is a telephone **near** my bed.
내 침대 근처에는 전화기가 있다.

05 nurse
[nəːrs]
n 간호사   a person who is trained to look after sick people
She wants to become a **nurse**.
그녀는 간호사가 되고 싶다.

06 only
[óunli]
ad 단지, 오직   with no other existing or present
In elementary school I had **only** one teacher.
초등학교에서는 선생님이 오직 한 분이었다.

07 person
[páːrsən]
n 사람, 인물   a man or woman; a human being
Who is that **person** over there?
저기 있는 저 사람은 누구예요?

08 pet
[pet]
n 애완동물   an animal that you keep in your home for pleasure
The debate was about how to keep **pets**.
그 토론은 애완동물을 키우는 방법에 관한 것이었다.

09 pool
[puːl]
n 물웅덩이   a small amount of liquid lying on a surface
There's a huge **pool** of water on the kitchen floor.
부엌 바닥에 큰 물웅덩이가 있다.

key words
famous a 유명한 / train v 가르치다 / existing a 현존하는
elementary a 기본의, 초등 학교의 / debate n 토론, 논쟁

🎧 Listen and repeat. Track 80

10　post　　**n** 우편 / **v** 부치다　letters or packages that are brought to your home
[poust]　　Hasn't the **post** come yet?
아직 우편물 안 왔어요?

11　question　**n** 질문, 물음　a sentence or phrase that asks for an answer
[kwéstʃən]　That is a hard **question** to answer.
그것은 대답하기 어려운 질문이네요.

12　quick　**a** 빠른　done with speed; taking a short time
[kwik]　This dish is **quick** and easy to make.
이 요리는 빠르고 쉽게 만들 수 있어요.

13　return　**v** 돌아오다, 돌아가다　to come or go back to a place
[ritə́:rn]　I need to **return** because my brother is sick.
남동생이 아프기 때문에 나는 돌아가야 한다.

14　ride　**v** 타다　to sit on a bicycle, etc and control it as it moves
[raid]　Young children often **ride** tricycles.
어린 아이들은 종종 세발자전거를 탄다.

15　same　**a** 같은, 동일한　not different, not another; exactly the one
[seim]　The twins look exactly the **same**.
그 쌍둥이는 정말 똑같아요.

16　sand　**n** 모래　a powder consisting of very small grains of rock
[sænd]　They were mixing cement with **sand**.
그들은 시멘트를 모래와 섞고 있었다.

17　shoot　**v** 쏘다, 발사하다　to fire a gun or another weapon
[ʃu:t]　Did he **shoot** the bird, and kill it?
그가 그 새를 쏘아 죽였니?

18　shop　**n** 가게, 상점　a building where things are bought and sold
[ʃap]　There are many **shops** on both sides of the road.
그 길 양쪽에는 가게들이 많이 있다.

key words
sentence **n** 문장 / phrase **n** 구 / control **v** 조절하다 / tricycle **n** 세발자전거
twins **n** 쌍둥이 / powder **n** 가루, 분말 / grain **n** 미량 / cement **n** 시멘트 / weapon **n** 무기

Exercise

A. Complete the sentence.

1. _____ I use your bathroom?
   내가 너의 욕실을 사용해도 되니?

2. They were mixing cement with _____.
   그들은 시멘트를 모래와 섞고 있었다.

3. Please _____ the desk and chair.
   책상과 의자를 옮겨 주세요.

4. She wants to become a _____.
   그녀는 간호사가 되고 싶다.

5. In elementary school I had _____ one teacher.
   초등학교에서는 선생님이 오직 한 분이었다.

6. The debate was about how to keep _____.
   그 토론은 애완동물을 키우는 방법에 관한 것이었다.

7. That is a hard _____ to answer.
   그것은 대답하기 어려운 질문이네요.

8. The twins look exactly the _____.
   그 쌍둥이는 정말 똑같아요.

9. There's a huge _____ of water on the kitchen floor.
   부엌 바닥에 큰 물웅덩이가 있다.

10. This city is famous for a big fish _____.
    이 도시는 큰 생선시장으로 유명하다.

11. Hasn't the _____ come yet?
    아직 우편물 안 왔어요?

12. This dish is _____ and easy to make.
    이 요리는 빠르고 쉽게 만들 수 있어요.

13. I need to _____ because my brother is sick.
    남동생이 아프기 때문에 나는 돌아가야 한다.

14. Who is that _____ over there?
    저기 있는 저 사람은 누구예요?

15. Young children often _____ tricycles.
    어린 아이들은 종종 세발자전거를 탄다.

16. Did he _____ the bird, and kill it?
    그가 그 새를 쏘아 죽였니?

17. There is a telephone _____ my bed.
    내 침대 근처에는 전화기가 있다.

18. There are many _____ on both sides of the road.
    그 길 양쪽에는 가게들이 많이 있다.

Hint

| pet | move | market | may | sand | near | nurse | only | person |
| pool | post | question | quick | shoot | shop | ride | return | same |

Exercise

B. Fill in the word and meaning.

	Word	Meaning
01	near	
02	post	
03	return	
04	market	
05	question	
06	same	
07	shoot	
08	only	
09	quick	
10	may	
11	pool	
12	move	
13	pet	
14	sand	
15	shop	
16	ride	
17	person	
18	nurse	

	Meaning	Word
01	시장	
02	~해도 좋다	
03	움직이다, 옮기다	
04	~의 가까이에	
05	간호사	
06	단지, 오직	
07	사람, 인물	
08	애완동물	
09	물웅덩이	
10	우편, 부치다	
11	질문, 물음	
12	빠른	
13	돌아오다, 돌아가다	
14	타다	
15	같은, 동일한	
16	모래	
17	쏘다, 발사하다	
18	가게, 상점	

C. Listen, write the word and meaning. (Track 81)

	Word	Meaning		Word	Meaning
01			10		
02			11		
03			12		
04			13		
05			14		
06			15		
07			16		
08			17		
09			18		

Unit 27

Unit 28

🎧 Listen and repeat. (Track 82)

01 smell [smel]
v (냄새를) 맡다 to become aware of it when you breathe in through your nose
It stopped to **smell** a flower.
그것은 꽃 냄새를 맡으려고 멈췄다.

02 smoke [smouk]
v 담배를 피우다 to breathe through a cigarette
I will not **smoke** anymore.
나는 더 이상 담배를 피우지 않겠다.

03 spend [spend]
v 쓰다, 소비하다 to pass time, to pay money for something
Do you **spend** your day at a desk?
하루를 책상에서 보냅니까?

04 spring [spriŋ]
n 봄 the season of the year when the weather gets warmer
Summer comes after **spring**.
여름은 봄 다음에 온다.

05 store [stɔːr]
n 가게, 상점 a large shop
There are many beautiful pencils in the **store**.
그 가게에는 예쁜 연필이 많이 있다.

06 stove [stouv]
n 난로 a closed metal box in which you burn wood, coal
When can you deliver the **stove**?
난로를 언제 배달해 주실 수 있어요?

07 sweet [swiːt]
a 달콤한 tasting as if it contains a lot of sugar
Did you eat any cake or **sweet** cookie?
너는 케이크나 달콤한 과자를 먹었니?

08 swing [swiŋ]
n 그네 a seat that is hung from above so that you can go back and forth
He is pushing the baby's **swing**.
그는 아이의 그네를 밀고 있다.

09 thank [θæŋk]
v 감사하다 to tell somebody that you are grateful
Thank you for telling me about the Korean language.
한국어에 대해 말해 줘서 고마워.

---

key words
aware **a** 깨닫고 / breathe **v** 빨아들이다 / anymore **ad** 더 이상 / season **n** 계절
coal **n** 석탄 / deliver **v** 배달하다 / taste **v** 맛보다 / contain **v** 포함하다 / forth **ad** 앞으로

🎧 Listen and repeat. Track 83

10 thin [θin]
a 마른, 얇은   having a small distance between the opposite sides
The ice seems too **thin** to skate on.
얼음이 너무 얇아 스케이트를 탈 수 없을 것 같아요.

11 tomorrow [təmɔ́:rou]
ad 내일   the day after today
I won't be in class **tomorrow** because I have to see a doctor.
나는 병원에 가야 하기 때문에 내일 수업에 갈 수 없어.

12 top [tap]
n 꼭대기, 정상   the highest part of something
The cat was sitting on the **top** of the house.
고양이가 집 꼭대기에 앉아 있다.

13 wall [wɔ:l]
n 벽   a solid, vertical structure made of stone, brick, etc
A man is painting the **wall** of a flower shop.
한 남자가 꽃 가게의 벽을 칠하고 있다.

14 warm [wɔ:rm]
a 따뜻한   having a pleasant temperature between cool and hot
Put two spoons of powder in **warm** water.
가루 두 스푼을 따뜻한 물에 넣으세요.

15 water [wɔ́:tər]
n 물   the clear liquid that is in rivers, seas and lakes
We have polluted the land, air, and **water**.
우리가 땅, 공기 및 물을 오염시켜 놓았어.

16 wear [wɛər]
v 입고 있다, 쓰고 있다   to have clothes or shoes on your body
He was **wearing** a suit and tie.
그는 정장을 입고 넥타이를 하고 있었다.

17 west [west]
n 서쪽   the direction you look towards to see the sun go down
China is to the **west** of Korea.
중국은 한국의 서쪽에 있습니다.

18 wet [wet]
a 젖은   covered in a liquid, especially water
It grows well in hot and **wet** places.
그것은 덥고 비가 많이 오는 지역에서 잘 자란다.

key words
opposite **a** 맞은편의 / seem **v** ~인 듯하다, ~인 것 같은 생각이 들다 / vertical **a** 수직의
brick **n** 벽돌 / pollute **v** 오염시키다 / suit **n** (정장) 한 벌 / especially **ad** 특히

Exercise

A. Complete the sentence.

1. I will not _____ anymore.
   나는 더 이상 담배를 피우지 않겠다.

2. Do you _____ your day at a desk?
   하루를 책상에서 보냅니까?

3. Summer comes after _____.
   여름은 봄 다음에 온다.

4. We have polluted the land, air, and _____.
   우리가 땅, 공기 및 물을 오염시켜 놓았어.

5. When can you deliver the _____?
   난로를 언제 배달해 주실 수 있어요?

6. He was _____ a suit and tie.
   그는 정장을 입고 넥타이를 하고 있었다.

7. He is pushing the baby's _____.
   그는 아이의 그네를 밀고 있다.

8. The ice seems too _____ to skate on.
   얼음이 너무 얇아 스케이트를 탈 수 없을 것 같아요.

9. A man is painting the _____ of a flower shop.
   한 남자가 꽃 가게의 벽을 칠하고 있다.

10. I won't be in class _____ because I have to see a doctor.
    나는 병원에 가야 하기 때문에 내일 수업에 갈 수 없어.

11. Did you eat any cake or _____ cookie?
    너는 케이크나 달콤한 과자를 먹었니?

12. The cat was sitting on the _____ of the house.
    고양이가 집 꼭대기에 앉아 있다.

13. Put two spoons of powder in _____ water.
    가루 두 스푼을 따뜻한 물에 넣으세요.

14. It stopped to _____ a flower.
    그것은 꽃 냄새를 맡으려고 멈췄다.

15. _____ you for telling me about the Korean language.
    한국어에 대해 말해 줘서 고마워.

16. China is to the _____ of Korea.
    중국은 한국의 서쪽에 있습니다.

17. There are many beautiful pencils in the _____.
    그 가게에는 예쁜 연필이 많이 있다.

18. It grows well in hot and _____ places.
    그것은 덥고 비가 많이 오는 지역에서 잘 자란다.

Hint

| smell | tomorrow | spend | wear | spring | thank | sweet | wet | top |
| stove | wall | | smoke | warm | store | water | swing | thin | west |

Exercise

B. Fill in the word and meaning.

	Word	Meaning
01	smoke	
02	thank	
03	swing	
04	spring	
05	top	
06	stove	
07	tomorrow	
08	water	
09	smell	
10	warm	
11	west	
12	sweet	
13	wet	
14	wear	
15	spend	
16	wall	
17	thin	
18	store	

	Meaning	Word
01	(냄새를) 맡다	
02	담배를 피우다	
03	쓰다, 소비하다	
04	봄	
05	가게, 상점	
06	난로	
07	달콤한	
08	그네	
09	감사하다	
10	마른, 얇은	
11	내일	
12	꼭대기, 정상	
13	벽	
14	따뜻한	
15	물	
16	입고 있다, 쓰고 있다	
17	서쪽	
18	젖은	

🎧 C. Listen, write the word and meaning. (Track 84)

	Word	Meaning		Word	Meaning
01			10		
02			11		
03			12		
04			13		
05			14		
06			15		
07			16		
08			17		
09			18		

Review 14

A. Read and fill in the word and meaning.

word	definition	meaning
	a person who is trained to look after sick people	
	used for saying that something is possible	
	a sentence or phrase that asks for an answer	
	not far away in time or distance	
	to come or go back to a place	
	a man or woman; a human being	
	a building where things are bought and sold	
	a place where people buy and sell things	
	done with speed; taking a short time	
	with no other existing or present	
	a powder consisting of very small grains of rock	
	an animal that you keep in your home for pleasure	
	to change position or to put in a different place	
	to sit on a bicycle, etc and control it as it moves	
	letters or packages that are brought to your home	
	not different, not another; exactly the one	
	a small amount of liquid lying on a surface	
	to fire a gun or another weapon	

Hint
may   move   ride   pet   sand   shoot   shop   only   person
pool   quick   same   post   near   return   market   nurse   question

B. Read and fill in the word and meaning.

word	definition	meaning
	to breathe through a cigarette	
	a closed metal box in which you burn wood, coal	
	having a small distance between the opposite sides	
	to become aware of it when you breathe in through your nose	
	covered in a liquid, especially water	
	a large shop	
	the day after today	
	to pass time, to pay money for something	
	to tell somebody that you are grateful	
	the direction you look towards to see the sun go down	
	the season of the year when the weather gets warmer	
	the highest part of something	
	to have clothes or shoes on your body	
	having a pleasant temperature between cool and hot	
	tasting as if it contains a lot of sugar	
	a solid, vertical structure made of stone, brick, etc	
	a seat that is hung from above so that you can go back and forth	
	the clear liquid that is in rivers, seas and lakes	

Hint
smell   west   spend   wear   swing   thank   sweet   wet   smoke
water   store   top   warm   wall   stove   spring   thin   tomorrow

Unit 29

🎧 Listen and repeat. Track 85

01 air
[εər]
n 공기, 공중   the mixture of gases that surrounds the earth
I'm enjoying the blue sea and the fresh **air**.
나는 푸른 바다와 상쾌한 공기를 즐기고 있어.

02 alien
[éiljən]
n 외국인, 우주인   a person who comes from another country
All the **aliens** feel homesick.
모든 외국인은 고향을 그리워한다.

03 ask
[æsk]
v 묻다, 물어보다   to put a question to find out some information
You **asked** me what languages are spoken in Korea.
네가 한국에서는 어떤 언어가 쓰이는지 나에게 물었잖아.

04 author
[ɔ́:θər]
n 저자, 작가   a person who writes a book, play, etc
He is a well-known **author** of detective novels.
그는 유명한 탐정소설 작가이다.

05 before
[bifɔ́:r]
prep ~전에   ealier than the time, in front of something
Read the questions **before** listening to the tape.
테이프를 듣기 전에 질문을 읽어보세요.

06 behind
[biháind]
prep ~뒤에   at or towards the back of somebody / something
He parked his car **behind** the building.
그는 빌딩 뒤에 차를 주차해 놨어요.

07 board
[bɔ:rd]
n 널, 판자   a long, thin, flat piece of wood, etc
Dad sawed the **board** in two.
아빠는 톱으로 그 판자를 둘로 잘랐다.

08 candle
[kǽndl]
n 양초   a round stick of solid oil or fat
I think one **candle** is enough for us.
촛불 하나면 충분하다고 생각해요.

09 card
[ka:rd]
n 카드   thick rigid paper; a piece of plastic that has information on it
You can come here with your student **card**.
학생 카드를 가지고 여기에 와야 합니다.

---

key words
mixture **n** 혼합물 / homesick **v** 고향을 그리워하는 / saw **v** 톱질하다 / rigid **a** 단단한

🎧 Listen and repeat. Track 86

10 chest [tʃest]
n 가슴, 대형 상자   the top part of the front of your body
He measures 37 inches around the **chest**.
그의 가슴둘레는 37인치이다.

11 chopsticks [tʃɑ́pstiks]
n 젓가락   two thin sticks used for picking up food to eat
Try to pick up food with **chopsticks**.
젓가락으로 음식을 먹도록 해보세요.

12 coin [kɔin]
n 동전   a piece of money made of metal
The old man put the **coins** in the pot.
노인이 냄비 안에 동전들을 넣었다.

13 comb [koum]
v 빗다 / n 빗   to make your hair tidy
I dry my hair and **comb** it every morning.
나는 매일 아침 머리를 말리고 빗질한다.

14 crayon [kréiən]
n 크레용   a soft, thick, colored pencil used for drawing
The picture is drawn with a **crayon**.
그 그림은 크레용으로 그려진 것이다.

15 cream [kri:m]
n 크림   the thick white liquid that rises to the top of milk
Coffee with **cream** and sugar, please.
설탕과 크림 넣은 커피를 주세요.

16 dial [dáiəl]
v 다이얼을 돌리다 / n 다이얼   to push the buttons on a telephone to call
Are you sure you **dialed** it right?
다이얼을 맞게 돌리셨나요?

17 dialogue [dáiəlɔ̀:g]
n 대화   conversation or discussion between people
Listen to each **dialogue** and choose the right answer.
대화를 듣고 올바른 답을 고르세요.

18 down [daun]
ad 아래로, 낮은 쪽으로   to a lower level or place; towards the bottom
Suddenly, I lost my balance and fell **down**.
갑자기, 나는 균형을 잃고 쓰러졌다.

---

key words
measure v 치수를 재다 / pot n 냄비 / tidy a 정돈된 / conversation n 대화
discussion n 토론 / bottom n 바닥

Exercise

A. Complete the sentence.

1. All the _____ feel homesick.
   모든 외국인은 고향을 그리워한다.

2. Dad sawed the _____ in two.
   아빠는 톱으로 그 판자를 둘로 잘랐다.

3. You _____ me what languages are spoken in Korea.
   네가 한국에서는 어떤 언어가 쓰이는지 나에게 물었잖아.

4. He measures 37 inches around the _____.
   그의 가슴둘레는 37인치이다.

5. I'm enjoying the blue sea and the fresh _____.
   나는 푸른 바다와 상쾌한 공기를 즐기고 있어.

6. He is a well-known _____ of detective novels.
   그는 유명한 탐정소설 작가이다.

7. Read the questions _____ listening to the tape.
   테이프를 듣기 전에 질문을 읽어보세요.

8. I think one _____ is enough for us.
   촛불 하나면 충분하다고 생각해요.

9. You can come here with your student _____.
   학생 카드를 가지고 여기에 와야 합니다.

10. He parked his car _____ the building.
    그는 빌딩 뒤에 차를 주차해 놨어요.

11. Try to pick up food with _____.
    젓가락으로 음식을 먹도록 해보세요.

12. The old man put the _____ in the pot.
    노인이 냄비 안에 동전들을 넣었다.

13. Suddenly, I lost my balance and fell _____.
    갑자기, 나는 균형을 잃고 쓰러졌다.

14. I dry my hair and _____ it every morning.
    나는 매일 아침 머리를 말리고 빗질한다.

15. Are you sure you _____ it right?
    다이얼을 맞게 돌리셨나요?

16. The picture is drawn with a _____.
    그 그림은 크레용으로 그려진 것이다.

17. Listen to each _____ and choose the right answer.
    각 대화를 듣고 올바른 답을 고르세요.

18. Coffee with _____ and sugar, please.
    설탕과 크림 넣은 커피를 주세요.

Hint

| alien | ask | coin | dialogue | behind | comb | board | card | author |
| chest | air | crayon | before | cream | dial | candle | down | chopsticks |

Unit 29

Exercise

B. Fill in the word and meaning.

	Word	Meaning
01	before	
02	candle	
03	down	
04	air	
05	card	
06	alien	
07	coin	
08	board	
09	comb	
10	ask	
11	dialogue	
12	chopsticks	
13	cream	
14	author	
15	crayon	
16	dial	
17	chest	
18	behind	

	Meaning	Word
01	공기, 공중	
02	외계인, 우주인	
03	묻다, 물어보다	
04	저자, 작가	
05	~전에	
06	~뒤에	
07	널, 판자	
08	양초	
09	카드	
10	가슴, 대형상자	
11	젓가락	
12	동전	
13	빗다, 빗	
14	크레용	
15	크림	
16	다이얼을 돌리다, 다이얼	
17	대화	
18	아래로, 낮은 쪽으로	

C. Listen, write the word and meaning. (Track 87)

	Word	Meaning		Word	Meaning
01			10		
02			11		
03			12		
04			13		
05			14		
06			15		
07			16		
08			17		
09			18		

Unit 30

🎧 Listen and repeat. Track 88

01 drive [draiv]
v 운전하다   to control or operate a car, bus, etc
Computers will **drive** cars in the future.
미래에는 컴퓨터가 차를 운전하게 될 것입니다.

02 drop [drap]
v 떨어뜨리다   to let something fall
I **dropped** a cup of coffee on the floor.
나는 커피를 바닥에 떨어뜨렸다.

03 example [igzǽmpəl]
n 본보기, 모범   something which shows, explains what you say
Can you give me an **example**?
예를 하나 들어볼래?

04 excuse [ikskjúːz]
v 용서하다, 변명하다   to forgive somebody; to explain one's bad behavior
Please **excuse** me for being careless.
제 부주의를 용서해 주십시오.

05 feel [fiːl]
v 느끼다   to be in the state that is mentioned
Take a rest and you'll **feel** better.
휴식을 취해라, 그러면 더 나은 기분이 느껴질거야.

06 few [fjuː]
a 조금의, 다소의   a small number of; some
We'll meet in a **few** hours, right?
몇 시간 후에 우리 만나는 것 맞죠?

07 fool [fuːl]
n 바보   a person who acts in a silly way
He makes me a **fool**.
그는 날 바보로 만들었다.

08 for [fɔːr]
prep ~을 위해, ~동안   in order to do something; showing a length of time
This monument was built **for** the founder.
이 기념비는 창립자를 위해 세워졌다.

09 grass [græs]
n 풀, 잔디   the common green plant with thin leaves
The cat crept silently through the **grass**.
고양이가 살금살금 잔디밭을 기어갔다.

key words
explain v 설명하다 / careless a 부주의한 / state n 상태 / mention v 언급하다
silly a 바보 같은 / monument n 기념비 / founder n 창립자 / creep v 기어가다

🎧 Listen and repeat. (Track 89)

10 ground [graund]
n 땅, 지면   the solid surface of the earth
There is a wallet on the **ground**.
땅에 지갑이 떨어져 있다.

11 hen [hen]
n 암탉   a female bird that is kept for its eggs or meat
The **hen** has five chicks.
그 암탉에게는 병아리가 다섯 마리 있다.

12 hike [haik]
v 하이킹하다   to go for a long walk in the country
I love to **hike** and be outdoors.
나는 하이킹과 야외 활동 하는 것을 좋아한다.

13 hotel [houtél]
n 호텔   a place where you pay to stay when you are on traveling
The **hotels** are full of tourists.
그 호텔은 여행객으로 가득 차 있다.

14 hungry [hʌ́ŋgri]
a 배고픈   wanting to eat
Hungry babies cried for their mothers' milk.
배고픈 아기들은 젖을 달라고 울어댔다.

15 lake [leik]
n 호수   a large area of water that is surrounded by land
The **lake** is twenty meters deep.
그 호수는 깊이가 20 미터나 된다.

16 land [lænd]
n 육지   an area of ground
This means that 30% of the earth's surface is **land**.
이것은 지면의 30%가 육지라는 것을 의미한다.

17 line [lain]
n 줄, 선   a row of things; a long thin mark on the surface
Draw two **lines** on the paper.
종이에 선을 두 개 그으세요.

18 lip [lip]
n 입술   either of the two soft edges at the opening of your mouth
A bright smile came to his **lips**.
그의 입가에는 밝은 미소가 떠돌고 있었다.

key words

solid a 고체의 / wallet n 지갑 / outdoor a 야외의 / pay v 지불하다 / surround v 에워싸다

Exercise

A. Complete the sentence.

1. There is a wallet on the _____.
   땅에 지갑이 떨어져 있다.

2. Take a rest and you'll _____ better.
   휴식을 취해라, 그러면 더 나은 기분이 느껴질거야.

3. I _____ a cup of coffee on the floor.
   나는 커피를 바닥에 떨어뜨렸다.

4. Please _____ me for being careless.
   제 부주의를 용서해 주십시오.

5. We'll meet in a _____ hours, right?
   몇 시간 후에 우리 만나는 것 맞죠?

6. Draw two _____ on the paper.
   종이에 선을 두 개 그으세요.

7. He makes me a _____.
   그는 날 바보로 만들었다.

8. This monument was built _____ the founder.
   이 기념비는 창립자를 위해 세워졌다.

9. Computers will _____ cars in the future.
   미래에는 컴퓨터가 차를 운전하게 될 것입니다.

10. The cat crept silently through the _____.
    고양이가 살금살금 잔디밭을 기어갔다.

11. The _____ has five chicks.
    그 암탉에게는 병아리가 다섯 마리 있다.

12. A bright smile came to his _____.
    그의 입가에는 밝은 미소가 떠돌고 있었다.

13. I love to _____ and be outdoors.
    나는 하이킹과 야외 활동 하는 것을 좋아한다.

14. The _____ is full of tourists.
    그 호텔은 여행객으로 가득 차 있다.

15. Can you give me an _____?
    예를 하나 들어볼래?

16. _____ babies cried for their mothers' milk.
    배고픈 아기들은 젖을 달라고 울어댔다.

17. The _____ is twenty meters deep.
    그 호수는 깊이가 20 미터나 된다.

18. This means that 30% of the earth's surface is _____.
    이것은 지면의 30%가 육지라는 것을 의미한다.

Hint

| fool | example | drop | excuse | hike | few | ground | feel | hen |
| hotel | land | for | lake | drive | line | grass | lip | hungry |

Exercise

B. Fill in the word and meaning.

	Word	Meaning
01	drop	
02	feel	
03	drive	
04	hen	
05	grass	
06	for	
07	hungry	
08	ground	
09	line	
10	few	
11	land	
12	fool	
13	lip	
14	lake	
15	hotel	
16	excuse	
17	hike	
18	example	

	Meaning	Word
01	운전하다	
02	떨어뜨리다	
03	본보기, 모범	
04	용서하다, 변명하다	
05	느끼다	
06	조금의, 다소의	
07	바보	
08	~을 위해, ~동안	
09	풀, 잔디	
10	땅, 지면	
11	암탉	
12	하이킹하다	
13	호텔	
14	배고픈	
15	호수	
16	육지	
17	줄, 선	
18	입술	

C. Listen, write the word and meaning. (Track 90)

	Word	Meaning		Word	Meaning
01			10		
02			11		
03			12		
04			13		
05			14		
06			15		
07			16		
08			17		
09			18		

Review 15

A. Read and fill in the word and meaning.

word	definition	meaning
	the mixture of gases that surrounds the earth	
	a piece of money made of metal	
	thick rigid paper; a piece of plastic that has information on it	
	to a lower level or place; towards the bottom	
	a person who comes from another country	
	a round stick of solid oil or fat	
	conversation or discussion between people	
	the top part of the front of your body	
	to put a question to find out some information	
	two thin sticks used for picking up food to eat	
	to push the buttons on a telephone to call	
	a person who writes a book, play, etc	
	a long, thin, flat piece of wood, etc	
	to make your hair tidy	
	earlier than the time, in front of something	
	the thick white liquid that rises to the top of milk	
	at or towards the back of somebody / something	
	a soft, thick, colored pencil used for drawing	

Hint
alien   ask   coin   dialogue   behind   comb   board   card   author
chest   air   crayon   before   cream   dial   candle   down   chopsticks

B. Read and fill in the word and meaning.

word	definition	meaning
	a small number of; some	
	to control or operate a car, bus, etc	
	in order to do something; showing a length of time	
	a place where you pay to stay when you are on traveling	
	to be in the state that is mentioned	
	a large area of water that is surrounded by land	
	a person who acts in a silly way	
	an area of ground	
	to forgive somebody; to explain one's bad behavior	
	wanting to eat	
	either of the two soft edges at the opening of your mouth	
	the common green plant with thin leaves	
	something which shows, explains what you say	
	to go for a long walk in the country	
	the solid surface of the earth	
	to let something fall	
	a row of things; a long thin mark on the surface	
	a female bird that is kept for its eggs or meat	

Hint
fool   example   drop   excuse   hike   few   ground   feel   hen
hotel   land   for   lake   drive line   grass   lip   hungry

Unit 31

🎧 Listen and repeat. Track 91

01 meal
[miːl]
n 식사   the food that is eaten when you eat
I want to have a light **meal**.
나는 가볍게 식사를 하고 싶다.

02 medal
[médl]
n 메달, 상패   a small flat metal given to somebody as a prize
A gold **medal** was awarded to the winner.
우승자에게 금메달이 수여되었다.

03 need
[niːd]
v ~할 필요가 있다   it is necessary or must be done
I **need** your help.
난 당신의 도움이 필요해요.

04 never
[névəːr]
ad 결코 ~하지 않다   at no time; not ever
I will **never** do that again.
난 다시는 그 일을 하지 않을 것이다.

05 other
[ʌ́ðər]
a 다른, 그 밖의   in addition to the one that has already mentioned
Look at the **other** side of the box.
그 상자의 다른 쪽을 보세요.

06 outside
[áutsáid]
ad 밖에   in or at a place that is not in a room or a building
I asked him to wait **outside**.
난 그에게 밖에서 기다리도록 요구했다.

07 peace
[piːs]
n 평화   a period of time in which there is no war or violence
His prime concern is world **peace**.
그의 주된 관심사는 세계 평화이다.

08 piano
[piǽnou]
n 피아노   a musical instrument that you play by pressing down keys
Do you want to learn how to play the **piano**?
너는 피아노 치는 법을 배우고 싶니?

09 piece
[piːs]
n 조각, 단편   one of the parts that something is made of
The plate fell on the floor and broke into small **pieces**.
접시가 마룻바닥에 떨어져 산산조각 났다.

key words
prize n 상 / award v 수여하다 / addition n 추가, 부가 / already ad 이미, 벌써
violence n 격렬함, 폭력 / prime a 첫째의, 가장 중요한 / instrument n 악기, 기구

🎧 Listen and repeat. Track 92

10 poster
[póustər]
n 전단, 포스터   a printed picture in a public place used to advertise
There is a **poster** on the wall.
벽에는 포스터가 붙어있다.

11 rabbit
[rǽbit]
n 토끼   a small animal with long ears
The **rabbit** looked around for something to eat.
토끼는 먹을 것을 찾아 주위를 둘러보았다.

12 read
[ri:d]
v 읽다   to look at words and understand them
Have you **read** his memo yet?
그가 남긴 메모 읽었어요?

13 road
[roud]
n 길, 도로   a way which cars and buses can drive along
There are many trees on the **road**.
그 길에는 나무들이 많이 있다.

14 rocket
[rákit]
n 로켓   a vehicle that is used for travel into space
The **rocket** soared into orbit.
그 로켓은 궤도 속으로 높이 치솟았다.

15 sandwich
[sǽndwitʃ]
n 샌드위치   two slices of bread with food between them
The man usually has **sandwiches** for lunch.
그 남자는 점심으로 대개 샌드위치를 먹는다.

16 schedule
[skédʒu(:)l]
n 예정, 스케줄   a plan that will happen or work that must be done
I have a problem with my **schedule** this weekend.
이번 주 나의 스케줄에 문제가 있어.

17 shoulder
[ʃóuldər]
n 어깨   the part of your body between your neck and the top of your arm
A bird is sitting on Bob's **shoulder**.
새 한 마리가 밥의 어깨에 앉아있다.

18 show
[ʃou]
v 보여주다   to let somebody see something
Show me your catalog, please.
카탈로그 좀 보여 주세요.

---

key words
print v 인쇄하다 / advertise v 광고하다 / soar v 높이 날아오르다
orbit n 궤도 / usually ad 보통, 일반적으로 / catalog n 카탈로그, 목록

Unit 31   157

Exercise

A. Complete the sentence.

1. I will _____ do that again.
   난 다시는 그 일을 하지 않을 것이다.

2. I want to have a light _____.
   나는 가볍게 식사를 하고 싶다.

3. The man usually has _____ for lunch.
   그 남자는 점심으로 대개 샌드위치를 먹는다.

4. I _____ your help.
   난 당신의 도움이 필요해요.

5. Look at the _____ side of the box.
   그 상자의 다른 쪽을 보세요.

6. I asked him to wait _____.
   난 그에게 밖에서 기다리도록 요구했다.

7. A bird is sitting on Bob's _____.
   새 한 마리가 밥의 어깨에 앉아있다.

8. There are many trees on the _____.
   그 길에는 나무들이 많이 있다.

9. I have a problem with my _____ this weekend.
   이번 주 나의 스케줄에 문제가 있어.

10. His prime concern is world _____.
    그의 주된 관심사는 세계 평화이다.

11. Do you want to learn how to play the _____?
    너는 피아노 치는 법을 배우고 싶니?

12. The _____ looked around for something to eat.
    토끼는 먹을 것을 찾아 주위를 둘러보았다.

13. A gold _____ was awarded to the winner.
    우승자에게 금메달이 수여되었다.

14. The plate fell on the floor and broke into small _____.
    접시가 마룻바닥에 떨어져 산산조각 났다.

15. There is a _____ on the wall.
    벽에는 포스터가 붙어있다.

16. Have you _____ his memo yet?
    그가 남긴 메모 읽었어요?

17. The _____ soared into orbit.
    그 로켓은 궤도 속으로 높이 치솟았다.

18. _____ me your catalog, please.
    카탈로그 좀 보여 주세요.

Hint

| piano | meal | rabbit | shoulder | medal | poster | road | show | need |
| sandwich | piece | never | read | | other | schedule | outside | rocket | peace |

Unit 31

Exercise

B. Fill in the word and meaning.

	Word	Meaning
01	medal	
02	never	
03	read	
04	peace	
05	road	
06	meal	
07	sandwich	
08	rocket	
09	poster	
10	need	
11	shoulder	
12	piano	
13	show	
14	outside	
15	piece	
16	schedule	
17	rabbit	
18	other	

	Meaning	Word
01	식사	
02	메달, 상패	
03	~할 필요가 있다	
04	결코 ~하지 않다	
05	다른, 그 밖의	
06	밖에	
07	평화	
08	피아노	
09	조각, 단편	
10	전단, 포스터	
11	토끼	
12	읽다	
13	길, 도로	
14	로켓	
15	샌드위치	
16	예정, 스케줄	
17	어깨	
18	보여주다	

C. Listen, write the word and meaning. Track 93

	Word	Meaning		Word	Meaning
01			10		
02			11		
03			12		
04			13		
05			14		
06			15		
07			16		
08			17		
09			18		

Unit 32

🎧 Listen and repeat. (Track 94)

01 snake [sneik] — **n** 뱀   a long thin animal with no legs moving its body
Snakes do not have arms or legs.
뱀은 팔이나 다리가 없습니다.

02 so [sou] — **conj** 그래서   with the result that; therefore
So you have to stay in New York two or three more days.
그래서 너는 뉴욕에 이삼일 정도 더 머물러야 한다.

03 square [skwɛəːr] — **n** 정사각형   a shape that has four sides of the same length and angles
A **square** has four equal sides.
정사각형은 4변이 똑같습니다.

04 stairs [stɛəːrz] — **n** 계단   a series of steps inside a building leading from one level to another
The boy had fallen down the **stairs**.
소년은 계단 아래로 떨어졌다.

05 street [striːt] — **n** 거리   a road in a town or city that has shops and houses
Cars run on the right side of the **street** in Korea.
한국의 차들은 거리에서 오른쪽으로 달린다.

06 strong [strɔ(ː)ŋ] — **a** 힘센, 강한   having great physical power to act
It helps to make the muscles **strong**.
그것은 근육을 강하게 만들어 주는데 도움이 된다.

07 take [teik] — **v** 잡다, 가지고 가다   to carry or move something
Would you help me **take** it to the post office?
이것을 우체국까지 가져가도록 도와주시겠어요?

08 talk [tɔːk] — **v** 말하다   to say things; to speak to give information
In our club, we **talk** to each other in English.
클럽에서 우리는 서로 영어로 대화를 합니다.

09 thing [θiŋ] — **n** 물건, 것   an object that is not named; a fact, subject
There are many fun **things** in the trunk.
트렁크 안에 재미있는 것들이 많이 있어.

---

key words
result **n** 결과 / therefore **ad** 그러므로, 그 결과 / length **n** 길이 / angle **n** 각도, 각
equal **a** 동등한, 같은 / series **n** 연속 / physical **a** 육체적인 / muscle **n** 근육 / trunk **n** 여행용 큰가방

🎧 Listen and repeat. Track 95

10 throw [θrou] — **v** 던지다 — to send something from your hand through the air
You have to **throw** the ball through a basket.
공을 던져 바구니를 통과시켜야 한다.

11 toy [tɔi] — **n** 장난감 — an object for a child to play with
Games and **toys** are everywhere.
게임기와 장난감들이 사방에 널려 있다.

12 truck [trʌk] — **n** 트럭 — a large strong motor vehicle used for carrying goods
The **truck** is overloaded.
그 트럭에는 너무 짐이 많이 실려 있다.

13 will [wil] — **aux** ~할 것이다 — used in forming the future tenses
I'm afraid it **will** rain.
비가 올 것 같다.

14 win [win] — **v** 이기다 — to be the best or first in a game, competition, etc
We can't **win** this game without him.
그가 없이는 시합에서 이길 수 없어.

15 window [wíndou] — **n** 창문 — the opening that you can see through and that lets light in
A girl was standing near the **window**.
한 소녀가 창문 근처에 서 있었다.

16 wing [wiŋ] — **n** 날개 — one of the two parts that a bird and insect uses for flying
The bird spread its **wings** and flew away.
그 새는 날개를 펼치고 날아갔다.

17 winter [wíntər] — **n** 겨울 — the coldest season of the year between autumn and spring
In **winter**, we go skating or skiing.
겨울에는 스케이트 또는 스키를 타러 갑니다.

18 wood [wud] — **n** 나무, 목재 — the hard substance that trees are made of
That was an old **wood** structure.
그것은 오래된 목재 구조물이다.

key words
everywhere **ad** 어디에나 / overload **v** 짐을 너무 많이 싣다 / tense **n** 시제 / afraid **a** 걱정하여, 근심하여 / competition **n** 시합, 경쟁 / stand **v** 서 있다 / spread **v** 펼치다 / structure **n** 건물, 구조

Unit 32

Exercise

A. Complete the sentence.

1. _____ you have to stay in New York two or three more days.
   그래서 너는 뉴욕에 이삼일 정도 더 머물러야 한다.

2. A _____ has four equal sides.
   정사각형은 4변이 똑같습니다.

3. That was an old _____ structure.
   그것은 오래된 목재 구조물이다.

4. The boy had fallen down the _____.
   소년은 계단 아래로 떨어졌다.

5. The _____ is overloaded.
   그 트럭에는 너무 짐이 많이 실려 있다.

6. Cars run on the right side of the _____ in Korea.
   한국의 차들은 거리에서 오른쪽으로 달린다.

7. It helps to make the muscles _____.
   그것은 근육을 강하게 만들어 주는데 도움이 된다.

8. We can't _____ this game without him.
   그가 없이는 시합에서 이길 수 없어.

9. In our club, we _____ to each other in English.
   클럽에서 우리는 서로 영어로 대화를 합니다.

10. There are many fun _____ in the trunk.
    트렁크 안에 재미있는 것들이 많이 있어.

11. _____ do not have arms or legs.
    뱀은 팔이나 다리가 없습니다.

12. You have to _____ the ball through a basket.
    공을 던져 바구니를 통과시켜야 한다.

13. In _____, we go skating or skiing.
    겨울에는 스케이트 또는 스키를 타러 갑니다.

14. Games and _____ are everywhere.
    게임기와 장난감들이 사방에 널려 있다.

15. I'm afraid it _____ rain.
    비가 올 것 같다.

16. A girl was standing near the _____.
    한 소녀가 창문 근처에 서 있었다.

17. Would you help me _____ it to the post office?
    이것을 우체국까지 가져가도록 도와주시겠어요?

18. The bird spread its _____ and flew away.
    그 새는 날개를 펼치고 날아갔다.

Hint

toy	snake	will	take	wing	square	thing	window	stairs
wood	throw	win	street	strong	talk	so	truck	winter

Unit 32

Exercise

B. Fill in the word and meaning.

	Word	Meaning
01	take	
02	snake	
03	truck	
04	win	
05	so	
06	thing	
07	street	
08	talk	
09	will	
10	winter	
11	stairs	
12	throw	
13	wood	
14	wing	
15	strong	
16	toy	
17	window	
18	square	

	Meaning	Word
01	뱀	
02	그래서	
03	정사각형	
04	계단	
05	거리	
06	강한	
07	잡다, 가지고 가다	
08	말하다	
09	물건, 것	
10	던지다	
11	장난감	
12	트럭	
13	~할 것이다	
14	이기다	
15	창문	
16	날개	
17	겨울	
18	나무, 목재	

C. Listen, write the word and meaning. Track 96

	Word	Meaning		Word	Meaning
01			10		
02			11		
03			12		
04			13		
05			14		
06			15		
07			16		
08			17		
09			18		

Review 16

A. Read and fill in the word and meaning.

word	definition	meaning
	a small animal with long ears	
	a printed picture in a public place used to advertise	
	the part of your body between your neck and the top of your arm	
	a small flat metal given to somebody as a prize	
	one of the parts that something is made of	
	to look at words and understand them	
	it is necessary or must be done	
	a way which cars and buses can drive along	
	the food that is eaten when you eat	
	to let somebody see something	
	a vehicle that is used for travel into space	
	a musical instrument that you play by pressing down keys	
	in or at a place that is not in a room or a building	
	two slices of bread with food between them	
	at no time; not ever	
	a period of time in which there is no war or violence	
	in addition to the one that has already mentioned	
	a plan that will happen or work that must be done	

Hint
piano   show   other   shoulder   medal   read   road   meal   sandwich
need   piece   never   poster   rabbit   schedule   outside   rocket   peace

B. Read and fill in the word and meaning.

word	definition	meaning
	the opening that you can see through and that lets light in	
	to say things; to speak to give information	
	one of the two parts that a bird and insect uses for flying	
	a long thin animal with no legs moving its body	
	the coldest season of the year between autumn and spring	
	an object that is not named; a fact, subject	
	the hard substance that trees are made of	
	to send something from your hand through the air	
	having great physical power to act	
	a series of steps inside a building leading from one level to another	
	used in forming the future tenses	
	to carry or move something	
	with the result that; therefore	
	an object for a child to play with	
	a road in a town or city that has shops and houses	
	a large strong motor vehicle used for carrying goods	
	a shape that has four sides of the same length and angles	
	to be the best or first in a game, competition, etc	

Hint

thing   snake   talk   take   wing   square   toy   window   throw
wood   truck   win   winter   strong   will   so   stairs   street

Unit 33

🎧 Listen and repeat. Track 97

01 album
[ǽlbəm]
n 앨범, 사진첩   a book in which you can keep photographs
I've always wanted this kind of **album**.
나는 늘 이런 종류의 앨범이 갖고 싶었어.

02 appear
[əpíər]
v 나타나다   to give the impression of being
When will the stars **appear**?
언제 별들이 나타날까요?

03 away
[əwéi]
ad 떨어져서   at a particular distance from a place
It's one block **away**.
한 구역 떨어져 있어요.

04 backward
[bǽkwərd]
ad 뒤로, 거꾸로   in the direction that your back is facing
Don't lean **backward**, please.
뒤로 기대지 마세요.

05 below
[bilóu]
prep ~의 아래에   at or to a lower position than something
We could see the valley **below** the mountain.
우리는 산 아래쪽으로 계곡을 볼 수 있었다.

06 both
[bouθ]
a 둘 다의, 양쪽의   the two; the one as well as the other
It looks good on **both** men and women.
그것은 여자와 남자 둘 다에게 잘 어울린다.

07 bridge
[bridʒ]
n 다리   a structure that is built over a road
They are building a **bridge** across a river.
그들은 강에 다리를 놓고 있다.

08 carry
[kǽri]
v 나르다, 운반하다   to hold something while you are moving
It's heavy, but I can manage to **carry** it.
그것은 무겁지만, 내가 그럭저럭 운반할 수 있다.

09 case
[keis]
n 경우, 사례   a situation of a particular type
In this **case**, what would you say?
이런 경우에 당신은 뭐라고 말하겠는가?

---

key words
impression n 인상, 감명 / lean v 기대다 / valley n 계곡 / manage v (이럭저럭) 잘 해내다 / situation n 상황

🎧 Listen and repeat. (Track 98)

10 Christmas n 크리스마스   the period of time before and after 25 December
[krísməs]
Let's make a **Christmas** tree.
크리스마스트리를 만들자.

11 circle n 원   a completely round flat shape
[sə́:rkl]
Using thick pens, draw a dot in the middle of each **circle**.
굵은 펜을 사용하여 각각의 원 중앙에 점을 하나 그려라.

12 computer n 컴퓨터   a machine that can store, find and arrange information
[kəmpjú:tər]
They are looking at a **computer** screen.
그들은 컴퓨터 화면을 보고 있다.

13 cool a 시원한   fairly cold; not hot or warm
[ku:l]
It is quite **cool** in the shade.
그늘은 매우 시원하다.

14 cross v 가로지르다   to go from one side to the other
[krɔ:s]
Let's **cross** the street at the crosswalk.
횡단보도에서 길을 건너자.

15 curtain n 커튼   a piece of fabric that is hung to cover a window
[kə́:rtən]
He found a one hundred dollar bill behind the **curtain**.
그는 커튼 뒤에서 100달러 지폐를 찾았다.

16 dictionary n 사전   a book that contains a list of the words in a language
[díkʃənèri]
Look up this word in the **dictionary**.
이 단어를 사전에서 찾아봐라.

17 die v 죽다   to stop living
[dai]
When you **die**, your soul goes to Heaven.
죽으면 영혼은 천국에 간다.

18 drum n 북, 드럼   a musical instrument played by hitting with hands or sticks
[drʌm]
The man is playing the **drum**.
남자가 드럼을 연주하고 있다.

---

key words

arrange v 정리하다 / fairly ad 꽤 / shade n 그늘 / crosswalk n 횡단보도 / fabric n 직물 / soul n 영혼

Unit 33

Exercise

A. Complete the sentence.

1. It is quite _____ in the shade.
   그늘은 매우 시원하다.

2. Look up this word in the _____.
   이 단어를 사전에서 찾아봐라.

3. It looks good on _____ men and women.
   그것은 여자와 남자 둘 다에게 잘 어울린다.

4. When will the stars _____?
   언제 별들이 나타날까요?

5. It's one block _____.
   한 구역 떨어져 있어요.

6. We could see the valley _____ the mountain.
   우리는 산 아래쪽으로 계곡을 볼 수 있었다.

7. I've always wanted this kind of _____.
   나는 늘 이런 종류의 앨범이 갖고 싶었어.

8. They are building a _____ across a river.
   그들은 강에 다리를 놓고 있다.

9. It's heavy, but I can manage to _____ it.
   그것은 무겁지만, 내가 그럭저럭 운반할 수 있다.

10. In this _____, what would you say?
    이런 경우에 당신은 뭐라고 말하겠는가?

11. He found a one hundred dollar bill behind the _____.
    그는 커튼 뒤에서 100달러 지폐를 찾았다.

12. When you _____, your soul goes to Heaven.
    죽으면 영혼은 천국에 간다.

13. Let's make a _____ tree.
    크리스마스트리를 만들자.

14. Using thick pens, draw a dot in the middle of each _____.
    굵은 펜을 사용하여 각각의 원 중앙에 점을 하나 그려라.

15. Don't lean _____, please.
    뒤로 기대지 마세요.

16. Let's _____ the street at the crosswalk.
    횡단보도에서 길을 건너자.

17. They are looking at a _____ screen.
    그들은 컴퓨터 화면을 보고 있다.

18. The man is playing the _____.
    남자가 드럼을 연주하고 있다.

Hint

| cross | backward | carry | die | album | computer | Christmas | below | drum |
| curtain | appear | case | both | away | bridge | circle | dictionary | cool |

Exercise

B. Fill in the word and meaning.

	Word	Meaning
01	backward	
02	carry	
03	cross	
04	album	
05	die	
06	Christmas	
07	appear	
08	computer	
09	drum	
10	below	
11	curtain	
12	case	
13	dictionary	
14	bridge	
15	cool	
16	circle	
17	both	
18	away	

	Meaning	Word
01	앨범, 사진첩	
02	나타나다	
03	떨어져서	
04	거꾸로, 뒤로	
05	~의 아래에	
06	둘 다의, 양쪽의	
07	다리	
08	나르다, 운반하다	
09	경우, 사례	
10	크리스마스	
11	원	
12	컴퓨터	
13	시원한	
14	가로지르다	
15	커튼	
16	사전	
17	죽다	
18	북, 드럼	

C. Listen, write the word and meaning. (Track 99)

	Word	Meaning		Word	Meaning
01			10		
02			11		
03			12		
04			13		
05			14		
06			15		
07			16		
08			17		
09			18		

Unit 34

🎧 Listen and repeat. (Track 100)

01 each [iːtʃ]
a 각각의   considering every member of the group as individuals
Each team has five players.
각 팀에는 5명의 선수가 있습니다.

02 exercise [éksərsàiz]
v 운동하다 / **n** 운동   physical activity that keeps you healthy and strong
Why don't you do **exercises** regularly?
운동을 규칙적으로 하는 게 어떠니?

03 fact [fækt]
n 사실, 진실   used to refer to a particular situation that exists
Many advertisers often use this simple **fact**.
많은 광고주들이 이 단순한 사실을 종종 이용한다.

04 field [fiːld]
n 들판, 벌판   an area of land on farm, used for growing crops
The **field** of corn waved in the breeze.
옥수수 밭이 산들바람에 물결쳤다.

05 fight [fait]
v 싸우다   to take part in a war
They began to **fight** over the rabbit.
그들은 토끼를 두고 싸우기 시작했다.

06 form [fɔːrm]
n 형태, 모양   the shape of something
The articles will be published in book **form**.
기사들은 책의 형태로 출간될 것이다.

07 fox [faks]
n 여우   a wild animal of the dog family, with reddish brown fur
The tiger is more dangerous than the **fox**.
호랑이는 여우보다 더 위험하다.

08 grow [grou]
v 키우다, 재배하다   to make plants grow by giving them water, etc
We can't **grow** palm trees in a cold climate.
추운 기후에서는 야자수를 키울 수 없다.

09 guitar [gitáːr]
n 기타   a musical instrument with six strings and a long neck
A boy was playing the **guitar**.
한 소년이 기타를 치고 있었다.

key words
individual **n** 개인 / exist **v** 존재하다 / advertiser **n** 광고주 / wave **v** 물결치다
breeze **n** 산들바람 / article **n** 기사 / publish **v** 출간하다 / climate **n** 기후, 날씨 / string **n** 줄, 선

🎧 Listen and repeat. (Track 101)

10 gun
[gʌn]
n 총, 대포   a weapon that is used for firing bullets
The bank was robbed by two men with **guns**.
그 은행은 총을 가진 두 사람에 의해 강도당했다.

11 hill
[hil]
n 언덕   a high area of land that is not as high as a mountain
The **hill** has a pine forest.
그 언덕에는 소나무 숲이 있다.

12 hit
[hit]
v 치다, 때리다   to make sudden, violent contract with somebody / something
A car almost **hit** him.
그는 하마터면 자동차에 치일 뻔했다.

13 hurt
[həːrt]
v 상처를 내다   to cause somebody physical pain or injury
I **hurt** my leg while playing soccer yesterday.
어제 축구를 하다가 다리를 다쳤다.

14 large
[laːrdʒ]
a 큰, 넓은   greater in size, amount, etc than usual
Do you have it in a **large** size?
큰 사이즈도 있나요?

15 last
[læst]
a 지난번의, 최후의   the most recent one, only remaining
This is my **last** chance to take the exam.
이번이 시험을 볼 수 있는 최후의 기회이다.

16 leaf
[liːf]
n 나뭇잎   a flat green part of a plant
Three ants are carrying a **leaf**.
개미 세 마리가 나뭇잎을 나르고 있다.

17 list
[list]
n 목록, 명단   a series of names, figures, items, etc
The **list** included her name.
그 명단에는 그녀의 이름도 들어 있었다.

18 little
[litl]
a 작은   not big; small; smaller than others
His fat **little** body is covered with soft gray fur.
그의 통통하고 작은 몸은 부드러운 회색 털로 덮여 있습니다.

---

key words
bullet n 탄알 / injury n 상해, 상처 / remain v 남아있다 / chance n 기회 / include v 포함하다 / fur n 털

Unit 34 171

Exercise

A. Complete the sentence.

1. Many advertisers often use this simple _____.
   많은 광고주들이 이 단순한 사실을 종종 이용한다.

2. _____ team has five players.
   각 팀에는 5명의 선수가 있습니다.

3. The _____ included her name.
   그 명단에는 그녀의 이름도 들어 있었다.

4. We can't _____ palm trees in a cold climate.
   추운 기후에서는 야자수를 키울 수 없다.

5. The tiger is more dangerous than the _____.
   호랑이는 여우보다 더 위험하다.

6. The _____ of corn waved in the breeze.
   옥수수 밭이 산들바람에 물결쳤다.

7. A boy was playing the _____.
   한 소년이 기타를 치고 있었다.

8. The bank was robbed by two men with _____.
   그 은행은 총을 가진 두 사람에 의해 강도당했다.

9. The _____ has a pine forest.
   그 언덕에는 소나무 숲이 있다.

10. Three ants are carrying a _____.
    개미 세 마리가 나뭇잎을 나르고 있다.

11. A car almost _____ him.
    그는 하마터면 자동차에 치일 뻔했다.

12. I _____ my leg while playing soccer yesterday.
    어제 축구를 하다가 다리를 다쳤다.

13. They began to _____ over the rabbit.
    그들은 토끼를 두고 싸우기 시작했다.

14. Do you have it in a _____ size?
    큰 사이즈도 있나요?

15. Why don't you do _____ regularly?
    운동을 규칙적으로 하는 게 어떠니?

16. This is my _____ chance to take the exam.
    이번이 시험을 볼 수 있는 최후의 기회이다.

17. The articles will be published in book _____.
    기사들은 책의 형태로 출간될 것이다.

18. His fat _____ body is covered with soft gray fur.
    그의 통통하고 작은 몸은 부드러운 회색 털로 덮여 있습니다.

Hint

| fact | leaf | grow | fox | each | list | field | guitar | last |
| hit | exercise | fight | hill | form | gun | little | hurt | large |

Unit 34

Exercise

B. Fill in the word and meaning.

	Word	Meaning
01	exercise	
02	field	
03	grow	
04	hit	
05	fox	
06	each	
07	hill	
08	large	
09	form	
10	list	
11	little	
12	gun	
13	fight	
14	leaf	
15	last	
16	hurt	
17	guitar	
18	fact	

	Meaning	Word
01	각각의	
02	운동하다, 운동	
03	사실, 진실	
04	들판, 벌판	
05	싸우다	
06	형태, 모양	
07	여우	
08	키우다, 재배하다	
09	기타	
10	총, 대포	
11	언덕	
12	치다, 때리다	
13	상처를 내다	
14	큰, 넓은	
15	지난번의, 최후의	
16	나뭇잎	
17	목록, 명단	
18	작은	

🎧 C. Listen, write the word and meaning. (Track 102)

	Word	Meaning		Word	Meaning
01			10		
02			11		
03			12		
04			13		
05			14		
06			15		
07			16		
08			17		
09			18		

Review 17

A. Read and fill in the word and meaning.

word	definition	meaning
	a situation of a particular type	
	a structure that is built over a road	
	a book in which you can keep photographs	
	a piece of fabric that is hung to cover a window	
	to hold something while you are moving	
	to give the impression of being	
	a book that contains a list of the words in a language	
	the period of time before and after 25 December	
	at or to a lower position than something	
	to go from one side to the other	
	the two; the one as well as the other	
	a completely round flat shape	
	to stop living	
	in the direction that your back is facing	
	fairly cold; not hot or warm	
	at a particular distance from a place	
	a machine that can store, find and arrange information	
	a musical instrument played by hitting with hands or sticks	

Hint

cross backward carry die album computer Christmas curtain drum
bridge appear case cool away below circle dictionary both

B. Read and fill in the word and meaning.

word	definition	meaning
	to make sudden, violent contract with somebody / something	
	used to refer to a particular situation that exists	
	to cause somebody physical pain or injury	
	physical activity that keeps you healthy and strong	
	a high area of land that is not as high as a mountain	
	to take part in a war	
	considering every member of the group as individuals	
	a weapon that is used for firing bullets	
	an area of land on farm, used for growing crops	
	greater in size, amount, etc than usual	
	a musical instrument with six strings and a long neck	
	the most recent one, only remaining	
	the shape of something	
	a series of names, figures, items, etc	
	a wild animal of the dog family, with reddish brown fur	
	a flat green part of a plant	
	to make plants grow by giving them water, etc	
	not big; small; smaller than others	

Hint

gun   hill   grow   fox   each   list   fight   guitar   exercise
hit   last   field   leaf   form   fact   little   hurt   large

Unit 35

🎧 Listen and repeat. Track 103

01 meter [míːtər]
n 미터   a unit of length in the metric system
The tower is ten **meters** high.
그 탑은 10미터이다.

02 middle [mídl]
n 중앙, 한가운데   the part of something that is furthest from its ends
Look at the second picture in the **middle**.
가운데에 있는 두 번째 사진을 보세요.

03 news [njuːz]
n 뉴스, 기사   new information about something that has happen recently
The **news** article reported only the tip of the iceberg.
그 뉴스 기사는 빙산의 일각만 보도했다.

04 next [nekst]
a 다음의   the one that comes after the present one
You should visit here **next** time.
다음에 너도 한 번 와 봐야 해.

05 paint [peint]
v (페인트를) 칠하다   to cover a surface with paint
He **painted** the door white.
그는 문을 흰색으로 칠했다.

06 pair [pɛər]
n 한 쌍, 한 벌   two things of the same type
She lost a **pair** of earrings that is given from her husband.
그녀는 남편이 준 귀걸이 한 쌍을 잃어버렸다.

07 penguin [péŋgwin]
n 펭귄   a black and white seabird
What are the **penguins** looking at?
펭귄들이 무엇을 보고 있나요?

08 pineapple [páinæpl]
n 파인애플   a tropical fruit with thick rough skin
I ordered a glass of **pineapple** juice.
나는 파인애플 주스 한 잔을 주문했다.

09 pipe [paip]
n 관, 파이프   a tube through which liquids and gases can flow
The water **pipe** is leaking.
수도관이 새고 있다.

---

key words
furthest a 가장 먼 / second n 둘째의, 2등의 / iceberg n 빙산
tropical a 열대지방의 / skin n 껍질, 피부 / order v 주문하다 / leak v 새다

🎧 Listen and repeat. (Track 104)

10 prince [prins]
n 왕자   a male member of a royal family
The princess and **prince** didn't get married.
공주와 왕자는 결혼하지 않았다.

11 real [ríːəl]
a 진실의, 실제의   actually existing of happening
I don't know the **real** reason about the problem.
나는 그 문제에 대한 진짜 이유를 모르겠다.

12 regular [régjələːr]
a 규칙적인, 보통의   following a pattern
Eating **regular** meals is good for health.
규칙적인 식사를 하는 것은 건강에 좋다.

13 roll [roul]
v 구르다   to move along a surface, turning over many times
The apples fell out and **rolled** everywhere.
사과들이 떨어져서 사방으로 굴러갔다.

14 roof [ruːf]
n 지붕   the structure that covers the top of a building
This house has a flat **roof**.
이 집은 지붕이 평평하다.

15 score [skɔːr]
n 점수, 성적   the number of points, goals, etc.
What was the final **score**?
최종 점수는 몇이었나요?

16 seat [siːt]
n 좌석, 자리   a place where you can sit
I want a **seat** for the rock concert.
그 록 콘서트의 좌석이 필요해요.

17 shut [ʃʌt]
v 닫다   to make something close; to become closed
Shut the door behind you.
당신 뒤의 문을 닫으세요.

18 side [said]
n 쪽, 측면   a position to the left or right of something
The **side** of the car was damaged.
차의 측면이 손상 되었다.

---

key words
royal **a** 왕족의 / actually **ad** 실제로 / pattern **n** 양식, 모범 / position **n** 위치 / damaged **a** 손상을 입은

Exercise

A. Complete the sentence.

1. I don't know the _____ reason about the problem.
   나는 그 문제에 대한 진짜 이유를 모르겠다.

2. What are the _____ looking at?
   펭귄들이 무엇을 보고 있나요?

3. What was the final _____?
   최종 점수는 몇 이었나요?

4. The tower is ten _____ high.
   그 탑은 10미터이다.

5. The _____ article reported only the tip of the iceberg.
   그 뉴스 기사는 빙산의 일각만 보도했다.

6. You should visit here _____ time.
   다음에 너도 한 번 와 봐야 해.

7. I want a _____ for the rock concert.
   그 록 콘서트의 좌석이 필요해요.

8. He _____ the door white.
   그는 문을 흰색으로 칠했다.

9. Look at the second picture in the _____.
   가운데에 있는 두 번째 사진을 보세요.

10. She lost a _____ of earrings that is given from her husband.
    그녀는 남편이 준 귀걸이 한 쌍을 잃어버렸다.

11. This house has a flat _____.
    이 집은 지붕이 평평하다.

12. The water _____ is leaking.
    수도관이 새고 있다.

13. The princess and _____ didn't get married.
    공주와 왕자는 결혼하지 않았다.

14. Eating _____ meals is good for health.
    규칙적인 식사를 하는 것은 건강에 좋다.

15. I ordered a glass of _____ juice.
    나는 파인애플 주스 한 잔을 주문했다.

16. _____ the door behind you.
    당신 뒤의 문을 닫으세요.

17. The apples fell out and _____ everywhere.
    사과들이 떨어져서 사방으로 굴러갔다.

18. The _____ of the car was damaged.
    차의 측면이 손상 되었다.

Hint

| penguin | news | seat | regular | meter | roll | paint | side | pipe |
| middle | pair | next | score | pineapple | real | prince | roof | shut |

Exercise

B. Fill in the word and meaning.

	Word	Meaning
01	middle	
02	paint	
03	real	
04	next	
05	roof	
06	pipe	
07	side	
08	meter	
09	roll	
10	pineapple	
11	shut	
12	news	
13	prince	
14	seat	
15	pair	
16	score	
17	regular	
18	penguin	

	Meaning	Word
01	미터	
02	중앙, 한가운데	
03	뉴스, 기사	
04	다음의	
05	(페인트를) 칠하다	
06	한 쌍, 한 벌	
07	펭귄	
08	파인애플	
09	관, 파이프	
10	왕자	
11	진실의, 실제의	
12	규칙적인, 보통의	
13	구르다	
14	지붕	
15	점수, 성적	
16	좌석, 자리	
17	닫다	
18	쪽, 측면	

C. Listen, write the word and meaning. (Track 105)

	Word	Meaning
01		
02		
03		
04		
05		
06		
07		
08		
09		

	Word	Meaning
10		
11		
12		
13		
14		
15		
16		
17		
18		

Unit 36

🎧 Listen and repeat. Track 106

01 soft [sɔ(ː)ft]
a 부드러운   less hard than average
He asked her in a **soft** voice.
그는 그녀에게 부드러운 목소리로 물었다.

02 some [sʌm]
a 약간의, 얼마간의   a quantity of something when you are not stating the number precisely
I need **some** chocolate and **some** butter.
초콜릿과 버터가 약간 필요해.

03 stamp [stæmp]
n 우표   a small piece of paper which you stick on an envelope
These **stamps** will surely decorate the envelope.
이 우표들은 틀림없이 봉투를 꾸며 줄거야.

04 station [stéiʃən]
n 정거장   a place where trains stop so that people can get on or off
Let's go to a nearby **station**.
가까운 정거장으로 가자.

05 subway [sʌ́bwèi]
n 지하철   an underground railway system in a city
The **subway** fare has gone up.
지하철 요금이 인상되었다.

06 summer [sʌ́mər]
n 여름   the season between spring and autumn
I went to Australia this **summer**.
이번 여름에 호주에 갔었어.

07 tall [tɔːl]
a 키 큰   having a greater than average height
He was **tall** and thin.
그는 키가 크고 말랐었다.

08 taste [teist]
v 맛이 나다   to have a particular flavor
It **tastes** great.
정말 맛있다.

09 ticket [tíkit]
n 표, 입장권   a paper that gives you the right to travel on a bus, train
How much does the student **ticket** cost?
학생 표는 얼마죠?

key words
less **a** 보다 작은 / average **n** 평균 / precisely **ad** 정확히 / envelope **n** 봉투
decorate **v** 꾸미다 / nearby **a** 가까운 / fare **n** 요금 / cost **n** 비용

🎧 Listen and repeat. (Track 107)

10 tiger [táigə:r]
n 호랑이 a large wild animal that has yellowish fur with black
A **tiger** is bigger than a cat, but it's smaller than a bear.
호랑이는 고양이보다는 크다. 그러나 곰보다는 작다.

11 true [tru:]
a 진실한, 정말의 be based on facts rather than being imagined
It is **true** that he loves Jane.
그가 제인을 사랑한다는 것은 정말이다.

12 tulip [tjú:lip]
n 튤립 brightly colored flowers, shaped like a cup
The man is preparing to plant **tulips**.
남자가 튤립을 심을 준비를 하고 있다.

13 when [hwen]
ad 언제 at what time
When are they to arrive?
그들은 언제 도착할 예정인가?

14 which [hwitʃ]
a 어느, 어떤 used in question to ask somebody to be exact about things
Which animal do you like the most?
네가 가장 좋아하는 동물은 어떤 동물이니?

15 why [hwai]
ad 왜, 어째서 used in question to ask the reason for
Tell me **why** you did it.
왜 그렇게 했는지 그 이유를 말해 주세요.

16 word [wə:rd]
n 말, 낱말 a single unit of language that can be spoken or written
These two characters can form a **word**.
이 두 글자가 하나의 낱말을 형성한다.

17 work [wə:rk]
n 일 / v 일하다 something that involves physical or mental effort
There is so much **work** to do.
할 일이 너무 많다.

18 world [wə:rld]
n 세계 the earth, with all its countries
The **world** after the year 2050 will be just fantastic.
2050년 이후의 세계는 정말 환상적일 것이다.

key words
yellowish a 황색을 띤 / base v ~에 바탕을 두다 / rather ad 오히려 / prepare v 준비하다
most a 가장, 최대의 / character n 문자 / involve v 수반하다 / mental a 정신의 / fantastic a 환상적인

Exercise

A. Complete the sentence.

1. _____ animal do you like the most?
   네가 가장 좋아하는 동물은 어떤 동물이니?

2. These _____ will surely decorate the envelope.
   이 우표들은 틀림없이 봉투를 꾸며 줄거야.

3. It is _____ that he loves Jane.
   그가 제인을 사랑한다는 것은 정말이다.

4. These two characters can form a _____.
   이 두 글자가 하나의 낱말을 형성한다.

5. The _____ fare has gone up.
   지하철 요금이 인상되었다.

6. I went to Australia this _____.
   이번 여름에 호주에 갔었어.

7. He was _____ and thin.
   그는 키가 크고 말랐었다.

8. There is so much _____ to do.
   할 일이 너무 많다.

9. It _____ great.
   정말 맛있다.

10. I need _____ chocolate and _____ butter.
    초콜릿과 버터가 약간 필요해.

11. How much does the student _____ cost?
    학생 표는 얼마죠?

12. He asked her in a _____ voice.
    그는 그녀에게 부드러운 목소리로 물었다.

13. Tell me _____ you did it.
    왜 그렇게 했는지 그 이유를 말해 주세요.

14. A _____ is bigger than a cat, but it's smaller than a bear.
    호랑이는 고양이보다는 크다. 그러나 곰보다는 작다.

15. The man is preparing to plant _____.
    남자가 튤립을 심을 준비를 하고 있다.

16. _____ are they to arrive?
    그들은 언제 도착할 예정인가?

17. Let's go to a nearby _____.
    가까운 정거장으로 가자.

18. The _____ after the year 2050 will be just fantastic.
    2050년 이후의 세계는 정말 환상적일 것이다.

Hint

| tall | subway | word | true | soft | which | some | taste | summer |
| why | world | tiger | stamp | work | tulip | station | ticket | when |

Exercise

B. Fill in the word and meaning.

	Word	Meaning
01	subway	
02	tall	
03	some	
04	tulip	
05	taste	
06	when	
07	soft	
08	why	
09	true	
10	work	
11	word	
12	stamp	
13	world	
14	ticket	
15	which	
16	summer	
17	tiger	
18	station	

	Meaning	Word
01	부드러운	
02	약간의, 얼마간의	
03	우표	
04	정거장	
05	지하철	
06	여름	
07	키 큰	
08	맛이 나다	
09	표, 입장권	
10	호랑이	
11	진실한, 정말의	
12	튤립	
13	언제	
14	어느, 어떤	
15	왜, 어째서	
16	말, 낱말	
17	일, 일하다	
18	세계	

C. Listen, write the word and meaning. (Track 108)

	Word	Meaning		Word	Meaning
01			10		
02			11		
03			12		
04			13		
05			14		
06			15		
07			16		
08			17		
09			18		

Review 18

A. Read and fill in the word and meaning.

word	definition	meaning
	to cover a surface with paint	
	the one that comes after the present one	
	the part of something that is furthest from its ends	
	following a pattern	
	the number of points, goals, etc.	
	to move along a surface, turning over many times	
	new information about something that has happen recently	
	a place where you can sit	
	two things of the same type	
	the structure that covers the top of a building	
	a black and white seabird	
	to make something close; to become closed	
	a tube through which liquids and gases can flow	
	actually existing of happening	
	a tropical fruit with thick rough skin	
	a position to the left or right of something	
	a unit of length in the metric system	
	a male member of a royal family	

Hint

penguin news seat regular meter roll paint side pipe
middle pair next score pineapple real prince roof shut

B. Read and fill in the word and meaning.

word	definition	meaning
	the earth, with all its countries	
	a large wild animal that has yellowish fur with black	
	a single unit of language that can be spoken or written	
	less hard than average	
	something that involves physical or mental effort	
	a paper that gives you the right to travel on a bus, train	
	a quantity of something when you are not stating the number precisely	
	be based on facts rather than being imagined	
	a small piece of paper which you stick on an envelope	
	used in question to ask the reason for	
	brightly colored flowers, shaped like a cup	
	a place where trains stop so that people can get on or off	
	having a greater than average height	
	at what time	
	an underground railway system in a city	
	used in question to ask somebody to be exact about things	
	to have a particular flavor	
	the season between spring and autumn	

Hint

| tall | subway | word | true | soft | which | some | taste | summer |
| why | world | tiger | stamp | work | tulip | station | ticket | when |

Unit 37

🎧 **Listen and repeat.** Track 109

01 address n 주소 details of where somebody lives
[ədrés]
He wrote a message with his **address** and phone number.
그는 쪽지에 주소와 전화번호를 썼다.

02 alphabet n 알파벳 a set of symbols in a fixed order used for writing a language
[ǽlfəbèt]
There are twenty-six letters in the English **alphabet**.
영어 알파벳에는 26자가 있어요.

03 ambulance n 구급차 a vehicle for taking people to hospital
[ǽmbjuləns]
I asked for the **ambulance** service to the hospital.
나는 그 병원에 구급차를 보내달라고 요청했다.

04 band n 악단, 무리 a small group of musicians who play music together
[bænd]
They listen to the music and dance to the **band**.
그들은 음악을 듣고 악단에 맞춰 춤을 춘다.

05 beside prep ~의 옆에 next to somebody / something
[bisáid]
He saw there was another piece of paper **beside** his plate.
그는 접시 옆에 있는 또 다른 종이를 보았다.

06 between prep ~의 사이에 into the space separating two or more things
[bitwí:n]
There are a lot of little differences **between** America and Korea.
미국과 한국 사이에는 작은 차이점들이 많이 있어.

07 burn v 타다 to be on fire
[bə:rn]
The steaks started to **burn**.
스테이크가 타기 시작했다.

08 cassette n 카세트 a small flat plastic case containing tape for playing music
[kæsét]
I'll buy the **cassette** recorder.
나는 그 카세트 녹음기를 살 것이다.

09 center n 중앙, 중심 the middle point or part of something
[séntər]
Why is the boy in the **center** crying?
가운데 있는 소년은 왜 울고 있니?

---

key words
detail n 세부사항 / fixed a 고정된 / letter n 글자 / musician n 음악가
separate v 분리하다 / difference n 차이점

🎧 Listen and repeat. (Track 110)

10 classmate [klǽsmèit] — **n** 급우 — students who are in the same class at school
All of her **classmates** were very sad.
그녀의 급우들 모두가 매우 슬펐다.

11 climb [klaim] — **v** 오르다 — to go up something towards the top
Monkeys **climb** well.
원숭이는 잘 오른다.

12 copy [kápi] — **n** 복사 — to produce something that looks like the original thing
This is a **copy** of a famous picture.
이것은 유명한 그림의 복사본이다.

13 corn [kɔ:rn] — **n** 옥수수 — used to refer to crops such as wheat
The container is full of **corns**.
그 그릇에는 옥수수가 가득 들어있다.

14 danger [déindʒər] — **n** 위험 — the possibility that someone may be harmed or killed
The bodyguard protected her against **danger**.
경호원은 위험으로부터 그녀를 보호했다.

15 date [deit] — **n** 날짜 — a specific time that can be named
What was the **date** on the poster?
포스터 위에 적힌 날짜는 언제였습니까?

16 daughter [dɔ́:tər] — **n** 딸 — a person's female child
You are my **daughter's** friend.
네가 내 딸아이의 친구구나.

17 different [dífərənt] — **a** 다른, 각각의 — not like each other in one or more ways
Teenage culture is **different** from adult culture.
십대 문화는 성인문화와 다르다.

18 doctor [dáktər] — **n** 의사 — someone who is qualified in medicine and treats people
A **doctor** and a nurse take care of him.
한 의사와 간호원이 그를 돌보고 있습니다.

key words
original **a** 원래의, 최초의 / harm **v** 상처를 입히다 / specific **a** 명확한, 일정한 / teenage **a** 10대의 / culture **a** 문화 / qualified **a** 자격 있는 / medicine **n** 의학, 의술 / treat **v** 치료하다

Exercise

A. Complete the sentence.

1. There are twenty-six letters in the English _____.
   영어 알파벳에는 26자가 있어요.

2. The bodyguard protected her against _____.
   경호원은 위험으로부터 그녀를 보호했다.

3. I asked for the _____ service to the hospital.
   나는 그 병원에 구급차를 보내달라고 요청했다.

4. He saw there was another piece of paper _____ his plate.
   그는 접시 옆에 있는 또 다른 종이를 보았다.

5. Teenage culture is _____ from adult culture.
   십대 문화는 성인문화와 다르다.

6. Monkeys _____ well.
   원숭이는 잘 오른다.

7. The steaks started to _____.
   스테이크가 타기 시작했다.

8. Why is the boy in the _____ crying?
   가운데 있는 소년은 왜 울고 있니?

9. All of her _____ were very sad.
   그녀의 급우들 모두가 매우 슬펐다.

10. He wrote a message with his _____ and phone number.
    그는 쪽지에 주소와 전화번호를 썼다.

11. This is a _____ of a famous picture.
    이것은 유명한 그림의 복사본이다.

12. The container is full of _____.
    그 그릇에는 옥수수가 가득 들어있다.

13. What was the _____ on the poster?
    포스터 위에 적힌 날짜는 언제였습니까?

14. They listen to the music and dance to the _____.
    그들은 음악을 듣고 악단에 맞춰 춤을 춘다.

15. There are a lot of little differences _____ America and Korea.
    미국과 한국 사이에는 작은 차이점들이 많이 있어.

16. I'll buy the _____ recorder.
    나는 그 카세트 녹음기를 살 것이다.

17. You are my _____'s friend.
    네가 내 딸아이의 친구구나.

18. A _____ and a nurse take care of him.
    한 의사와 간호원이 그를 돌보고 있습니다.

Hint

| burn | alphabet | classmate | daughter | band | cassette | doctor | address | center |
| beside | ambulance | different | copy | date | between | climb | corn | danger |

Exercise

B. Fill in the word and meaning.

	Word	Meaning
01	band	
02	classmate	
03	burn	
04	danger	
05	address	
06	copy	
07	daughter	
08	alphabet	
09	different	
10	corn	
11	doctor	
12	ambulance	
13	date	
14	cassette	
15	between	
16	climb	
17	center	
18	beside	

	Meaning	Word
01	주소	
02	알파벳	
03	구급차	
04	악단, 무리	
05	~의 옆에	
06	~의 사이에	
07	타다	
08	카세트	
09	중앙, 중심	
10	급우	
11	오르다	
12	복사	
13	옥수수	
14	위험	
15	날짜	
16	딸	
17	다른, 각각의	
18	의사	

C. Listen, write the word and meaning. Track 111

	Word	Meaning		Word	Meaning
01			10		
02			11		
03			12		
04			13		
05			14		
06			15		
07			16		
08			17		
09			18		

Unit 38

🎧 **Listen and repeat.** (Track 112)

01 earth [ə:rθ] — n 지구 — the planet on which we live
The sun is bigger than the **earth**.
태양이 지구보다 더 크다.

02 east [i:st] — n 동쪽 — the direction where the sun rises
The sun rises in the **east**.
해는 동쪽에서 뜹니다.

03 fair [fɛər] — a 공평한 / ad 정정 당당하게 — treating everyone equally to the rules
That's not **fair**.
그것은 공평하지 않아요.

04 fall [fɔ:l] — n 가을 — the season of the year between summer and winter
It is windy in the **fall**.
가을에는 바람이 많이 불어요.

05 fill [fil] — v 채우다 — to become full of something
The bottle is **filled** with water.
그 병은 물로 가득 차 있다.

06 film [film] — n 영화, 필름 — moving pictures recorded with sound
The **film** was boring, so I fell asleep.
그 영화가 지루해서 나는 잠이 들었다.

07 frog [frɔ:g] — n 개구리 — a small creature with smooth skin
The **frog** is jumping.
개구리가 뛰어오르고 있다.

08 front [frʌnt] — n 앞, 앞쪽 — the part of something that faces forward
There is a church in **front** of the school.
학교 앞에는 교회가 있다.

09 half [hæf] — n 반, 절반 — something can be divided into two equal parts
Half of this money is yours.
이 돈의 반은 당신 것입니다.

key words
planet n 행성 / equally ad 똑같이, 동등하게 / windy a 바람이 부는
bottle n 병 / boring a 지루한 / creature n 생물 / smooth a 매끄러운

🎧 Listen and repeat. Track 113

10 hardly [háːrdli]
ad 거의 ~아니다   almost no; almost not
I can **hardly** believe it.
나는 그것이 거의 믿어지지 않는다.

11 hold [hould]
v 잡다, 갖고 있다   to take somebody / something and keep him / her / it in your hand
He **held** a gun in his hand.
그는 손에 총을 잡고 있었다.

12 hole [houl]
n 구멍   a hollow space in something solid
The girl is digging a **hole**.
소녀가 구멍을 파고 있다.

13 job [dʒab]
n 일, 직업   work for which you receive regular payment
I congratulate myself on finding a good **job**.
좋은 일자리를 구해서 기뻐요.

14 jungle [dʒʌ́ŋgl]
n 밀림   a forest in a tropical area where a lot of trees and plants
The lion is king of the **jungle**.
사자는 밀림의 왕입니다.

15 laugh [læf]
v 웃다, 비웃다   to make a sound with your throat while smiling
Try to **laugh** as much as possible.
가능한 한 많이 웃으려고 노력하세요.

16 lead [liːd]
v 안내하다, 인도하다   to make a person go in the right direction
A dog is **leading** the blind man.
한 마리 개가 눈먼 사람을 인도하고 있다.

17 lot [lat]
n 많음   a large amount of something
It snows a **lot** in winter.
겨울에는 눈이 많이 온다.

18 mail [meil]
n 우편물   the letters, etc that you receive
The **mail** was lost.
우편물이 분실되었다.

key words
almost **ad** 거의 / hollow **a** 우묵한 / dig **v** 파다 / payment **n** 보수
congratulate oneself on ~을 기뻐하다 / blind **a** 눈 먼

Unit 38 191

Exercise

A. Complete the sentence.

1. The sun rises in the _____.
   해는 동쪽에서 뜹니다.

2. The girl is digging a _____.
   소녀가 구멍을 파고 있다.

3. A dog is _____ the blind man.
   한 마리 개가 눈먼 사람을 인도하고 있다.

4. It is windy in the _____.
   가을에는 바람이 많이 불어요.

5. The _____ was boring, so I fell asleep.
   그 영화가 지루해서 나는 잠이 들었다.

6. The sun is bigger than the _____.
   태양이 지구보다 더 크다.

7. The _____ is jumping.
   개구리가 뛰어오르고 있다.

8. _____ of this money is yours.
   이 돈의 반은 당신 것입니다.

9. The _____ was lost.
   우편물이 분실되었다.

10. Try to _____ as much as possible.
    가능한 한 많이 웃으려고 노력하세요.

11. I can _____ believe it.
    나는 그것이 거의 믿어지지 않는다.

12. The bottle is _____ with water.
    그 병은 물로 가득 차 있다.

13. That's not _____.
    그것은 공평하지 않아요.

14. He _____ a gun in his hand.
    그는 손에 총을 잡고 있었다.

15. The lion is king of the _____.
    사자는 밀림의 왕입니다.

16. It snows a _____ in winter.
    겨울에는 눈이 많이 온다.

17. There is a church in _____ of the school.
    학교 앞에는 교회가 있다.

18. I congratulate myself on finding a good _____.
    좋은 일자리를 구해서 기뻐요.

Hint

| fair | east | half | jungle | front | laugh | film | lead | hole |
| fall | hold | earth | fill | job | lot | frog | hardly | mail |

Exercise

B. Fill in the word and meaning.

	Word	Meaning
01	east	
02	hardly	
03	front	
04	jungle	
05	fall	
06	lot	
07	earth	
08	mail	
09	hold	
10	laugh	
11	fill	
12	hole	
13	lead	
14	film	
15	job	
16	half	
17	frog	
18	fair	

	Meaning	Word
01	지구	
02	동쪽	
03	공평한, 정정 당당하게	
04	가을	
05	채우다	
06	영화, 필름	
07	개구리	
08	앞, 앞쪽	
09	반, 절반	
10	거의 ~아니다	
11	잡다, 갖고 있다	
12	구멍	
13	일, 직업	
14	밀림	
15	웃다, 비웃다	
16	안내하다, 인도하다	
17	많음	
18	우편물	

🎧 C. Listen, write the word and meaning. (Track 114)

	Word	Meaning		Word	Meaning
01			10		
02			11		
03			12		
04			13		
05			14		
06			15		
07			16		
08			17		
09			18		

Review 19

A. Read and fill in the word and meaning.

word	definition	meaning
	to go up something towards the top	
	details of where somebody lives	
	not like each other in one or more ways	
	students who are in the same class at school	
	a person's female child	
	a set of symbols in a fixed order used for writing a language	
	the middle point or part of something	
	someone who is qualified in medicine and treats people	
	to produce something that looks like the original thing	
	a vehicle for taking people to hospital	
	used to refer to crops such as wheat	
	to be on fire	
	the possibility that someone may be harmed or killed	
	a small group of musicians who play music together	
	a small flat plastic case containing tape for playing music	
	next to somebody / something	
	a specific time that can be named	
	into the space separating two or more things	

Hint

burn   alphabet   classmate   corn   band   cassette   doctor   center   address
climb   different   ambulance   copy   date   between   beside   danger   daughter

B. Read and fill in the word and meaning.

word	definition	meaning
	to take somebody / something and keep him / her / it in your hand	
	a small creature with smooth skin	
	almost no; almost not	
	the part of something that faces forward	
	the letters, etc that you receive	
	moving pictures recorded with sound	
	a large amount of something	
	something can be divided into two equal parts	
	the planet on which we live	
	to make a person go in the right direction	
	to become full of something	
	the direction where the sun rises	
	to make a sound with your throat while smiling	
	the season of the year between summer and winter	
	a hollow space in something solid	
	work for which you receive regular payment	
	treating everyone equally to the rules	
	a forest in a tropical area where a lot of trees and plants	

Hint
frog   earth   half   jungle   lead   fill   film   front   hole
mail   hold   east   laugh   job   lot   fair   hardly   fall

Unit 39

🎧 Listen and repeat. Track 115

01 million [míljən]
n 백만   the number 1,000,000
The population of this country is about one **million**.
이 나라의 인구는 약 1백만 명이다.

02 minute [mínit]
n 분, 잠시   each of the 60 parts of an hour
We'll be there in ten **minutes**.
10분 후면 우리는 거기에 도착할거야.

03 niece [ni:s]
n 조카딸   the daughter of someone's sister or brother
How old is your **niece**?
너희 조카딸은 몇 살이니?

04 north [nɔ:rθ]
n 북쪽 / a 북쪽의   the direction that is on your left when you watch the sun rise
Seoul is **north** of Busan.
서울은 부산의 북쪽에 있습니다.

05 parents [pέərənts]
n 부모   your mother and father
My **parents** are worried about our argument.
나의 부모님은 우리의 논쟁에 대해 걱정을 하신다.

06 photo [fóutou]
n 사진   a picture that is made using a camera
I'm looking for my grandpa's **photo** album.
나는 할아버지의 사진첩을 찾고 있는 중이야.

07 place [pleis]
n 장소, 곳   a particular position, point or area
The ambulance started to the **place**.
구급차가 그곳으로 출발했다.

08 plan [plæn]
n 계획 / v 계획하다   something that you intend to do or achieve
I have a **plan** to take a computer course.
컴퓨터 수업을 받을 계획이야.

09 problem [prábləm]
n 문제   a thing that is difficult to deal with
She discovered the **problem** by accident.
그녀는 그 문제를 우연히 발견했다.

key words
population n 인구 / about ad 대략 / worry v 걱정시키다 / argument n 논쟁
intend v ~할 작정이다 / achieve v 이루다 / course n 과정, 수업 / accident n 우연

🎧 Listen and repeat. Track 116

10 program [próugræm]
n 프로그램   a set of instructions in code that control the operation
Just click the **program** icon twice quickly.
그 프로그램 아이콘을 두 번 빨리 클릭하면 돼.

11 record [rékərd]
n 기록, 레코드   to keep a written account or photographs of something
He has a criminal **record**.
그는 전과기록이 있다.

12 rectangle [réktæŋgəl]
n 직사각형   a 4-sided shape whose corners are all 90 degree angles
Can you draw a **rectangle**?
직사각형을 그릴 수 있나요?

13 rose [rouz]
n 장미   a flower with a sweet smell that grows on a bush with thorns
The **rose** doesn't have thorns.
그 장미는 가시가 없습니다.

14 round [raund]
a 둥근   shaped like a circle or a ball
He knew that the earth is **round**.
그는 지구가 둥글다는 것을 알았다.

15 service [sə́ːrvis]
n 서비스, 봉사   something that the public needs
The clerk called to the Flying Doctors **Service** center at once.
그 사무원은 즉시 '비행 의료 봉사' 센터에 전화했다.

16 shall [ʃæl]
aux ~을 할까요   used for suggesting that you do something with people
Shall we go skiing?
스키 타러 갈까?

17 silver [sílvər]
n 은 / a 은으로 만든   a grayish-white metal used for making jewellery
She has a **silver** ball.
그녀는 은으로 된 공을 갖고 있다.

18 size [saiz]
n 크기, 치수   how large or small a thing is
The file is much smaller in **size** but still high quality.
그 파일은 크기는 훨씬 더 작지만, 그러나 좋은 음질을 유지한다.

---

key words
instruction n 지시, 명령 / operation n 작업,조작 / criminal a 범죄의 / degree n 도
bush n 덤불 / thorn n 가시 / suggest v 제안하다 / grayish a 회색빛 도는

Unit 39

Exercise

A. Complete the sentence.

1. I'm looking for my grandpa's _____ album.
   나는 할아버지의 사진첩을 찾고 있는 중이야.

2. We'll be there in ten _____.
   10분 후면 우리는 거기에 도착할거야.

3. She discovered the _____ by accident.
   그녀는 그 문제를 우연히 발견했다.

4. The _____ doesn't have thorns.
   그 장미는 가시가 없습니다.

5. How old is your _____?
   너희 조카딸은 몇 살이니?

6. _____ we go skiing?
   스키 타러 갈까?

7. My _____ are worried about our argument.
   나의 부모님은 우리의 논쟁에 대해 걱정을 하신다.

8. The ambulance started to the _____.
   구급차는 그곳으로 출발했다.

9. I have a _____ to take a computer course.
   컴퓨터 수업을 받을 계획이야.

10. She has a _____ ball.
    그녀는 은으로 된 공을 갖고 있다.

11. Just click the _____ icon twice quickly.
    그 프로그램 아이콘을 두 번 빨리 클릭하면 돼.

12. He has a criminal _____.
    그는 전과기록이 있다.

13. The population of this country is about one _____.
    이 나라의 인구는 약 1백만 명이다.

14. Can you draw a _____?
    직사각형을 그릴 수 있나요?

15. The clerk called to the Flying Doctors _____ center at once.
    그 사무원은 즉시 '비행 의료 봉사' 센터에 전화했다.

16. Seoul is _____ of Busan.
    서울은 부산의 북쪽에 있습니다.

17. He knew that the earth is _____.
    그는 지구가 둥글다는 것을 알았다.

18. The file is much smaller in _____ but still high quality.
    그 파일은 크기는 훨씬 더 작지만, 그러나 좋은 음질을 유지한다.

Hint

| north | size | plan | rectangle | photo | service | parents | silver | million |
| place | minute | niece | record | problem | round | program | shall | rose |

Exercise

B. Fill in the word and meaning.

	Word	Meaning
01	record	
02	niece	
03	round	
04	photo	
05	million	
06	rose	
07	parents	
08	shall	
09	place	
10	rectangle	
11	minute	
12	problem	
13	service	
14	silver	
15	plan	
16	size	
17	program	
18	north	

	Meaning	Word
01	백만	
02	분, 잠시	
03	조카딸	
04	북쪽, 북쪽의	
05	부모	
06	사진	
07	장소, 곳	
08	계획, 계획하다	
09	문제	
10	프로그램	
11	기록, 레코드	
12	직사각형	
13	장미	
14	둥근	
15	서비스, 봉사	
16	~을 할까요	
17	은, 은으로 만든	
18	크기, 치수	

C. Listen, write the word and meaning. Track 117

	Word	Meaning		Word	Meaning
01			10		
02			11		
03			12		
04			13		
05			14		
06			15		
07			16		
08			17		
09			18		

Unit 40

🎧 Listen and repeat. Track 118

01 son [sʌn] — n 아들 — a person's male child
He has two **sons** who became doctors.
그는 의사가 된 두 아들이 있다.

02 sour [sáuəːr] — a 시큼한, 신 — having an unpleasant taste like the taste of a lemon
These apples are **sour**.
이 사과들은 시다.

03 steam [stiːm] — n 스팀, 증기 — the hot mist that is formed when water boils
She put me in a room full of **steam**.
어머니께서 나를 증기로 가득한 방으로 데려가셨다.

04 step [step] — v 밟다, 걷다 — to put your foot on the thing
Be careful! You'll **step** on your laptop computer.
조심해! 너는 네 휴대용 컴퓨터를 밟게 될꺼야.

05 sunny [sʌ́ni] — a 밝게 비치는 — with a lot of bright light from the sun
This afternoon it will be **sunny**.
오늘 오후에는 날씨가 갤 것으로 보인다.

06 supermarket [súːpərmàːrkit] — n 슈퍼마켓 — a large shop which sells food and household goods
The man is looking at the fruit in a **supermarket**.
남자가 슈퍼마켓에서 과일을 보고 있다.

07 team [tiːm] — n 팀, 조 — a group of people who play a particular game
How many players does a baseball **team** have?
한 야구팀은 몇 명의 선수들로 이루어져 있나요?

08 terror [térəːr] — n 공포, 두려움 — very great fear
He screamed in **terror** as the rats came towards him.
그는 쥐들이 그를 향해 다가오자 공포로 비명을 질렀다.

09 till [til] — prep ~까지 — during the period before a particular time
They played **till** six.
그들은 6시까지 놀았다.

---

key words
mist n 연무, 안개 / boil v 끓다 / household a 가정의, 가사의
particular a 특정한 / scream v 비명을 지르다 / rat n 쥐

🎧 Listen and repeat. Track 119

10 today
[tədéi]
ad 오늘   on this day; at the present period
I need to send these letters **today**.
이 편지들을 오늘 보내야 해.

11 twice
[twais]
ad 두 번, 2회   two times; on two occasions
Half of students use the computer **twice** a week.
학생들의 절반은 한 주에 두 번씩 컴퓨터를 사용한다.

12 umpire
[ʌ́mpaiər]
n 심판 / **v** 심판하다   a person who watches a game to make sure that the players obey the rules
The **umpire** called him safe.
심판은 그에게 세이프를 선언했다.

13 worm
[wə:rm]
n 벌레   a long thin creature with no bones or legs
This apple has a **worm** in it.
이 사과 안에 벌레가 들어 있어요.

14 write
[rait]
v 쓰다   to make letters on surface, using a pen or a pencil
Hangeul is easy to read and **write**.
한글은 읽고 쓰기 쉽다.

15 wrong
[rɔ:ŋ]
a 잘못된, 나쁜   not right or not correct
It was **wrong** of you to laugh at him.
그를 비웃은 것은 네가 잘못했다.

16 yard
[ja:rd]
n 마당   an area outside a building
They all had a fun time in our **yard**.
그들 모두는 우리 집 마당에서 아주 즐거운 시간을 가졌다.

17 yesterday
[jéstə:rdi]
ad 어제   on the day before today
Dad fixed my chair **yesterday**.
어제 아빠가 내 의자를 고쳐주셨다.

18 zero
[zíərou]
n 영, 영도   nothing at all
To repeat this message, press **zero**.
메시지 반복 청취는 0번을 눌러 주십시오.

key words
occasion n 경우, 기회 / bone n 뼈 / fix v 수리하다 / repeat v 반복하다 / press v 누르다

Exercise

A. Complete the sentence.

1. They all had a fun time in our _____.
   그들 모두는 우리 집 마당에서 아주 즐거운 시간을 가졌다.

2. These apples are _____.
   이 사과들은 시다.

3. They played _____ six.
   그들은 6시까지 놀았다.

4. This afternoon it will be _____.
   오늘 오후에는 날씨가 갤 것으로 보인다.

5. How many players does a baseball _____ have?
   한 야구팀은 몇 명의 선수로 이루어져 있나요?

6. Dad fixed my chair _____.
   어제 아빠가 내 의자를 고쳐주셨다.

7. He screamed in _____ as the rats came towards him.
   그는 쥐들이 그를 향해 다가오자 공포로 비명을 질렀다.

8. To repeat this message, press _____.
   메시지 반복 청취는 0번을 눌러 주십시오.

9. Half of students use the computer _____ a week.
   학생들의 절반은 한 주에 두 번씩 컴퓨터를 사용한다.

10. The _____ called him safe.
    심판은 그에게 세이프를 선언했다.

11. The man is looking at the fruit in a _____.
    남자가 슈퍼마켓에서 과일을 보고 있다.

12. This apple has a _____ in it.
    이 사과 안에 벌레가 들어 있어요.

13. She put me in a room full of _____.
    어머니께서 나를 증기로 가득한 방으로 데려가셨다.

14. Hangeul is easy to read and _____.
    한글은 읽고 쓰기 쉽다.

15. He has two _____ who became doctors.
    그는 의사가 된 두 아들이 있다.

16. I need to send these letters _____.
    이 편지들을 오늘 보내야 해.

17. Be careful! You'll _____ on your laptop computer.
    조심해! 너는 네 휴대용 컴퓨터를 밟게 될꺼야.

18. It was _____ of you to laugh at him.
    그를 비웃은 것은 네가 잘못했다.

Hint

| worm | supermarket | till | steam | yesterday | write | son | today | umpire |
| team | yard | sunny | sour | step | twice | terror | wrong | zero |

Unit 40

Exercise

B. Fill in the word and meaning.

	Word	Meaning
01	sunny	
02	team	
03	umpire	
04	till	
05	son	
06	twice	
07	wrong	
08	sour	
09	yesterday	
10	supermarket	
11	worm	
12	zero	
13	steam	
14	yard	
15	write	
16	terror	
17	today	
18	step	

	Meaning	Word
01	아들	
02	시큼한, 신	
03	스팀, 증기	
04	밟다, 걷다	
05	밝게 비치는	
06	슈퍼마켓	
07	팀, 조	
08	공포, 두려움	
09	~까지	
10	오늘	
11	두 번, 2회	
12	심판, 심판하다	
13	벌레	
14	쓰다	
15	잘못된, 나쁜	
16	마당	
17	어제	
18	영, 영도	

🎧 C. Listen, write the word and meaning. (Track 120)

	Word	Meaning		Word	Meaning
01			10		
02			11		
03			12		
04			13		
05			14		
06			15		
07			16		
08			17		
09			18		

Review 20

A. Read and fill in the word and meaning.

word	definition	meaning
	a particular position, point or area	
	the direction that is on your left when you watch the sun rise	
	the number 1,000,000	
	your mother and father	
	each of the 60 parts of an hour	
	something that you intend to do or achieve	
	a picture that is made using a camera	
	used for suggesting that you do something with people	
	the daughter of someone's sister or brother	
	something that the public needs	
	a thing that is difficult to deal with	
	to keep a written account or photographs of something	
	a set of instructions in code that control the operation	
	a flower with a sweet smell that grows on a bush with thorns	
	how large or small a thing is	
	a 4-sided shape whose corners are all 90 degree angles	
	a grayish-white metal used for making jewellery	
	shaped like a circle or a ball	

Hint

north   silver   plan   problem   size   service   minute   photo   million
round   parents   niece   record   rose   place   program   shall   rectangle

B. Read and fill in the word and meaning.

word	definition	meaning
	two times; on two occasions	
	a person who watches a game to make sure that the players obey the rules	
	a person's male child	
	the hot mist that is formed when water boils	
	to make letters on surface, using a pen or a pencil	
	having an unpleasant taste like the taste of a lemon	
	on the day before today	
	a group of people who play a particular game	
	with a lot of bright light from the sun	
	a long thin creature with no bones or legs	
	during the period before a particular time	
	to put your foot on the thing	
	on this day; at the present period	
	a large shop which sells food and household goods	
	not right or not correct	
	very great fear	
	nothing at all	
	an area outside a building	

Hint

worm　umpire　yard　team　zero　write　wrong　twice　supermarket
steam　till　sunny　sour　step　today　terror　son　yesterday

 MEMO

Total Test

Test 1

Track 3

🎧 **Listen, write the word and meaning.**

	Word	Meaning
01		
02		
03		
04		
05		
06		
07		
08		
09		
10		
11		
12		
13		
14		
15		
16		
17		
18		

점수	점	확인	

Test 2

Track 6

🎧 **Listen, write the word and meaning.**

	Word	Meaning
01		
02		
03		
04		
05		
06		
07		
08		
09		
10		
11		
12		
13		
14		
15		
16		
17		
18		

점수	점	확인	

Test 3

Track 9

🎧 **Listen, write the word and meaning.**

	Word	Meaning
01		
02		
03		
04		
05		
06		
07		
08		
09		
10		
11		
12		
13		
14		
15		
16		
17		
18		

점수	점	확인	

Test 4

Track 12

🎧 **Listen, write the word and meaning.**

	Word	Meaning
01		
02		
03		
04		
05		
06		
07		
08		
09		
10		
11		
12		
13		
14		
15		
16		
17		
18		

점수	점	확인	

Test 5

Track 15

🎧 **Listen, write the word and meaning.**

	Word	Meaning
01		
02		
03		
04		
05		
06		
07		
08		
09		
10		
11		
12		
13		
14		
15		
16		
17		
18		

점수	점	확인	

Test 6

Track 18

🎧 **Listen, write the word and meaning.**

	Word	Meaning
01		
02		
03		
04		
05		
06		
07		
08		
09		
10		
11		
12		
13		
14		
15		
16		
17		
18		

점수	점	확인	

Test 7

Track 21

🎧 **Listen, write the word and meaning.**

	Word	Meaning
01		
02		
03		
04		
05		
06		
07		
08		
09		
10		
11		
12		
13		
14		
15		
16		
17		
18		

점수		점	확인	

Test 8

Track 24

🎧 **Listen, write the word and meaning.**

	Word	Meaning
01		
02		
03		
04		
05		
06		
07		
08		
09		
10		
11		
12		
13		
14		
15		
16		
17		
18		

점수		점	확인	

Test 9

Track 27

🎧 **Listen, write the word and meaning.**

	Word	Meaning
01		
02		
03		
04		
05		
06		
07		
08		
09		
10		
11		
12		
13		
14		
15		
16		
17		
18		

점수	점	확인	

Test 10

Track 30

🎧 **Listen, write the word and meaning.**

	Word	Meaning
01		
02		
03		
04		
05		
06		
07		
08		
09		
10		
11		
12		
13		
14		
15		
16		
17		
18		

점수	점	확인	

Test 11

Track 33

🎧 **Listen, write the word and meaning.**

	Word	Meaning
01		
02		
03		
04		
05		
06		
07		
08		
09		
10		
11		
12		
13		
14		
15		
16		
17		
18		

점수	점	확인

Test 12

Track 36

🎧 **Listen, write the word and meaning.**

	Word	Meaning
01		
02		
03		
04		
05		
06		
07		
08		
09		
10		
11		
12		
13		
14		
15		
16		
17		
18		

점수	점	확인

Test 13

Track 39

🎧 **Listen, write the word and meaning.**

	Word	Meaning
01		
02		
03		
04		
05		
06		
07		
08		
09		
10		
11		
12		
13		
14		
15		
16		
17		
18		

점수	점	확인	

Test 14

Track 42

🎧 **Listen, write the word and meaning.**

	Word	Meaning
01		
02		
03		
04		
05		
06		
07		
08		
09		
10		
11		
12		
13		
14		
15		
16		
17		
18		

점수	점	확인	

Test 15

Track 45

🎧 **Listen, write the word and meaning.**

	Word	Meaning
01		
02		
03		
04		
05		
06		
07		
08		
09		
10		
11		
12		
13		
14		
15		
16		
17		
18		

점수	점	확인	

Test 16

Track 48

🎧 **Listen, write the word and meaning.**

	Word	Meaning
01		
02		
03		
04		
05		
06		
07		
08		
09		
10		
11		
12		
13		
14		
15		
16		
17		
18		

점수	점	확인	

Test 17

Track 51

🎧 **Listen, write the word and meaning.**

	Word	Meaning
01		
02		
03		
04		
05		
06		
07		
08		
09		
10		
11		
12		
13		
14		
15		
16		
17		
18		

점수	점	확인

Test 18

Track 54

🎧 **Listen, write the word and meaning.**

	Word	Meaning
01		
02		
03		
04		
05		
06		
07		
08		
09		
10		
11		
12		
13		
14		
15		
16		
17		
18		

점수	점	확인

Test 19

Track 57

🎧 Listen, write the word and meaning.

	Word	Meaning
01		
02		
03		
04		
05		
06		
07		
08		
09		
10		
11		
12		
13		
14		
15		
16		
17		
18		

점수	점	확인

Test 20

Track 60

🎧 Listen, write the word and meaning.

	Word	Meaning
01		
02		
03		
04		
05		
06		
07		
08		
09		
10		
11		
12		
13		
14		
15		
16		
17		
18		

점수	점	확인

Test 21

Track 63

🎧 **Listen, write the word and meaning.**

	Word	Meaning
01		
02		
03		
04		
05		
06		
07		
08		
09		
10		
11		
12		
13		
14		
15		
16		
17		
18		

점수	점	확인

Test 22

Track 66

🎧 **Listen, write the word and meaning.**

	Word	Meaning
01		
02		
03		
04		
05		
06		
07		
08		
09		
10		
11		
12		
13		
14		
15		
16		
17		
18		

점수	점	확인

Test 23

Track 69

🎧 **Listen, write the word and meaning.**

	Word	Meaning
01		
02		
03		
04		
05		
06		
07		
08		
09		
10		
11		
12		
13		
14		
15		
16		
17		
18		

점수	점	확인	

Test 24

Track 72

🎧 **Listen, write the word and meaning.**

	Word	Meaning
01		
02		
03		
04		
05		
06		
07		
08		
09		
10		
11		
12		
13		
14		
15		
16		
17		
18		

점수	점	확인	

Test 25

Track 75

🎧 **Listen, write the word and meaning.**

	Word	Meaning
01		
02		
03		
04		
05		
06		
07		
08		
09		
10		
11		
12		
13		
14		
15		
16		
17		
18		

점수	점	확인	

Test 26

Track 78

🎧 **Listen, write the word and meaning.**

	Word	Meaning
01		
02		
03		
04		
05		
06		
07		
08		
09		
10		
11		
12		
13		
14		
15		
16		
17		
18		

점수	점	확인	

Test 27

Track 81

🎧 **Listen, write the word and meaning.**

	Word	Meaning
01		
02		
03		
04		
05		
06		
07		
08		
09		
10		
11		
12		
13		
14		
15		
16		
17		
18		

점수	점	확인

Test 28

Track 84

🎧 **Listen, write the word and meaning.**

	Word	Meaning
01		
02		
03		
04		
05		
06		
07		
08		
09		
10		
11		
12		
13		
14		
15		
16		
17		
18		

점수	점	확인

Test 29

Track 87

🎧 **Listen, write the word and meaning.**

	Word	Meaning
01		
02		
03		
04		
05		
06		
07		
08		
09		
10		
11		
12		
13		
14		
15		
16		
17		
18		

점수		확인	
	점		

Test 30

Track 90

🎧 **Listen, write the word and meaning.**

	Word	Meaning
01		
02		
03		
04		
05		
06		
07		
08		
09		
10		
11		
12		
13		
14		
15		
16		
17		
18		

점수		확인	
	점		

Test 31

Track 93

🎧 **Listen, write the word and meaning.**

	Word	Meaning
01		
02		
03		
04		
05		
06		
07		
08		
09		
10		
11		
12		
13		
14		
15		
16		
17		
18		

점수		점	확인	

Test 32

Track 96

🎧 **Listen, write the word and meaning.**

	Word	Meaning
01		
02		
03		
04		
05		
06		
07		
08		
09		
10		
11		
12		
13		
14		
15		
16		
17		
18		

점수		점	확인	

Test 33

Track 99

🎧 **Listen, write the word and meaning.**

	Word	Meaning
01		
02		
03		
04		
05		
06		
07		
08		
09		
10		
11		
12		
13		
14		
15		
16		
17		
18		

점수	점	확인	

Test 34

Track 102

🎧 **Listen, write the word and meaning.**

	Word	Meaning
01		
02		
03		
04		
05		
06		
07		
08		
09		
10		
11		
12		
13		
14		
15		
16		
17		
18		

점수	점	확인	

Test 35

Track 105

🎧 Listen, write the word and meaning.

	Word	Meaning
01		
02		
03		
04		
05		
06		
07		
08		
09		
10		
11		
12		
13		
14		
15		
16		
17		
18		

점수	점	확인	

Test 36

Track 108

🎧 Listen, write the word and meaning.

	Word	Meaning
01		
02		
03		
04		
05		
06		
07		
08		
09		
10		
11		
12		
13		
14		
15		
16		
17		
18		

점수	점	확인	

Test 37

Track 111

🎧 **Listen, write the word and meaning.**

	Word	Meaning
01		
02		
03		
04		
05		
06		
07		
08		
09		
10		
11		
12		
13		
14		
15		
16		
17		
18		

점수	점	확인	

Test 38

Track 114

🎧 **Listen, write the word and meaning.**

	Word	Meaning
01		
02		
03		
04		
05		
06		
07		
08		
09		
10		
11		
12		
13		
14		
15		
16		
17		
18		

점수	점	확인	

Test 39

(Track 117)

🎧 **Listen, write the word and meaning.**

	Word	Meaning
01		
02		
03		
04		
05		
06		
07		
08		
09		
10		
11		
12		
13		
14		
15		
16		
17		
18		

점수	점	확인	

Test 40

(Track 120)

🎧 **Listen, write the word and meaning.**

	Word	Meaning
01		
02		
03		
04		
05		
06		
07		
08		
09		
10		
11		
12		
13		
14		
15		
16		
17		
18		

점수	점	확인	

Answer Key

Unit 1

A
1. above
2. airplane
3. big
4. class
5. bicycle
6. chin
7. belt
8. church
9. city
10. across
11. after
12. birds
13. black
14. able
15. blanket
16. about
17. clean
18. clock

B
1. ~할 수 있는
2. 자전거
3. ~위에, ~의 위쪽에
4. 큰
5. 검정색, 검정색의
6. 비행기
7. 도시
8. 새
9. 담요
10. 시계
11. ~을 가로질러서
12. 수업, 학급
13. ~에 대하여
14. 교회
15. 띠, 벨트
16. 턱
17. 깨끗한
18. ~후에

1. able
2. about
3. above
4. across
5. after
6. airplane
7. belt
8. bicycle
9. big
10. bird
11. black
12. blanket
13. chin
14. church
15. city
16. class
17. clean
18. clock

C
1. bird 새
2. clock 시계
3. clean 깨끗한
4. city 도시
5. across ~을 가로질러서
6. black 검정색, 검정색의
7. about ~에 대하여
8. above ~위에, ~의 위쪽에
9. blanket 담요
10. belt 띠, 벨트
11. able ~할 수 있는
12. class 수업, 학급
13. airplane 비행기
14. after ~후에
15. big 큰
16. bicycle 자전거
17. church 교회
18. chin 턱

Unit 2

A
1. dolphin
2. hungry
3. draw
4. ill
5. ducks
6. dry
7. How
8. inside
9. ear
10. fun
11. gentleman
12. girl
13. door
14. gave
15. house
16. got
17. idea
18. garden

B
1. 그리다
2. 귀
3. 문
4. 사다, 얻다
5. 재미
6. 돌고래
7. 마른, 말리다
8. 어떻게, 얼마나
9. 생각, 의견
10. 오리
11. 주다
12. 소녀, 여자아이
13. 정원
14. 집
15. 안쪽에, 안쪽으로
16. 병든
17. 배고픈
18. 신사

1. dolphin
2. door
3. draw
4. dry
5. duck
6. ear
7. fun
8. garden
9. gentleman
10. get
11. girl
12. give
13. house
14. how
15. hungry
16. idea
17. ill
18. inside

C
1. ill 병든
2. duck 오리
3. get 사다, 얻다
4. fun 재미
5. dry 마른, 말리다
6. ear 귀
7. door 문
8. give 주다
9. dolphin 돌고래
10. draw 그리다
11. inside 안쪽에, 안쪽으로
12. girl 소녀, 여자아이
13. idea 생각, 의견
14. gentleman 신사
15. how 어떻게, 얼마나
16. garden 정원
17. hungry 배고픈
18. house 집

Review 1

A
1. bird 새
2. clock 시계
3. clean 깨끗한
4. city 도시
5. across ~을 가로질러서
6. black 검정색, 검정색의
7. about ~에 대하여
8. above ~위에, ~의 위쪽에
9. blanket 담요
10. belt 띠, 벨트
11. able ~할 수 있는
12. class 수업, 학급
13. airplane 비행기
14. after ~후에
15. big 큰
16. bicycle 자전거
17. church 교회
18. chin 턱

B
1. ill 병든
2. duck 오리
3. get 사다, 얻다
4. fun 재미
5. dry 마른, 말리다
6. ear 귀
7. door 문
8. give 주다
9. dolphin 돌고래
10. draw 그리다
11. inside 안쪽에, 안쪽으로
12. girl 소녀, 여자아이
13. idea 생각, 의견
14. gentleman 신사
15. how 어떻게, 얼마나
16. garden 정원
17. hungry 배고픈
18. house 집

Unit 3

A
1. lives
2. potatoes
3. long
4. listen
5. nephew
6. pork
7. nice
8. pretty
9. Look
10. name
11. room
12. new
13. night
14. poor
15. problem
16. neck
17. love
18. pulled

B
1. 살다
2. 목
3. 돼지고기
4. 방
5. 듣다
6. 좋은, 기쁜
7. 조카
8. 당기다, 끌다
9. 길이가 긴
10. 밤
11. 문제
12. 가난한
13. 새로운
14. 예쁜, 꽤
15. 감자
16. 보다
17. 이름
18. 사랑하다

C
1. listen
2. live
3. long
4. look
5. love
6. name
7. neck
8. nephew
9. new
10. nice
11. night
12. poor
13. pork
14. potato
15. pretty
16. problem
17. pull
18. room

D
1. problem — 문제
2. long — 길이가 긴
3. room — 방
4. live — 살다
5. love — 사랑하다
6. nephew — 조카
7. pull — 당기다, 끌다
8. neck — 목
9. listen — 듣다
10. name — 이름
11. look — 보다
12. pretty — 예쁜, 꽤
13. nice — 좋은, 기쁜
14. pork — 돼지고기
15. poor — 가난한
16. potato — 감자
17. new — 새로운
18. night — 밤

Unit 4

1. short
2. shoe
3. understand
4. sun
5. uncle
6. swim
7. under
8. switch
9. shoulders
10. sign
11. zoo
12. ugly
13. sugar
14. supper
15. table
16. vegetable
17. sick
18. use

B
1. 어깨
2. 삼촌
3. 태양
4. ~의 아래에
5. 신, 구두
6. 이해하다
7. 저녁 식사
8. 추한, 못생긴
9. 키가 작은
10. 수영하다
11. 사용하다
12. 설탕
13. 동물원
14. 야채
15. 신호,표지, 서명하다
16. 탁자
17. 스위치,스위치를 켜다, 끄다
18. 아픈

C
1. shoe
2. short
3. shoulder
4. sick
5. sign
6. sugar
7. sun
8. supper
9. swim
10. switch
11. table
12. ugly
13. uncle
14. under
15. understand
16. use
17. vegetable
18. zoo

D
1. sugar — 설탕
2. sun — 태양
3. short — 키가 작은
4. ugly — 추한, 못생긴
5. supper — 저녁 식사
6. shoe — 신, 구두
7. vegetable — 야채
8. sick — 아픈
9. sign — 신호, 표지, 서명하다
10. shoulder — 어깨
11. table — 탁자
12. switch — 스위치, 스위치를 켜다, 끄다
13. use — 사용하다
14. under — ~의 아래에
15. swim — 수영하다
16. zoo — 동물원
17. uncle — 삼촌
18. understand — 이해하다

Review 2

A
1. problem — 문제
2. long — 길이가 긴
3. room — 방
4. live — 살다
5. love — 사랑하다
6. nephew — 조카
7. pull — 당기다, 끌다
8. neck — 목
9. listen — 듣다
10. name — 이름
11. look — 보다
12. pretty — 예쁜, 꽤
13. nice — 좋은, 기쁜
14. pork — 돼지고기
15. poor — 가난한
16. potato — 감자
17. new — 새로운
18. night — 밤

B
1. sugar — 설탕
2. sun — 태양
3. short — 키가 작은
4. ugly — 추한, 못생긴
5. supper — 저녁 식사
6. shoe — 신, 구두
7. vegetable — 야채
8. sick — 아픈
9. sign — 신호, 표지, 서명하다
10. shoulder — 어깨
11. table — 탁자
12. switch — 스위치, 스위치를 켜다, 끄다
13. use — 사용하다
14. under — ~의 아래에
15. swim — 수영하다
16. zoo — 동물원
17. uncle — 삼촌
18. understand — 이해하다

Unit 5

A
1. closed
2. Again
3. always
4. angel
5. body
6. afternoon
7. clothes
8. early
9. cloud
10. boat
11. animal
12. apple
13. coat
14. bikes
15. cold
16. books
17. blue
18. bottle

B
1. 항상, 언제나
2. 보트, 배
3. 동물
4. 몸
5. 닫다
6. 오후
7. 구름
8. 파란색, 파란색의
9. 추운
10. 자전거
11. 외투, 코트
12. 일찍, 이른
13. 다시
14. 책
15. 옷, 의복
16. 사과
17. 병
18. 천사

1. afternoon
2. again
3. always
4. angel
5. animal
6. apple
7. bike
8. blue
9. boat
10. body
11. book
12. bottle
13. close
14. clothes
15. cloud
16. coat
17. cold
18. early

C
1. again   다시
2. book   책
3. apple   사과
4. afternoon   오후
5. animal   동물
6. close   닫다
7. body   몸
8. always   항상, 언제나
9. bottle   병
10. angel   천사
11. blue   파란색, 파란색의
12. cold   추운
13. early   일찍, 이른
14. boat   보트, 배
15. cloud   구름
16. bike   자전거
17. coat   외투, 코트
18. clothes   옷, 의복

Unit 6

A
1. free
2. horse
3. full
4. help
5. foot
6. here
7. jeans
8. lesson
9. friends
10. let
11. lie
12. from
13. lion
14. fruit
15. highest
16. home
17. light
18. like

B
1. 돕다
2. 친구, 벗
3. 청바지
4. 집, 집으로
5. 과일
6. 거짓말, 드러눕다
7. 여기에
8. 수업, 과
9. 발
10. 등불, 빛
11. 높은
12. 좋아하다
13. 한가한, 자유로운
14. 사자
15. ~시키다
16. ~로부터
17. 말
18. 배부른, 가득한

1. foot
2. free
3. friend
4. from
5. fruit
6. full
7. help
8. here
9. high
10. home
11. horse
12. jeans
13. lesson
14. let
15. lie
16. light
17. like
18. lion

C
1. help   돕다
2. let   ~시키다
3. lie   거짓말, 드러눕다
4. here   여기에
5. friend   친구, 벗
6. horse   말
7. high   높은
8. free   한가한, 자유로운
9. light   등불, 빛
10. home   집, 집으로
11. lesson   수업, 과
12. foot   발
13. like   좋아하다
14. fruit   과일
15. jeans   청바지
16. from   ~로부터
17. lion   사자
18. full   배부른, 가득한

Review 3

A
1. again   다시
2. book   책
3. apple   사과
4. afternoon   오후
5. animal   동물
6. close   닫다
7. body   몸
8. always   항상, 언제나
9. bottle   병
10. angel   천사
11. blue   파란색, 파란색의
12. cold   추운
13. early   일찍, 이른
14. boat   보트, 배
15. cloud   구름
16. bike   자전거
17. coat   외투, 코트
18. clothes   옷, 의복

B
1. help   돕다
2. let   ~시키다
3. lie   거짓말, 드러눕다
4. here   여기에
5. friend   친구, 벗
6. horse   말
7. high   높은
8. free   한가한, 자유로운
9. light   등불, 빛
10. home   집, 집으로
11. lesson   수업, 과
12. foot   발
13. like   좋아하다
14. fruit   과일
15. jeans   청바지
16. from   ~로부터
17. lion   사자
18. full   배부른, 가득한

Unit 7

A
1. must
2. played
3. sea
4. point
5. music
6. running
7. sad
8. much
9. say
10. mouth
11. movie
12. people
13. picked
14. school
15. pocket
16. pepper
17. mouse
18. see

B
1. 사람들
2. 연주하다, 놀다
3. 달리다
4. 영화
5. 따다, 꺾다
6. 학교
7. 생쥐
8. 호주머니
9. 보다, 만나다
10. 음악
11. 바다
12. 입
13. 끝, 점수, 가리키다
14. 말하다
15. ~해야 한다
16. 슬픈
17. 후추
18. (양이) 많은

1. mouse
2. mouth
3. movie
4. much
5. music
6. must
7. people
8. pepper
9. pick
10. play
11. pocket
12. point
13. run
14. sad
15. say
16. school
17. sea
18. see

C
1. much — (양이) 많은
2. movie — 영화
3. mouse — 생쥐
4. people — 사람들
5. pepper — 후추
6. mouth — 입
7. run — 달리다
8. must — ~해야 한다
9. see — 보다, 만나다
10. sad — 슬픈
11. music — 음악
12. pocket — 호주머니
13. say — 말하다
14. play — 연주하다, 놀다
15. sea — 바다
16. pick — 따다, 꺾다
17. school — 학교
18. point — 끝, 점수, 가리키다

Unit 8

A
1. study
2. trees
3. strong
4. turned
5. stopped
6. yellow
7. student
8. Try
9. young
10. zebra
11. stayed
12. story
13. woman
14. town
15. window
16. train
17. towel
18. years

B
1. 이야기
2. 기차
3. 창문
4. 젊은, 어린
5. 머무르다
6. 나무
7. 공부하다
8. 노란색, 노란색의
9. 멈추다
10. 여자
11. 도시
12. 해, 년
13. 타월, 수건
14. 얼룩말
15. 돌리다
16. 학생
17. 시도하다
18. 힘센, 강한

1. stay
2. stop
3. story
4. strong
5. student
6. study
7. towel
8. town
9. train
10. tree
11. try
12. turn
13. window
14. woman
15. year
16. yellow
17. young
18. zebra

C
1. window — 창문
2. stay — 머무르다
3. strong — 힘센, 강한
4. woman — 여자
5. turn — 돌리다
6. stop — 멈추다
7. year — 해, 년
8. story — 이야기
9. yellow — 노란색, 노란색의
10. towel — 타월, 수건
11. try — 시도하다
12. town — 도시
13. student — 학생
14. tree — 나무
15. young — 젊은, 어린
16. study — 공부하다
17. train — 기차
18. zebra — 얼룩말

Review 4

A
1. much — (양이) 많은
2. movie — 영화
3. mouse — 생쥐
4. people — 사람들
5. pepper — 후추
6. mouth — 입
7. run — 달리다
8. must — ~해야 한다
9. see — 보다, 만나다
10. sad — 슬픈
11. music — 음악
12. pocket — 호주머니
13. say — 말하다
14. play — 연주하다, 놀다
15. sea — 바다
16. pick — 따다, 꺾다
17. school — 학교
18. point — 끝, 점수, 가리키다

B
1. window — 창문
2. stay — 머무르다
3. strong — 힘센, 강한
4. woman — 여자
5. turn — 돌리다
6. stop — 멈추다
7. year — 해, 년
8. story — 이야기
9. yellow — 노란색, 노란색의
10. towel — 타월, 수건
11. try — 시도하다
12. town — 도시
13. student — 학생
14. tree — 나무
15. young — 젊은, 어린
16. study — 공부하다
17. train — 기차
18. zebra — 얼룩말

Answer Key

Unit 9

A
1. arms
2. bowl
3. arrived
4. boy
5. around
6. bread
7. can
8. dinner
9. aunt
10. dirty
11. back
12. breaks
13. everybody
14. breakfast
15. day
16. backwards
17. Bring
18. desk

B
1. 숙모
2. 뒤로, 등
3. 가져오다, 데려오다
4. ~할 수 있다
5. 도착하다
6. 깨다
7. 날, 하루
8. 팔
9. 빵
10. 더러운
11. 소년, 남자아이
12. 모두
13. 저녁식사, 정찬
14. 사발, 공기
15. ~의 주위에, ~의 둘레를
16. 아침식사
17. 책상
18. 뒤로, 거꾸로

1. arm
2. around
3. arrive
4. aunt
5. back
6. backwards
7. bowl
8. boy
9. bread
10. break
11. breakfast
12. bring
13. can
14. day
15. desk
16. dinner
17. dirty
18. everybody

C
1. can — ~할 수 있다
2. arm — 팔
3. day — 날, 하루
4. dinner — 저녁 식사, 정찬
5. arrive — 도착하다
6. around — ~의 주위에, ~의 둘레를
7. desk — 책상
8. back — 뒤로, 등
9. dirty — 더러운
10. everybody — 모두
11. aunt — 숙모
12. boy — 소년, 남자아이
13. bread — 빵
14. breakfast — 아침 식사
15. backwards — 뒤로, 거꾸로
16. bring — 가져오다, 데려오다
17. bowl — 사발, 공기
18. break — 깨다

Unit 10

1. fly
2. have
3. legs
4. flowers
5. head
6. jacket
7. food
8. left
9. fine
10. learn
11. finger
12. hard
13. laughed
14. hate
15. into
16. lamp
17. finished
18. late

B
1. 끝내다
2. 어려운
3. 식량, 식품
4. 머리
5. 좋은, 훌륭한
6. 배우다
7. 가지고 있다
8. 다리
9. 손가락
10. 램프
11. 왼쪽
12. 웃다
13. 재킷, 윗옷
14. 늦은, 늦게
15. 꽃
16. ~안으로
17. 몹시 싫어하다
18. 날다, 파리

1. fine
2. finger
3. finish
4. flower
5. fly
6. food
7. hard
8. hate
9. have
10. head
11. into
12. jacket
13. lamp
14. late
15. laugh
16. learn
17. left
18. leg

C
1. into — ~안으로
2. leg — 다리
3. late — 늦은, 늦게
4. finish — 끝내다
5. jacket — 재킷, 윗옷
6. fine — 좋은, 훌륭한
7. laugh — 웃다
8. lamp — 램프
9. flower — 꽃
10. finger — 손가락
11. hate — 몹시 싫어하다
12. food — 식량, 식품
13. learn — 배우다
14. hard — 어려운
15. fly — 날다, 파리
16. head — 머리
17. left — 왼쪽
18. have — 가지고 있다

Review 5

A
1. can — ~할 수 있다
2. arm — 팔
3. day — 날, 하루
4. dinner — 저녁 식사, 정찬
5. arrive — 도착하다
6. around — ~의 주위에, ~의 둘레를
7. desk — 책상
8. back — 뒤로, 등
9. dirty — 더러운
10. everybody — 모두
11. aunt — 숙모
12. boy — 소년, 남자아이
13. bread — 빵
14. breakfast — 아침 식사
15. backwards — 뒤로, 거꾸로
16. bring — 가져오다, 데려오다
17. bowl — 사발, 공기
18. break — 깨다

B
1. into — ~안으로
2. leg — 다리
3. late — 늦은, 늦게
4. finish — 끝내다
5. jacket — 재킷, 윗옷
6. fine — 좋은, 훌륭한
7. laugh — 웃다
8. lamp — 램프
9. flower — 꽃
10. finger — 손가락
11. hate — 몹시 싫어하다
12. food — 식량, 식품
13. learn — 배우다
14. hard — 어려운
15. fly — 날다, 파리
16. head — 머리
17. left — 왼쪽
18. have — 가지고 있다

Unit 11

A
1. morning
2. pears
3. month
4. pencil
5. sending
6. mother
7. set
8. missed
9. ship
10. monkey
11. pay
12. pants
13. paper
14. parks
15. river
16. sells
17. money
18. sheep

B
1. 원숭이
2. 바지
3. 팔다
4. 놓치다
5. 연필
6. 어머니
7. 배
8. 보내다
9. 돈
10. 양
11. 종이
12. (큰)배
13. 놓다, 넣다
14. 공원
15. 달
16. 강
17. 지불하다
18. 아침, 오전

1. miss
2. money
3. monkey
4. month
5. morning
6. mother
7. pants
8. paper
9. park
10. pay
11. pear
12. pencil
13. river
14. sell
15. send
16. set
17. sheep
18. ship

C
1. paper — 종이
2. money — 돈
3. mother — 어머니
4. miss — 놓치다
5. pencil — 연필
6. month — 달
7. park — 공원
8. pants — 바지
9. monkey — 원숭이
10. ship — (큰)배
11. morning — 아침, 오전
12. send — 보내다
13. pear — 배
14. sell — 팔다
15. sheep — 양
16. pay — 지불하다
17. set — 놓다, 넣다
18. river — 강

Unit 12

A
1. stand
2. starts
3. wide
4. too
5. star
6. tooth
7. Who
8. wind
9. sorry
10. tonight
11. white
12. speaks
13. What
14. spoon
15. together
16. toilet
17. Where
18. toe

B
1. 숟가락
2. 함께
3. 발가락
4. 무엇, 무슨
5. 미안한
6. 어디에, 어디로
7. 너무
8. 말하다
9. 넓은
10. 바람
11. 함께
12. 누구, 누가
13. 별
14. 화장실
15. 흰색, 흰색의
16. 시작하다
17. 이
18. 서다, 서 있다

1. sorry
2. speak
3. spoon
4. stand
5. star
6. start
7. toe
8. together
9. toilet
10. tonight
11. too
12. tooth
13. what
14. where
15. white
16. who
17. wide
18. wind

C
1. speak — 말하다
2. what — 무엇, 무슨
3. white — 흰색, 흰색의
4. sorry — 미안한
5. where — 어디에, 어디로
6. tooth — 이
7. spoon — 숟가락
8. start — 시작하다
9. who — 누구, 누가
10. stand — 서다, 서 있다
11. wind — 바람
12. star — 별
13. wide — 넓은
14. together — 함께
15. tonight — 오늘 밤, 오늘밤에
16. toilet — 화장실
17. toe — 발가락
18. too — 너무

Review 6

A
1. paper — 종이
2. money — 돈
3. mother — 어머니
4. miss — 놓치다
5. pencil — 연필
6. month — 달
7. park — 공원
8. pants — 바지
9. monkey — 원숭이
10. ship — (큰)배
11. morning — 아침, 오전
12. send — 보내다
13. pear — 배
14. sell — 팔다
15. sheep — 양
16. pay — 지불하다
17. set — 놓다, 넣다
18. river — 강

B
1. speak — 말하다
2. what — 무엇, 무슨
3. white — 흰색, 흰색의
4. sorry — 미안한
5. where — 어디에, 어디로
6. tooth — 이
7. spoon — 숟가락
8. start — 시작하다
9. who — 누구, 누가
10. stand — 서다, 서 있다
11. wind — 바람
12. star — 별
13. wide — 넓은
14. together — 함께
15. tonight — 오늘 밤, 오늘밤에
16. toilet — 화장실
17. toe — 발가락
18. too — 너무

Unit 13

A
1. bad
2. balloons
3. brother
4. Brown
5. ball
6. brush
7. dance
8. dark
9. bank
10. do
11. basket
12. cute
13. beans
14. cuts
15. buy
16. called
17. cousin
18. crying

B
1. 닦다, 빗, 솔
2. 풍선
3. 사다, 얻다
4. 콩
5. 전화를 걸다, 통화
6. 나쁜
7. 울다
8. 귀여운
9. 형제
10. 갈색, 갈색의
11. 춤추다
12. 공
13. 어두운, 어둠
14. 하다
15. 바구니
16. 자르다, 베다
17. 사촌
18. 은행

1. bad
2. ball
3. balloon
4. bank
5. basket
6. bean
7. brother
8. brown
9. brush
10. buy
11. call
12. cousin
13. cry
14. cut
15. cute
16. dance
17. dark
18. do

C
1. buy — 사다, 얻다
2. cousin — 사촌
3. bad — 나쁜
4. call — 전화를 걸다, 통화
5. cut — 자르다, 베다
6. ball — 공
7. bank — 은행
8. cry — 울다
9. balloon — 풍선
10. cute — 귀여운
11. brother — 형제
12. brush — 닦다, 빗, 솔
13. dark — 어두운, 어둠
14. basket — 바구니
15. dance — 춤추다
16. bean — 콩
17. do — 하다
18. brown — 갈색, 갈색의

Unit 14

A
1. find
2. happy
3. hair
4. knife
5. father
6. know
7. lady
8. enjoying
9. hands
10. knees
11. fat
12. evening
13. face
14. green
15. gray
16. king
17. great
18. kitchen

B
1. 얼굴
2. 즐기다
3. 큰, 위대한
4. 저녁
5. 손
6. 부엌
7. 살찐, 뚱뚱한
8. 칼
9. 알고 있다
10. 아버지
11. 숙녀
12. 왕
13. 머리카락
14. 무릎
15. 회색, 회색의
16. 행복한
17. 녹색, 녹색의
18. 찾다, 알다

1. enjoy
2. evening
3. face
4. fat
5. father
6. find
7. gray
8. great
9. green
10. hair
11. hand
12. happy
13. king
14. kitchen
15. knee
16. knife
17. know
18. lady

C
1. hand — 손
2. lady — 숙녀
3. happy — 행복한
4. kitchen — 부엌
5. enjoy — 즐기다
6. king — 왕
7. evening — 저녁
8. knee — 무릎
9. father — 아버지
10. hair — 머리카락
11. fat — 살찐, 뚱뚱한
12. green — 녹색, 녹색의
13. find — 찾다, 알다
14. face — 얼굴
15. knife — 칼
16. great — 큰, 위대한
17. know — 알고 있다
18. gray — 회색, 회색의

Review 7

A
1. buy — 사다, 얻다
2. cousin — 사촌
3. bad — 나쁜
4. call — 전화를 걸다, 통화
5. cut — 자르다, 베다
6. ball — 공
7. bank — 은행
8. cry — 울다
9. balloon — 풍선
10. cute — 귀여운
11. brother — 형제
12. brush — 닦다, 빗, 솔
13. dark — 어두운, 어둠
14. basket — 바구니
15. dance — 춤추다
16. bean — 콩
17. do — 하다
18. brown — 갈색, 갈색의

B
1. hand — 손
2. lady — 숙녀
3. happy — 행복한
4. kitchen — 부엌
5. enjoy — 즐기다
6. king — 왕
7. evening — 저녁
8. knee — 무릎
9. father — 아버지
10. hair — 머리카락
11. fat — 살찐, 뚱뚱한
12. green — 녹색, 녹색의
13. find — 찾다, 알다
14. face — 얼굴
15. knife — 칼
16. great — 큰, 위대한
17. know — 알고 있다
18. gray — 회색, 회색의

Unit 15

A
1. market
2. orange
3. Milk
4. minutes
5. meat
6. Open
7. outside
8. rich
9. over
10. ox
11. page
12. meet
13. Rain
14. mirror
15. ready
16. ring
17. rice
18. right

B
1. 열다
2. ~의 위에, ~의 위로
3. 시장
4. 쪽, 페이지
5. 고기
6. 준비가 된
7. 반지, 울리다
8. 분, 잠시
9. 수소
10. 쌀, 밥, 벼
11. 거울
12. 바깥쪽에, 바깥쪽으로
13. 오른쪽, 오른쪽의
14. 만나다
15. 부유한
16. 비
17. 오렌지, 오렌지색
18. 우유

1. market
2. meat
3. meet
4. milk
5. minute
6. mirror
7. open
8. orange
9. outside
10. over
11. ox
12. page
13. rain
14. ready
15. rice
16. rich
17. right
18. ring

C
1. open 열다
2. meet 만나다
3. ox 수소
4. market 시장
5. rain 비
6. minute 분, 잠시
7. page 쪽, 페이지
8. mirror 거울
9. meat 고기
10. over ~의 위에, ~의 위로
11. right 오른쪽, 오른쪽의
12. ring 반지, 울리다
13. milk 우유
14. rich 부유한
15. rice 쌀, 밥, 벼
16. outside 바깥쪽에, 바깥쪽으로
17. orange 오렌지, 오렌지색
18. ready 준비가 된

Unit 16

A
1. snow
2. soap
3. soccer
4. well
5. smiled
6. there
7. think
8. thumb
9. tie
10. time
11. Welcome
12. week
13. tired
14. socks
15. watched
16. way
17. song
18. wear

B
1. 양말
2. 생각하다
3. 묶다, 넥타이
4. 미소짓다
5. 지친
6. 길, 방법
7. 눈
8. 환영, 환영하다
9. 엄지손가락
10. 주
11. 비누
12. 보다, 시계
13. 잘
14. 축구
15. 입고(쓰고) 있다
16. 시간, 시각
17. 거기에
18. 노래

1. smile
2. snow
3. soap
4. soccer
5. socks
6. song
7. there
8. think
9. thumb
10. tie
11. time
12. tired
13. watch
14. way
15. wear
16. week
17. welcome
18. well

C
1. tie 묶다, 넥타이
2. soap 비누
3. way 길, 방법
4. smile 미소 짓다
5. time 시간, 시각
6. thumb 엄지손가락
7. snow 눈
8. think 생각하다
9. wear 입고(쓰고) 있다
10. watch 보다, 시계
11. soccer 축구
12. well 잘
13. welcome 환영, 환영하다
14. song 노래
15. tired 지친
16. week 주
17. there 거기에
18. socks 양말

Review 8

A
1. open 열다
2. meet 만나다
3. ox 수소
4. market 시장
5. rain 비
6. minute 분, 잠시
7. page 쪽, 페이지
8. mirror 거울
9. meat 고기
10. over ~의 위에, ~의 위로
11. right 오른쪽, 오른쪽의
12. ring 반지, 울리다
13. milk 우유
14. rich 부유한
15. rice 쌀, 밥, 벼
16. outside 바깥쪽에, 바깥쪽으로
17. orange 오렌지, 오렌지색
18. ready 준비가 된

B
1. tie 묶다, 넥타이
2. soap 비누
3. way 길, 방법
4. smile 미소짓다
5. time 시간, 시각
6. thumb 엄지손가락
7. snow 눈
8. think 생각하다
9. wear 입고(쓰고) 있다
10. watch 보다, 시계
11. soccer 축구
12. well 잘
13. welcome 환영, 환영하다
14. song 노래
15. tired 지친
16. week 주
17. there 거기에
18. socks 양말

Unit 17

A
1. beautiful
2. beef
3. belong
4. catches
5. country
6. chair
7. chest
8. begins
9. chickens
10. baseball
11. child
12. count
13. color
14. come
15. behind
16. cookie
17. chalk
18. cook

B
1. 잡다
2. ~의 뒤에
3. 의자
4. 야구, 야구공
5. 쿠키
6. 닭, 닭고기
7. 쇠고기
8. 오다
9. 색, 빛깔
10. 아름다운, 예쁜
11. 세다, 계산하다
12. 가슴
13. 나라, 시골
14. 시작하다
15. 어린이, 아이
16. 요리사, 요리하다
17. 분필
18. ~에 속하다

1. baseball
2. beautiful
3. beef
4. begin
5. behind
6. belong
7. catch
8. chair
9. chalk
10. chest
11. chicken
12. child
13. color
14. come
15. cook
16. cookie
17. count
18. country

C
1. chalk — 분필
2. baseball — 야구, 야구공
3. chair — 의자
4. color — 색, 빛깔
5. beautiful — 아름다운, 예쁜
6. catch — 잡다
7. come — 오다
8. beef — 쇠고기
9. country — 나라, 시골
10. child — 어린이, 아이
11. begin — 시작하다
12. chest — 가슴
13. behind — ~의 뒤에
14. count — 세다, 계산하다
15. cookie — 쿠키
16. belong — ~에 속하다
17. chicken — 닭, 닭고기
18. cook — 요리사, 요리하다

Unit 18

A
1. just
2. easy
3. kind
4. eat
5. eggs
6. grandmother
7. elephant
8. end
9. hot
10. glad
11. hour
12. doll
13. glass
14. hospital
15. goat
16. jumped
17. good
18. grandfather

B
1. 달걀
2. 할아버지
3. 병원
4. 쉬운
5. 친절한, 종류
6. 바로, 꼭, 막
7. 코끼리
8. 뛰다
9. 기쁜
10. 할머니
11. 염소
12. 인형
13. 유리(잔)
14. 시각, 한 시간
15. 끝, 끝나다
16. 더운
17. 먹다
18. 좋은, 즐거운

1. doll
2. easy
3. eat
4. egg
5. elephant
6. end
7. glad
8. glass
9. goat
10. good
11. grandfather
12. grandmother
13. hospital
14. hot
15. hour
16. jump
17. just
18. kind

C
1. good — 좋은, 즐거운
2. goat — 염소
3. hospital — 병원
4. easy — 쉬운
5. grandfather — 할아버지
6. eat — 먹다
7. grandmother — 할머니
8. egg — 달걀
9. doll — 인형
10. kind — 친절한, 종류
11. glass — 유리(잔)
12. just — 바로, 꼭, 막
13. glad — 기쁜
14. hour — 시각, 한 시간
15. elephant — 코끼리
16. jump — 뛰다
17. end — 끝, 끝나다
18. hot — 더운

Review 9

A
1. chalk — 분필
2. baseball — 야구, 야구공
3. chair — 의자
4. color — 색, 빛깔
5. beautiful — 아름다운, 예쁜
6. catch — 잡다
7. come — 오다
8. beef — 쇠고기
9. country — 나라, 시골
10. child — 어린이, 아이
11. begin — 시작하다
12. chest — 가슴
13. behind — ~의 뒤에
14. count — 세다, 계산하다
15. cookie — 쿠키
16. belong — ~에 속하다
17. chicken — 닭, 닭고기
18. cook — 요리사, 요리하다

B
1. good — 좋은, 즐거운
2. goat — 염소
3. hospital — 병원
4. easy — 쉬운
5. grandfather — 할아버지
6. eat — 먹다
7. grandmother — 할머니
8. egg — 달걀
9. doll — 인형
10. kind — 친절한, 종류
11. glass — 유리(잔)
12. just — 바로, 꼭, 막
13. glad — 기쁜
14. hour — 시각, 한 시간
15. elephant — 코끼리
16. jump — 뛰다
17. end — 끝, 끝나다
18. hot — 더운

Unit 19

A
1. lunch
2. low
3. man
4. Push
5. Queen
6. map
7. noon
8. quiet
9. nose
10. many
11. number
12. often
13. once
14. puppy
15. old
16. make
17. purple
18. put

B
1. 점심 식사
2. (수가)많은
3. 정오, 한낮
4. 종종, 자주
5. 낮은
6. 한 번
7. 밀다
8. 코
9. 조용한
10. 번호, 수
11. 만들다
12. 보라색, 보라색의
13. 여왕, 왕비
14. 지도
15. 놓다, 넣다
16. 강아지
17. 늙은, ~살의
18. 남자, 사람

1. low
2. lunch
3. make
4. man
5. many
6. map
7. noon
8. nose
9. number
10. often
11. old
12. once
13. puppy
14. purple
15. push
16. put
17. queen
18. quiet

C
1. noon — 정오, 한낮
2. quiet — 조용한
3. low — 낮은
4. nose — 코
5. lunch — 점심 식사
6. map — 지도
7. once — 한 번
8. many — (수가) 많은
9. puppy — 강아지
10. man — 남자, 사람
11. purple — 보라색, 보라색의
12. make — 만들다
13. queen — 여왕, 왕비
14. put — 놓다, 넣다
15. old — 늙은, ~살의
16. push — 밀다
17. number — 번호, 수
18. often — 종종, 자주

Unit 20

A
1. skirts
2. sky
3. small
4. teaches
5. telephone
6. slow
7. sister
8. Tell
9. sing
10. tennis
11. want
12. televisio
13. then
14. very
15. Wash
16. visit
17. wait
18. walk

B
1. 느린
2. 전화기
3. 방문하다
4. 노래하다
5. 기다리다
6. 텔레비전
7. 씻다
8. 원하다
9. 스커트, 치마
10. 가르치다
11. 테니스
12. 하늘
13. 걷다
14. 그 때에
15. 작은
16. 대단히, 몹시
17. 말하다
18. 여자형제, 자매

1. sing
2. sister
3. skirt
4. sky
5. slow
6. small
7. teach
8. telephone
9. television
10. tell
11. tennis
12. then
13. very
14. visit
15. wait
16. walk
17. want
18. wash

C
1. sing — 노래하다
2. tell — 말하다
3. want — 원하다
4. tennis — 테니스
5. sister — 여자형제, 자매
6. then — 그 때에
7. slow — 느린
8. skirt — 스커트, 치마
9. television — 텔레비전
10. walk — 걷다
11. sky — 하늘
12. very — 대단히, 몹시
13. telephone — 전화기
14. wait — 기다리다
15. small — 작은
16. visit — 방문하다
17. teach — 가르치다
18. wash — 씻다

Review 10

A
1. noon — 정오, 한낮
2. quiet — 조용한
3. low — 낮은
4. nose — 코
5. lunch — 점심 식사
6. map — 지도
7. once — 한 번
8. many — (수가) 많은
9. puppy — 강아지
10. man — 남자, 사람
11. purple — 보라색, 보라색의
12. make — 만들다
13. queen — 여왕, 왕비
14. put — 놓다, 넣다
15. often — 종종, 자주
16. push — 밀다
17. number — 번호, 수
18. old — 늙은, ~살의

B
1. sing — 노래하다
2. tell — 말하다
3. want — 원하다
4. tennis — 테니스
5. sister — 여자형제, 자매
6. then — 그 때에
7. slow — 느린
8. skirt — 스커트, 치마
9. television — 텔레비전
10. walk — 걷다
11. sky — 하늘
12. very — 대단히, 몹시
13. telephone — 전화기
14. wait — 기다리다
15. small — 작은
16. visit — 방문하다
17. teach — 가르치다
18. wash — 씻다

Unit 21

A
1. checked
2. accept
3. club
4. absent
5. crane
6. any
7. beach
8. Dear
9. birth
10. butter
11. action
12. button
13. cheap
14. clothes
15. corner
16. bath
17. dead
18. bill

B
1. 받아들이다
2. 목욕
3. 값이 싼
4. 결석의, 부재의
5. 단추, 버튼
6. 두루미, 기중기
7. 얼마간의
8. 옷, 의복
9. 죽은
10. 행동, 활동
11. 계산서, 지폐
12. 곤봉, 동호회
13. 버터
14. 구석, 길모퉁이
15. 출생, 탄생
16. 귀여운, 친애하는
17. 체크하다, 대조하다
18. 해변, 바닷가

1. absent
2. accept
3. action
4. any
5. bath
6. beach
7. bill
8. birth
9. butter
10. button
11. cheap
12. check
13. clothes
14. club
15. corner
16. crane
17. dead
18. dear

C
1. beach — 해변, 바닷가
2. crane — 두루미, 기중기
3. action — 행동, 활동
4. check — 체크하다, 대조하다
5. cheap — 값이 싼
6. any — 얼마간의
7. butter — 버터
8. club — 곤봉, 동호회
9. absent — 결석의, 부재의
10. corner — 구석, 길모퉁이
11. bath — 목욕
12. clothes — 옷, 의복
13. button — 단추, 버튼
14. accept — 받아들이다
15. birth — 출생, 탄생
16. dear — 귀여운, 친애하는
17. bill — 계산서, 지폐
18. dead — 죽은

Unit 22

A
1. dream
2. enjoyment
3. dollar
4. engine
5. family
6. fire
7. fix
8. hear
9. jealous
10. kids
11. goes
12. handle
13. holiday
14. huge
15. husband
16. far
17. keep
18. gloves

B
1. 엔진, 기관
2. 꿈
3. 장갑, 글러브
4. 손잡이
5. 달러
6. 가족
7. 휴가, 휴일
8. 기르다, 유지하다
9. 질투하는
10. 불, 화재
11. 아이
12. 거대한
13. 고치다, 붙이다
14. 남편
15. 듣다
16. 멀리
17. 가다
18. 즐거움, 기쁨

1. dollar
2. dream
3. engine
4. enjoyment
5. family
6. far
7. fire
8. fix
9. glove
10. go
11. handle
12. hear
13. holiday
14. huge
15. husband
16. jealous
17. keep
18. kid

C
1. far — 멀리
2. fix — 고치다, 붙이다
3. family — 가족
4. huge — 거대한
5. fire — 불, 화재
6. glove — 장갑, 글러브
7. enjoyment — 즐거움, 기쁨
8. husband — 남편
9. go — 가다
10. engine — 엔진, 기관
11. keep — 기르다, 유지하다
12. jealous — 질투하는
13. kid — 아이
14. handle — 손잡이
15. dream — 꿈
16. hear — 듣다
17. holiday — 휴가, 휴일
18. dollar — 달러

Review 11

A
1. beach — 해변, 바닷가
2. crane — 두루미, 기중기
3. action — 행동, 활동
4. check — 체크하다, 대조하다
5. cheap — 값이 싼
6. any — 얼마간의
7. butter — 버터
8. club — 곤봉, 동호회
9. accept — 받아들이다
10. corner — 구석, 길모퉁이
11. bath — 목욕
12. clothes — 옷, 의복
13. button — 단추, 버튼
14. absent — 결석의, 부재의
15. birth — 출생, 탄생
16. dear — 귀여운, 친애하는
17. bill — 계산서, 지폐
18. dead — 죽은

B
1. far — 멀리
2. fix — 고치다, 붙이다
3. family — 가족
4. huge — 거대한
5. fire — 불, 화재
6. glove — 장갑, 글러브
7. enjoyment — 즐거움, 기쁨
8. husband — 남편
9. go — 가다
10. engine — 엔진, 기관
11. keep — 기르다, 유지하다
12. jealous — 질투하는
13. kid — 아이
14. handle — 손잡이
15. dream — 꿈
16. hear — 듣다
17. holiday — 휴가, 휴일
18. dollar — 달러

Unit 23

A
1. luck
2. note
3. number
4. mad
5. salt
6. pen
7. Please
8. leave
9. police
10. purse
11. rest
12. letter
13. restaurant
14. safe
15. puzzle
16. sheep
17. peel
18. sheet

B
1. 제발, 부디
2. 화난, 미친
3. 편지, 글자
4. 떠나다
5. 휴식
6. 지갑
7. 운, 행운
8. 번호, 숫자
9. 퍼즐, 수수께끼
10. 양
11. 안전한
12. 펜, 우리
13. 시트, 커버
14. 경찰
15. 소금
16. 음식점, 레스토랑
17. 껍질을 벗기다
18. 기록, 노트

1. leave
2. letter
3. luck
4. mad
5. note
6. number
7. peel
8. pen
9. please
10. police
11. purse
12. puzzle
13. rest
14. restaurant
15. safe
16. salt
17. sheep
18. sheet

C
1. number 번호, 숫자
2. rest 휴식
3. safe 안전한
4. purse 지갑
5. letter 편지, 글자
6. peel 껍질을 벗기다
7. mad 화난, 미친
8. sheep 양
9. salt 소금
10. luck 운, 행운
11. note 기록, 노트
12. restaurant 음식점, 레스토랑
13. pen 펜, 우리
14. sheet 시트, 커버
15. please 제발, 부디
16. police 경찰
17. leave 떠나다
18. puzzle 퍼즐, 수수께끼

Unit 24

A
1. until
2. spell
3. sleep
4. video
5. south
6. stick
7. together
8. supper
9. visit
10. sure
11. test
12. stone
13. than
14. slide
15. tomato
16. understands
17. vegetables
18. woke

B
1. 저녁 식사
2. 시험
3. 잠자다
4. ~할 때까지
5. (미끄럼틀을) 타다
6. 방문하다
7. ~보다
8. 막대기, 지팡이
9. 일어나다
10. 비디오
11. 철자를 쓰다
12. 토마토
13. 확신한
14. 야채
15. 돌
16. 이해하다
17. 함께, 같이
18. 남쪽, 남쪽으로

1. sleep
2. slide
3. south
4. spell
5. stick
6. stone
7. supper
8. sure
9. test
10. than
11. together
12. tomato
13. understand
14. until
15. vegetable
16. video
17. visit
18. wake

C
1. slide (미끄럼틀을) 타다
2. than ~보다
3. tomato 토마토
4. south 남쪽, 남쪽으로
5. together 함께, 같이
6. sleep 잠자다
7. test 시험
8. visit 방문하다
9. spell 철자를 쓰다
10. sure 확신한
11. wake 일어나다
12. video 비디오
13. stone 돌
14. understand 이해하다
15. vegetable 야채
16. supper 저녁식사
17. stick 막대기, 지팡이
18. until ~할 때까지

Review 12

A
1. number 번호, 숫자
2. rest 휴식
3. safe 안전한
4. purse 지갑
5. letter 편지, 글자
6. peel 껍질을 벗기다
7. mad 화난, 미친
8. sheep 양
9. salt 소금
10. luck 운, 행운
11. note 기록, 노트
12. restaurant 음식점, 레스토랑
13. pen 펜, 우리
14. sheet 시트, 커버
15. please 제발, 부디
16. police 경찰
17. leave 떠나다
18. puzzle 퍼즐, 수수께끼

B
1. slide (미끄럼틀을) 타다
2. than ~보다
3. tomato 토마토
4. south 남쪽, 남쪽으로
5. together 함께, 같이
6. sleep 잠자다
7. test 시험
8. visit 방문하다
9. spell 철자를 쓰다
10. sure 확신한
11. wake 일어나다
12. video 비디오
13. stone 돌
14. understand 이해하다
15. vegetable 야채
16. supper 저녁식사
17. stick 막대기, 지팡이
18. until ~할 때까지

Unit 25

A
1. age
2. deer
3. cake
4. apartment
5. beating
6. blocks
7. camera
8. courage
9. cheese
10. as
11. chess
12. birthday
13. cock
14. beggar
15. covered
16. ago
17. coffee
18. deep

B
1. 거지
2. 나이, 연령
3. 생일
4. ~전에
5. 수탉
6. 때리다, 부딪치다
7. 커피
8. 깊은
9. 카메라
10. ~로서
11. 용기, 담력
12. 덮다, 씌우다
13. 치즈
14. 사슴
15. 체스
16. 블록, 한 구획
17. 케이크
18. 아파트

1. age
2. ago
3. apartment
4. as
5. beat
6. beggar
7. birthday
8. block
9. cake
10. camera
11. cheese
12. chess
13. cock
14. coffee
15. courage
16. cover
17. deep
18. deer

C
1. apartment — 아파트
2. beggar — 거지
3. block — 블록, 한 구획
4. ago — ~전에
5. birthday — 생일
6. cock — 수탉
7. age — 나이, 연령
8. coffee — 커피
9. beat — 때리다, 부딪치다
10. chess — 체스
11. as — ~로서
12. cover — 덮다, 씌우다
13. cheese — 치즈
14. deep — 깊은
15. cake — 케이크
16. deer — 사슴
17. camera — 카메라
18. courage — 용기, 담력

Unit 26

A
1. fast
2. drink
3. every
4. farm
5. flag
6. hospital
7. library
8. floor
9. dress
10. grandparents
11. heart
12. gold
13. helicopter
14. killed
15. exam
16. knock
17. hose
18. life

B
1. 마시다
2. 깃발
3. 조부모
4. 죽이다
5. 심장, 가슴
6. 드레스, 의복
7. 노크, 두드림
8. 시험
9. 마루, 바닥
10. 병원
11. ~마다, 모두
12. 헬리콥터
13. 도서관
14. 금
15. 농장
16. 생명, 생물
17. 호스
18. 빠른, 빨리

1. dress
2. drink
3. every
4. exam
5. farm
6. fast
7. flag
8. floor
9. gold
10. grandparent
11. heart
12. helicopter
13. hose
14. hospital
15. kill
16. knock
17. library
18. life

C
1. heart — 심장, 가슴
2. fast — 빠른, 빨리
3. kill — 죽이다
4. floor — 마루, 바닥
5. dress — 드레스, 의복
6. helicopter — 헬리콥터
7. farm — 농장
8. hose — 호스
9. gold — 금
10. flag — 깃발
11. hospital — 병원
12. grandparent — 조부모
13. life — 생명, 생물
14. every — ~마다, 모두
15. library — 도서관
16. drink — 마시다
17. knock — 노크, 두드림
18. exam — 시험

Review 13

A
1. apartment — 아파트
2. beggar — 거지
3. block — 블록, 한 구획
4. ago — ~전에
5. birthday — 생일
6. cock — 수탉
7. age — 나이, 연령
8. coffee — 커피
9. beat — 때리다, 부딪치다
10. chess — 체스
11. as — ~로서
12. cover — 덮다, 씌우다
13. cheese — 치즈
14. deep — 깊은
15. cake — 케이크
16. deer — 사슴
17. camera — 카메라
18. courage — 용기, 담력

B
1. heart — 심장, 가슴
2. fast — 빠른, 빨리
3. kill — 죽이다
4. floor — 마루, 바닥
5. dress — 드레스, 의복
6. helicopter — 헬리콥터
7. farm — 농장
8. hose — 호스
9. gold — 금
10. flag — 깃발
11. hospital — 병원
12. grandparent — 조부모
13. life — 생명, 생물
14. every — ~마다, 모두
15. library — 도서관
16. drink — 마시다
17. knock — 노크, 두드림
18. exam — 시험

Unit 27

A
1. May
2. sand
3. move
4. nurse
5. only
6. pets
7. question
8. same
9. pool
10. market
11. post
12. quick
13. return
14. person
15. ride
16. shoot
17. near
18. shops

B
1. ~의 가까이에
2. 우편, 부치다
3. 돌아오다, 돌아가다
4. 시장
5. 질문, 물음
6. 같은, 동일한
7. 쏘다, 발사하다
8. 단지, 오직
9. 빠른
10. ~해도 좋다
11. 물웅덩이
12. 움직이다, 옮기다
13. 애완동물
14. 모래
15. 가게, 상점
16. 타다
17. 사람, 인물
18. 간호사

1. market
2. may
3. move
4. near
5. nurse
6. only
7. person
8. pet
9. pool
10. post
11. question
12. quick
13. return
14. ride
15. same
16. sand
17. shoot
18. shop

C
1. nurse — 간호사
2. may — ~해도 좋다
3. question — 질문, 물음
4. near — ~의 가까이에
5. return — 돌아오다, 돌아가다
6. person — 사람, 인물
7. shop — 가게, 상점
8. market — 시장
9. quick — 빠른
10. only — 단지, 오직
11. sand — 모래
12. pet — 애완동물
13. move — 움직이다, 옮기다
14. ride — 타다
15. post — 우편, 부치다
16. same — 같은, 동일한
17. pool — 물웅덩이
18. shoot — 쏘다, 발사하다

Unit 28

A
1. smoke
2. spend
3. spring
4. water
5. stove
6. wearing
7. swing
8. thin
9. wall
10. tomorrow
11. sweet
12. top
13. warm
14. smell
15. Thank
16. west
17. store
18. wet

B
1. 담배를 피우다
2. 감사하다
3. 그네
4. 봄
5. 꼭대기, 정상
6. 난로
7. 내일
8. 물
9. (냄새를) 맡다
10. 따뜻한
11. 서쪽
12. 달콤한
13. 젖은
14. 입고 있다, 쓰고 있다
15. 쓰다, 소비하다
16. 벽
17. 마른, 얇은
18. 가게, 상점

1. smell
2. smoke
3. spend
4. spring
5. store
6. stove
7. sweet
8. swing
9. thank
10. thin
11. tomorrow
12. top
13. wall
14. warm
15. water
16. wear
17. west
18. wet

C
1. smoke — 담배를 피우다
2. stove — 난로
3. thin — 마른, 얇은
4. smell — (냄새를) 맡다
5. wet — 젖은
6. store — 가게, 상점
7. tomorrow — 내일
8. spend — 쓰다, 소비하다
9. thank — 감사하다
10. west — 서쪽
11. spring — 봄
12. top — 꼭대기, 정상
13. wear — 입고 있다, 쓰고 있다
14. warm — 따뜻한
15. sweet — 달콤한
16. wall — 벽
17. swing — 그네
18. water — 물

Review 14

A
1. nurse — 간호사
2. may — ~해도 좋다
3. question — 질문, 물음
4. near — ~의 가까이에
5. return — 돌아오다, 돌아가다
6. person — 사람, 인물
7. shop — 가게, 상점
8. market — 시장
9. quick — 빠른
10. only — 단지, 오직
11. sand — 모래
12. pet — 애완동물
13. move — 움직이다, 옮기다
14. ride — 타다
15. post — 우편, 부치다
16. same — 같은, 동일한
17. pool — 물웅덩이
18. shoot — 쏘다, 발사하다

B
1. smoke — 담배를 피우다
2. stove — 난로
3. thin — 마른, 얇은
4. smell — (냄새를) 맡다
5. wet — 젖은
6. store — 가게, 상점
7. tomorrow — 내일
8. spend — 쓰다, 소비하다
9. thank — 감사하다
10. west — 서쪽
11. spring — 봄
12. top — 꼭대기, 정상
13. wear — 입고 있다, 쓰고 있다
14. warm — 따뜻한
15. sweet — 달콤한
16. wall — 벽
17. swing — 그네
18. water — 물

Unit 29

A
1. aliens
2. board
3. asked
4. chest
5. air
6. author
7. before
8. candle
9. card
10. behind
11. chopsticks
12. coins
13. down
14. comb
15. dialed
16. crayon
17. dialogue
18. cream

B
1. ~전에
2. 양초
3. 아래로, 낮은 쪽으로
4. 공기, 공중
5. 카드
6. 외국인, 우주인
7. 동전
8. 널, 판자
9. 빗다, 빗
10. 묻다, 물어보다
11. 대화
12. 젓가락
13. 크림
14. 저자, 작가
15. 크레용
16. 다이얼을 돌리다, 다이얼
17. 가슴, 대형상자
18. ~뒤에

1. air
2. alien
3. ask
4. author
5. before
6. behind
7. board
8. candle
9. card
10. chest
11. chopsticks
12. coin
13. comb
14. crayon
15. cream
16. dial
17. dialogue
18. down

C
1. air — 공기, 공중
2. coin — 동전
3. card — 카드
4. down — 아래로, 낮은 쪽으로
5. alien — 외국인, 우주인
6. candle — 양초
7. dialogue — 대화
8. chest — 가슴, 대형 상자
9. ask — 묻다, 물어보다
10. chopsticks — 젓가락
11. dial — 다이얼을 돌리다, 다이얼
12. author — 저자, 작가
13. board — 널, 판자
14. comb — 빗다, 빗
15. before — ~전에
16. cream — 크림
17. behind — ~뒤에
18. crayon — 크레용

Unit 30

A
1. ground
2. feel
3. dropped
4. excuse
5. few
6. lines
7. fool
8. for
9. drive
10. grass
11. hen
12. lips
13. hike
14. hotel
15. example
16. Hungry
17. lake
18. land

B
1. 떨어뜨리다
2. 느끼다
3. 운전하다
4. 암탉
5. 풀, 잔디
6. ~을 위해, ~동안
7. 배고픈
8. 땅, 지면
9. 줄, 선
10. 조금의, 다소의
11. 육지
12. 바보
13. 입술
14. 호수
15. 호텔
16. 용서하다, 변명하다
17. 하이킹하다
18. 본보기, 모범

1. drive
2. drop
3. example
4. excuse
5. feel
6. few
7. fool
8. for
9. grass
10. ground
11. hen
12. hike
13. hotel
14. hungry
15. lake
16. land
17. line
18. lip

C
1. few — 조금의, 다소의
2. drive — 운전하다
3. for — ~을 위해, ~동안
4. hotel — 호텔
5. feel — 느끼다
6. lake — 호수
7. fool — 바보
8. land — 육지
9. excuse — 용서하다, 변명하다
10. hungry — 배고픈
11. lip — 입술
12. grass — 풀, 잔디
13. example — 본보기, 모범
14. hike — 하이킹하다
15. ground — 땅, 지면
16. drop — 떨어뜨리다
17. line — 줄, 선
18. hen — 암탉

Review 15

A
1. air — 공기, 공중
2. coin — 동전
3. card — 카드
4. down — 아래로, 낮은 쪽으로
5. alien — 외국인, 우주인
6. candle — 양초
7. dialogue — 대화
8. chest — 가슴, 대형 상자
9. ask — 묻다, 물어보다
10. chopsticks — 젓가락
11. dial — 다이얼을 돌리다, 다이얼
12. author — 저자, 작가
13. board — 널, 판자
14. comb — 빗다, 빗
15. before — ~전에
16. cream — 크림
17. behind — ~뒤에
18. crayon — 크레용

B
1. few — 조금의, 다소의
2. drive — 운전하다
3. for — ~을 위해, ~동안
4. hotel — 호텔
5. feel — 느끼다
6. lake — 호수
7. fool — 바보
8. land — 육지
9. excuse — 용서하다, 변명하다
10. hungry — 배고픈
11. lip — 입술
12. grass — 풀, 잔디
13. example — 본보기, 모범
14. hike — 하이킹하다
15. ground — 땅, 지면
16. drop — 떨어뜨리다
17. line — 줄, 선
18. hen — 암탉

Answer Key

Unit 31

A
1. never
2. meal
3. sandwiches
4. need
5. other
6. outside
7. shoulder
8. road
9. schedule
10. peace
11. piano
12. rabbit
13. medal
14. pieces
15. poster
16. read
17. rocket
18. Show

B
1. 메달, 상패
2. 결코 ~하지 않다
3. 읽다
4. 평화
5. 길, 도로
6. 로켓
7. 샌드위치
8. 로켓
9. 전단, 포스터
10. ~할 필요가 있다
11. 어깨
12. 피아노
13. 보여주다
14. 밖에
15. 조각, 단편
16. 예정, 스케줄
17. 토끼
18. 다른, 그 밖의

1. meal
2. medal
3. need
4. never
5. other
6. outside
7. peace
8. piano
9. piece
10. poster
11. rabbit
12. read
13. road
14. rocket
15. sandwich
16. schedule
17. shoulder
18. show

C
1. rabbit — 토끼
2. poster — 전단, 포스터
3. shoulder — 어깨
4. medal — 메달, 상패
5. piece — 조각, 단편
6. read — 읽다
7. need — ~할 필요가 있다
8. road — 길, 도로
9. meal — 식사
10. show — 보여주다
11. rocket — 로켓
12. piano — 피아노
13. outside — 밖에
14. sandwich — 샌드위치
15. never — 결코 ~하지 않다
16. peace — 평화
17. other — 다른, 그 밖의
18. schedule — 예정, 스케줄

Unit 32

A
1. So
2. square
3. wood
4. stairs
5. truck
6. street
7. strong
8. win
9. talk
10. things
11. Snakes
12. throw
13. winter
14. toys
15. will
16. window
17. take
18. wings

B
1. 잡다, 가지고 가다
2. 뱀
3. 트럭
4. 이기다
5. 그래서
6. 물건, 것
7. 거리
8. 말하다
9. ~할 것이다
10. 겨울
11. 계단
12. 던지다
13. 나무, 목재
14. 날개
15. 강한
16. 장난감
17. 창문
18. 정사각형

1. snake
2. so
3. square
4. stairs
5. street
6. strong
7. take
8. talk
9. thing
10. throw
11. toy
12. truck
13. will
14. win
15. window
16. wing
17. winter
18. wood

C
1. window — 창문
2. talk — 말하다
3. wing — 날개
4. snake — 뱀
5. winter — 겨울
6. thing — 물건, 것
7. wood — 나무, 목재
8. throw — 던지다
9. strong — 강한
10. stairs — 계단
11. will — ~할 것이다
12. take — 잡다, 가지고 가다
13. so — 그래서
14. toy — 장난감
15. street — 거리
16. truck — 트럭
17. square — 정사각형
18. win — 이기다

Review 16

A
1. rabbit — 토끼
2. poster — 전단, 포스터
3. shoulder — 어깨
4. medal — 메달, 상패
5. piece — 조각, 단편
6. read — 읽다
7. need — ~할 필요가 있다
8. road — 길, 도로
9. meal — 식사
10. show — 보여주다
11. rocket — 로켓
12. piano — 피아노
13. outside — 밖에
14. sandwich — 샌드위치
15. never — 결코 ~하지 않다
16. peace — 평화
17. other — 다른, 그 밖의
18. schedule — 예정, 스케줄

B
1. window — 창문
2. talk — 말하다
3. wing — 날개
4. snake — 뱀
5. winter — 겨울
6. thing — 물건, 것
7. wood — 나무, 목재
8. throw — 던지다
9. strong — 강한
10. stairs — 계단
11. will — ~할 것이다
12. take — 잡다, 가지고 가다
13. so — 그래서
14. toy — 장난감
15. street — 거리
16. truck — 트럭
17. square — 정사각형
18. win — 이기다

Unit 33

A
1. cool
2. dictionary
3. both
4. appear
5. away
6. below
7. album
8. bridge
9. carry
10. case
11. curtain
12. die
13. Christmas
14. circle
15. backward
16. cross
17. computer
18. drum

B
1. 거꾸로, 뒤로
2. 나르다, 운반하다
3. 가로지르다
4. 앨범, 사진첩
5. 죽다
6. 크리스마스
7. 나타나다
8. 컴퓨터
9. 북, 드럼
10. ~의 아래에
11. 커튼
12. 경우, 사례
13. 사전
14. 다리
15. 시원한
16. 원
17. 둘 다의, 양쪽의
18. 떨어져서

1. album
2. appear
3. away
4. backward
5. below
6. both
7. bridge
8. carry
9. case
10. Christmas
11. circle
12. computer
13. cool
14. cross
15. curtain
16. dictionary
17. die
18. drum

C
1. case — 경우, 사례
2. bridge — 다리
3. album — 앨범, 사진첩
4. curtain — 커튼
5. carry — 나르다, 운반하다
6. appear — 나타나다
7. dictionary — 사전
8. Christmas — 크리스마스
9. below — ~의 아래에
10. cross — 가로지르다
11. both — 둘 다의, 양쪽의
12. circle — 원
13. die — 죽다
14. backward — 거꾸로, 뒤로
15. cool — 시원한
16. away — 떨어져서
17. computer — 컴퓨터
18. drum — 북, 드럼

Unit 34

A
1. fact
2. Each
3. list
4. grow
5. fox
6. field
7. guitar
8. guns
9. hill
10. leaf
11. hit
12. hurt
13. fight
14. large
15. exercises
16. last
17. form
18. little

B
1. 운동하다, 운동
2. 들판, 벌판
3. 키우다, 재배하다
4. 치다, 때리다
5. 여우
6. 각각의
7. 언덕
8. 큰, 넓은
9. 형태, 모양
10. 목록, 명단
11. 작은
12. 총, 대포
13. 싸우다
14. 나뭇잎
15. 지난번의, 최후의
16. 상처를 내다
17. 기타
18. 사실, 진실

1. each
2. exercise
3. fact
4. field
5. fight
6. form
7. fox
8. grow
9. guitar
10. gun
11. hill
12. hit
13. hurt
14. large
15. last
16. leaf
17. list
18. little

C
1. hit — 치다, 때리다
2. fact — 사실, 진실
3. hurt — 상처를 내다
4. exercise — 운동하다, 운동
5. hill — 언덕
6. fight — 싸우다
7. each — 각각의
8. gun — 총, 대포
9. field — 들판, 벌판
10. large — 큰, 넓은
11. guitar — 기타
12. last — 지난번의, 최후의
13. form — 형태, 모양
14. list — 목록, 명단
15. fox — 여우
16. leaf — 나뭇잎
17. grow — 키우다, 재배하다
18. little — 작은

Review 17

A
1. case — 경우, 사례
2. bridge — 다리
3. album — 앨범, 사진첩
4. curtain — 커튼
5. carry — 나르다, 운반하다
6. appear — 나타나다
7. dictionary — 사전
8. Christmas — 크리스마스
9. below — ~의 아래에
10. cross — 가로지르다
11. both — 둘 다의, 양쪽의
12. circle — 원
13. die — 죽다
14. backward — 거꾸로, 뒤로
15. cool — 시원한
16. away — 떨어져서
17. computer — 컴퓨터
18. drum — 북, 드럼

B
1. hit — 치다, 때리다
2. fact — 사실, 진실
3. hurt — 상처를 내다
4. exercise — 운동하다, 운동
5. hill — 언덕
6. fight — 싸우다
7. each — 각각의
8. gun — 총, 대포
9. field — 들판, 벌판
10. large — 큰, 넓은
11. guitar — 기타
12. last — 지난번의, 최후의
13. form — 형태, 모양
14. list — 목록, 명단
15. fox — 여우
16. leaf — 나뭇잎
17. grow — 키우다, 재배하다
18. little — 작은

Answer Key

Unit 35

A
1. real
2. penguins
3. score
4. meters
5. news
6. next
7. seat
8. painted
9. middle
10. pair
11. roof
12. pipe
13. prince
14. regular
15. pineapple
16. Shut
17. rolled
18. side

B
1. 중앙, 한가운데
2. (페인트를) 칠하다
3. 진실의, 실제의
4. 다음의
5. 지붕
6. 관, 파이프
7. 쪽, 측면
8. 미터
9. 구르다
10. 파인애플
11. 닫다
12. 뉴스, 기사
13. 왕자
14. 좌석, 자리
15. 한 쌍, 한 벌
16. 점수, 성적
17. 규칙적인, 보통의
18. 펭귄

1. meter
2. middle
3. news
4. next
5. paint
6. pair
7. penguin
8. pineapple
9. pipe
10. prince
11. real
12. regular
13. roll
14. roof
15. score
16. seat
17. shut
18. side

C
1. paint — (페인트를) 칠하다
2. next — 다음의
3. middle — 중앙, 한가운데
4. regular — 규칙적인, 보통의
5. score — 점수, 성적
6. roll — 구르다
7. news — 뉴스, 기사
8. seat — 좌석, 자리
9. pair — 한 쌍, 한 벌
10. roof — 지붕
11. penguin — 펭귄
12. shut — 닫다
13. pipe — 관, 파이프
14. real — 진실의, 실제의
15. pineapple — 파인애플
16. side — 쪽, 측면
17. meter — 미터
18. prince — 왕자

Unit 36

A
1. Which
2. stamps
3. true
4. word
5. subway
6. summer
7. tall
8. work
9. tastes
10. some / some
11. ticket
12. soft
13. why
14. tiger
15. tulips
16. When
17. station
18. world

B
1. 지하철
2. 키 큰
3. 약간의, 얼마간의
4. 툴립
5. 맛이 나다
6. 언제
7. 부드러운
8. 왜, 어째서
9. 진실한, 정말의
10. 일, 일하다
11. 말, 낱말
12. 우표
13. 세계
14. 표, 입장권
15. 어느, 어떤
16. 여름
17. 호랑이
18. 정거장

1. soft
2. some
3. stamp
4. station
5. subway
6. summer
7. tall
8. taste
9. ticket
10. tiger
11. true
12. tulip
13. when
14. which
15. why
16. word
17. work
18. world

C
1. world — 세계
2. tiger — 호랑이
3. word — 말, 낱말
4. soft — 부드러운
5. work — 일, 일하다
6. ticket — 표, 입장권
7. some — 약간의, 얼마간의
8. true — 진실한, 정말의
9. stamp — 우표
10. why — 왜, 어째서
11. tulip — 툴립
12. station — 정거장
13. tall — 키 큰
14. when — 언제
15. subway — 지하철
16. which — 어느, 어떤
17. taste — 맛이 나다
18. summer — 여름

Review 18

A
1. paint — (페인트를) 칠하다
2. next — 다음의
3. middle — 중앙, 한가운데
4. regular — 규칙적인, 보통의
5. score — 점수, 성적
6. roll — 구르다
7. news — 뉴스, 기사
8. seat — 좌석, 자리
9. pair — 한 쌍, 한 벌
10. roof — 지붕
11. penguin — 펭귄
12. shut — 닫다
13. pipe — 관, 파이프
14. real — 진실의, 실제의
15. pineapple — 파인애플
16. side — 쪽, 측면
17. meter — 미터
18. prince — 왕자

B
1. world — 세계
2. tiger — 호랑이
3. word — 말, 낱말
4. soft — 부드러운
5. work — 일, 일하다
6. ticket — 표, 입장권
7. some — 약간의, 얼마간의
8. true — 진실한, 정말의
9. stamp — 우표
10. why — 왜, 어째서
11. tulip — 툴립
12. station — 정거장
13. tall — 키 큰
14. when — 언제
15. subway — 지하철
16. which — 어느, 어떤
17. taste — 맛이 나다
18. summer — 여름

Unit 37

A
1. alphabet
2. danger
3. ambulance
4. beside
5. different
6. climb
7. burn
8. center
9. classmates
10. address
11. copy
12. corns
13. date
14. band
15. between
16. cassette
17. daughter
18. doctor

B
1. 악단, 무리
2. 급우
3. 타다
4. 위험
5. 주소
6. 복사
7. 딸
8. 알파벳
9. 다른, 각각의
10. 옥수수
11. 의사
12. 구급차
13. 날짜
14. 카세트
15. ~의 사이에
16. 오르다
17. 중앙, 중심
18. ~의 옆에

1. address
2. alphabet
3. ambulance
4. band
5. beside
6. between
7. burn
8. cassette
9. center
10. classmate
11. climb
12. copy
13. corn
14. danger
15. date
16. daughter
17. different
18. doctor

C
1. climb — 오르다
2. address — 주소
3. different — 다른, 각각의
4. classmate — 급우
5. daughter — 딸
6. alphabet — 알파벳
7. center — 중앙, 중심
8. doctor — 의사
9. copy — 복사
10. ambulance — 구급차
11. corn — 옥수수
12. burn — 타다
13. danger — 위험
14. band — 악단, 무리
15. cassette — 카세트
16. beside — ~의 옆에
17. date — 날짜
18. between — ~의 사이에

Unit 38

A
1. east
2. hole
3. leading
4. fall
5. film
6. earth
7. frog
8. Half
9. mail
10. laugh
11. hardly
12. filled
13. fair
14. held
15. jungle
16. lot
17. front
18. job

B
1. 동쪽
2. 거의 ~아니다
3. 앞, 앞쪽
4. 밀림
5. 가을
6. 많음
7. 지구
8. 우편물
9. 잡다, 갖고 있다
10. 웃다, 비웃다
11. 채우다
12. 구멍
13. 안내하다, 인도하다
14. 영화, 필름
15. 일, 직업
16. 반, 절반
17. 개구리
18. 공평한, 정정 당당하게

1. earth
2. east
3. fair
4. fall
5. fill
6. film
7. frog
8. front
9. half
10. hardly
11. hold
12. hole
13. job
14. jungle
15. laugh
16. lead
17. lot
18. mail

C
1. hold — 잡다, 갖고 있다
2. frog — 개구리
3. hardly — 거의 ~아니다
4. front — 앞, 앞쪽
5. mail — 우편물
6. film — 영화, 필름
7. lot — 많음
8. half — 반, 절반
9. earth — 지구
10. lead — 안내하다, 인도하다
11. fill — 채우다
12. east — 동쪽
13. laugh — 웃다, 비웃다
14. fall — 가을
15. hole — 구멍
16. job — 일, 직업
17. fair — 공평한, 정정 당당하게
18. jungle — 밀림

Review 19

A
1. climb — 오르다
2. address — 주소
3. different — 다른, 각각의
4. classmate — 급우
5. daughter — 딸
6. alphabet — 알파벳
7. center — 중앙, 중심
8. doctor — 의사
9. copy — 복사
10. ambulance — 구급차
11. corn — 옥수수
12. burn — 타다
13. danger — 위험
14. band — 악단, 무리
15. cassette — 카세트
16. beside — ~의 옆에
17. date — 날짜
18. between — ~의 사이에

B
1. hold — 잡다, 갖고 있다
2. frog — 개구리
3. hardly — 거의 ~아니다
4. front — 앞, 앞쪽
5. mail — 우편물
6. film — 영화, 필름
7. lot — 많음
8. half — 반, 절반
9. earth — 지구
10. lead — 안내하다, 인도하다
11. fill — 채우다
12. east — 동쪽
13. laugh — 웃다, 비웃다
14. fall — 가을
15. hole — 구멍
16. job — 일, 직업
17. fair — 공평한, 정정 당당하게
18. jungle — 밀림

Unit 39

A
1. photo
2. minutes
3. problem
4. rose
5. niece
6. Shall
7. parents
8. place
9. plan
10. silver
11. program
12. record
13. million
14. rectangle
15. Service
16. north
17. round
18. size

B
1. 기록, 레코드
2. 조카딸
3. 둥근
4. 사진
5. 백만
6. 장미
7. 부모
8. ~을 할까요
9. 장소, 곳
10. 직사각형
11. 분, 잠시
12. 문제
13. 서비스, 봉사
14. 은, 은으로 만든
15. 계획, 계획하다
16. 크기, 치수
17. 프로그램
18. 북쪽, 북쪽의

1. million
2. minute
3. niece
4. north
5. parents
6. photo
7. place
8. plan
9. problem
10. program
11. record
12. rectangle
13. rose
14. round
15. service
16. shall
17. silver
18. size

C
1. place — 장소, 곳
2. north — 북쪽, 북쪽의
3. million — 백만
4. parents — 부모
5. minute — 분, 잠시
6. plan — 계획, 계획하다
7. photo — 사진
8. shall — ~을 할까요
9. niece — 조카딸
10. service — 서비스, 봉사
11. problem — 문제
12. record — 기록, 레코드
13. program — 프로그램
14. rose — 장미
15. size — 크기, 치수
16. rectangle — 직사각형
17. silver — 은, 은으로 만든
18. round — 둥근

Unit 40

A
1. yard
2. sour
3. till
4. sunny
5. team
6. yesterday
7. terror
8. zero
9. twice
10. umpire
11. supermarket
12. worm
13. steam
14. write
15. sons
16. today
17. step
18. wrong

B
1. 밝게 비치는
2. 팀, 조
3. 심판, 심판하다
4. ~까지
5. 아들
6. 두 번, 2회
7. 잘못된, 나쁜
8. 시큼한, 신
9. 어제
10. 슈퍼마켓
11. 벌레
12. 영, 영도
13. 스팀, 증기
14. 마당
15. 쓰다
16. 공포, 두려움
17. 오늘
18. 밟다, 걷다

1. son
2. sour
3. steam
4. step
5. sunny
6. supermarket
7. team
8. terror
9. till
10. today
11. twice
12. umpire
13. worm
14. write
15. wrong
16. yard
17. yesterday
18. zero

C
1. twice — 두 번, 2회
2. umpire — 심판, 심판하다
3. son — 아들
4. steam — 스팀, 증기
5. write — 쓰다
6. sour — 시큼한, 신
7. yesterday — 어제
8. zero — 영, 영도
9. sunny — 밝게 비치는
10. worm — 벌레
11. till — ~까지
12. step — 밟다, 걷다
13. today — 오늘
14. supermarket — 슈퍼마켓
15. wrong — 잘못된, 나쁜
16. terror — 공포, 두려움
17. team — 팀, 조
18. yard — 마당

Review 20

A
1. place — 장소, 곳
2. north — 북쪽, 북쪽의
3. million — 백만
4. parents — 부모
5. minute — 분, 잠시
6. plan — 계획, 계획하다
7. photo — 사진
8. shall — ~을 할까요
9. niece — 조카딸
10. service — 서비스, 봉사
11. problem — 문제
12. record — 기록, 레코드
13. program — 프로그램
14. rose — 장미
15. size — 크기, 치수
16. rectangle — 직사각형
17. silver — 은, 은으로 만든
18. round — 둥근

B
1. twice — 두 번, 2회
2. umpire — 심판, 심판하다
3. son — 아들
4. steam — 스팀, 증기
5. write — 쓰다
6. sour — 시큼한, 신
7. yesterday — 어제
8. team — 팀, 조
9. sunny — 밝게 비치는
10. worm — 벌레
11. till — ~까지
12. step — 밟다, 걷다
13. today — 오늘
14. supermarket — 슈퍼마켓
15. wrong — 잘못된, 나쁜
16. terror — 공포, 두려움
17. zero — 영, 영도
18. yard — 마당

Total Test 해당 Unit별 Exercise 3번 문제의 정답과 일치

 MEMO

MEMO